IMAGES
of America

SMYRNA, CLAYTON, AND WOODLAND BEACH

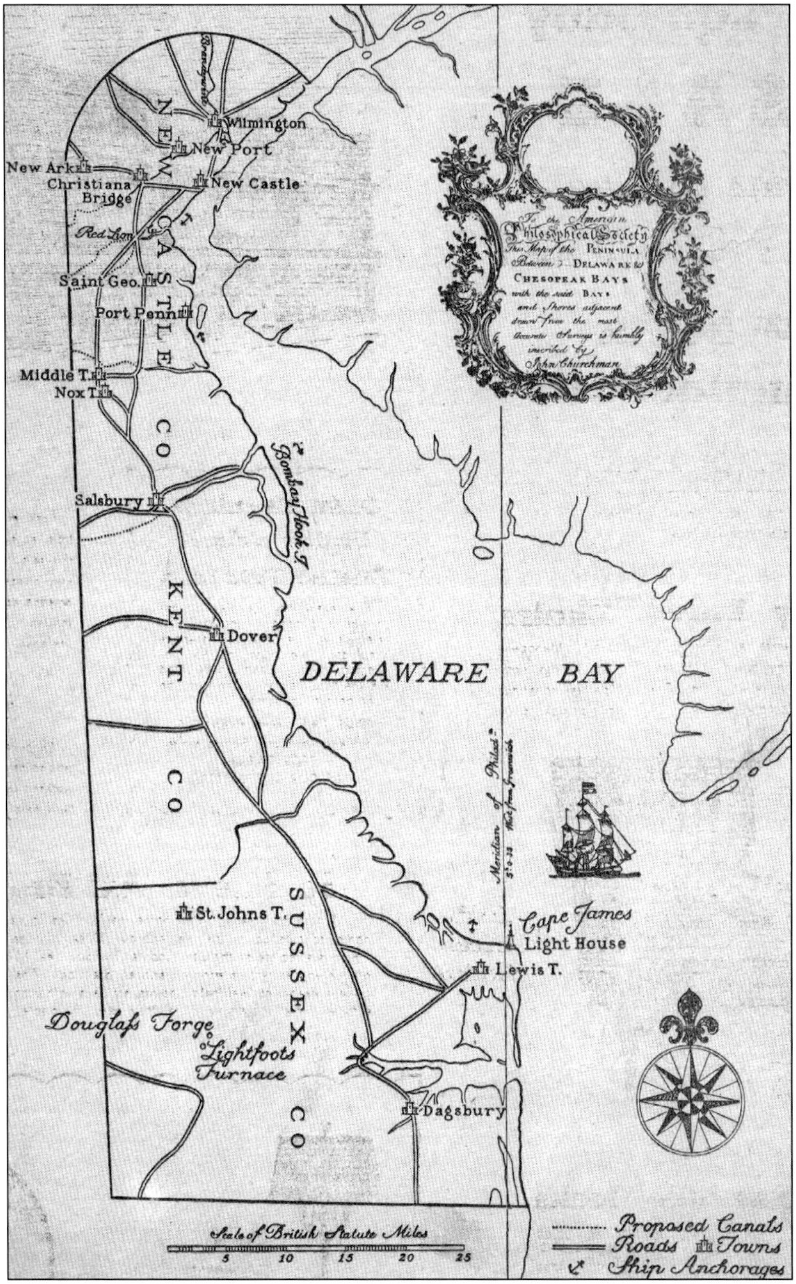

This map was drawn in 1787, the year that Delaware ratified the United States Constitution, by John Churchman for the American Philosophical Society. There were few towns at the inception of the newly created "First State." The village of Salisbury is shown at the northern edge of the otherwise very low-populated Kent County. (Courtesy of the Delaware Public Archives.)

On the Cover: This photograph shows William and James Clements outside of their hardware store in Clayton, Delaware, in 1925. The brothers created a lasting business that would continue in the town for many years, always occupying the same building on the corner of Main Street and Clayton Avenue. (Courtesy of the Delaware Public Archives.)

IMAGES
of America

SMYRNA, CLAYTON, AND WOODLAND BEACH

Jess Hansen

ARCADIA
PUBLISHING

Copyright © 2013 by Jess Hansen
ISBN 978-1-4671-2033-3

Published by Arcadia Publishing
Charleston, South Carolina

Printed in the United States of America

Library of Congress Control Number: 2013934310

For all general information, please contact Arcadia Publishing:
Telephone 843-853-2070
Fax 843-853-0044
E-mail sales@arcadiapublishing.com
For customer service and orders:
Toll-Free 1-888-313-2665

Visit us on the Internet at www.arcadiapublishing.com

To my beautiful daughter Elizabeth, may you always follow your dreams.

Contents

ACKNOWLEDGMENTS

I would like to sincerely thank Randy Goss, photograph archivist at the Delaware Public Archives, for his time and effort in helping locate pertinent photographs.

Special thanks to Brooks Keen and the Duck Creek Historical Society for their warm welcome and access to their collections; Fire Chief Isaac Hankins and the Citizens' Hose Company No. 1, Inc., of Smyrna, for their time and effort in finding great views of Smyrna; and to the Town of Clayton for their willingness to share their town pictures.

My sincere appreciation to Brian Hill, Virginia Cubbage, Roy James Jr., Heather Jones, Brooks Keen, Preston and Thelma Knight, Ruth Ogden, and Phil Voshell for sharing their personal photograph collections for this work. Thank you to all who pointed me in the right direction and assisted me on my search for these important pieces of history.

Unless otherwise noted, all images appear courtesy of the Delaware Public Archives.

INTRODUCTION

In 1681, William Penn was granted land from the Duke of York in what would become Pennsylvania and Delaware. A year later, under Penn's direction, vast acres of lands were granted to persons living in the three lower counties (New Castle, Kent, and Sussex). In the 1600s, northern Kent County was a heavily wooded, soil rich stretch of land situated between the Delaware Bay and the colony of Maryland. Duck Creek, a tributary to the Delaware Bay, ran across the northern dividing line for the county.

Along this river, a religious group called the Friends, or Quakers, from Pennsylvania began meeting as early as December 1705 on a tract of land referred to as Gravesend. This portion of the tract, owned by Benjamin Shurmer, provided an ideal location for a village, and Salisbury was soon founded. Prior to 1718, there are records of parcels being sold in the area. The village of Salisbury grew to include stores and other businesses before the center of the settlement shifted to the village of Duck Creek, located directly on its namesake river.

It is hard to envision when looking at it today, but the creek served as a major transportation route to the Delaware Bay. Ephram Herman, who in 1680 cut a thoroughfare at the mouth of Duck Creek where it met the Delaware Bay, made all of this possible. This allowed large boats to have access to the channel. The entire existence of Salisbury, Duck Creek Village, and modern-day Smyrna emerged from the importance of this waterway. Large boats traveled into the creek to load grains and other materials for export to Wilmington, Philadelphia, and other points north for farmers. As the village grew, additional land was cleared for agriculture and dwellings. Unfortunately, the growth of the community was also its downfall. By clearing the land around the creek, the composition of the riverbed was compromised. Silt crept into the waters and created a shallower passageway. Over time, this prohibited the ability of larger cargo vessels to maneuver and make safe travel all the way to Salisbury. This shifted the transportation hub east to Green's Landing (Smyrna Landing today).

William Green took ownership of a tract of land referred to as Gravesend in 1680. This land made up a significant portion of what would become the town of Smyrna. After Green's death in 1708, his sons took possession of his property. Later, his grandson James Green inherited these lands from his father, Thomas. In 1768, James sold 15 acres to Samuel Ball of Philadelphia. This land was located at the intersection of the King's Road and the Maryland Road. This 15-acre corner was then called Ball's Corner. Soon after, others purchased the three remaining corners of this intersection, and businesses were built out of necessity. To accommodate the rural travelers taking their grains to Greens Landing, the Indian King Hotel was built near the corner that Samuel Ball dubbed "Duck Creek Crossroads."

It did not take long for Duck Creek Crossroads to become a vital location in Delaware. In fact, legislators met at Belmont Hall (the then home of Thomas Collins) and considered making Duck Creek Crossroads the capital of the new state. Although not officially incorporated as a town until 1817, the name was changed to Smyrna in 1792. Local lore claims this name was chosen because of Smyrna's historical importance in the grain industry in Turkey; Smyrna, Delaware, mimicked that with the large quantities of grain production in the Duck Creek Crossroads Village.

Duck Creek Crossroads was a booming center of important industrial and agricultural activity. Greens Landing served as a very important shipping center for exports of grain, produce, and livestock headed to Philadelphia. The Kings Road (what would one day become Route 13) traveled north and south through the state. Maryland Road ran east from Greens Landing all the way to Maryland.

Several significant Delaware citizens came from or settled in Duck Creek Crossroads/Smyrna. These people played important roles in the Revolutionary War, War of 1812, and the Civil War. Duck Creek inhabitants Daniel Cummins, a tavern owner from Smyrna, and Allen McLane, a Revolutionary War captain and spy for the colonists under Gen. George Washington, both signed the ratification for the Constitution as representatives of Kent County, Delaware. Capt. Isaac Griffin, who owned land west of the crossroads (in what is now Clayton), played a role in the standoff and capture of Cheney Clow. Soon after, he moved with his wife to Fayette County, Pennsylvania. It was rumored that he was forced to move after receiving an onslaught of death threats from Cheney Clow's faithful followers.

Commodore Jacob Jones, famed hero of the War of 1812, was born just outside of the village of Duck Creek. He was educated in Dover before joining the Navy. He commanded the US sloop *Wisp*. Col. Edwin Wilmer, originally from Smyrna, locally rose to fame during the Civil War as he announced the draft lottery on the steps of his grandfather's (George Wilson) house, called the Barracks, in Smyrna in 1863. Although no battles were fought here, Smyrna offered its share of men into the Delaware militias for all three of the early wars.

As the use of the railroads became more popular and cost effective, less and less exporting business went to Smyrna Landing. With the introduction of the railroad just outside of Smyrna, the pathways for farmers selling their grain and produce changed from traveling to Smyrna Landing and Woodland Beach to traveling to Smyrna Station (Clayton).

Throughout the turn of the 20th century, life thrived in small-town Smyrna. Ever popular, merchants and businessmen moved to set up shop in the growing village. Confectioneries, carriage builders, general stores, drugstores, barbershops, and even banks soon sprang up. The effect of illnesses, war, and depression were certainly felt in Smyrna, and several businesses were stung with the changes in economy. As the years have passed, however, Smyrna continued to grow. Through all of the changes, the sense of community stayed ever vigilant with help from neighborhoods, town organizations, churches, theaters, volunteer fireman's association, and related clubs. As with most small towns, carnivals and parades help to celebrate the local and national heritage and history and bring the townspeople together.

In an attempt to better connect the state for farming, industry, and passenger travel purposes, the Delaware Railroad Company was organized in 1852 under the guidance of John Middleton Clayton, a well-known Delaware senator from Kent County. The town of Smyrna was not interested in allowing the railroad to impede upon their booming commerce and shipping industry in Smyrna Landing. So, looking elsewhere, the Delaware Railroad Company surveyed Richard Tibbitt's land to the west of Smyrna in 1854 and, with his permission, started laying tracks. The Tibbitt land went from wooded farmland to a bustling railroad town within five years. Richard's father, James Tibbitt, originally acquired pieces of tracts from other landowners like Isaac Griffin and William Cummins. The closest village was a cluster of houses referred to as Jimtown, just a mile to the south. The Jimtown community consisted of a few homes, including "Aunt Betsy's," who sold cakes and beer to weary travelers on their route to Smyrna Landing. Richard Tibbitt was living in this community in the census records of 1860 with George Hodgson's family.

According to records, no homes were on this Tibbitt tract of land sectioned by the railroad. By 1857, the Philadelphia, Wilmington and Baltimore Railroad Company began using the lines as well, allowing for more train traffic, passengers, and transportation of goods. By 1859, lots were sold by Richard Tibbitt for a small railroad depot, a hotel, and a store. This stopping point was called Smyrna Station.

The Civil War claimed men from Smyrna Station. George Hodgson went into the 2nd Delaware Infantry (also known as the "Crazy Delawares") at the age of 34. A tailor by trade who lived near Jimtown, he enlisted in Smyrna in February 1862 for a three-year term. In June 1864, Hodgson was captured as a prisoner of war near Petersburg, Virginia. He, like thousands of other Union POWs, was transferred to Andersonville, Georgia, were he ultimately died in September of that year. Disease and filth were rampant at the prison that was built to house 10,000 prisoners. At one time, nearly 33,000 soldiers were encamped on the 26-acre facility. In November 1862, Richard Tibbitt found himself in Company F of the 6th Delaware Regiment. He was assigned guard duty for the railroad crossings in Havre de Grace, among other places.

In 1860, Alexander McConaughy, a storeowner and real estate agent in the new village of Smyrna Station, decided that a post office was needed. Taking it upon himself, he wrote to the post office department asking that an office be granted in the name of "Clayton" after the adored John M. Clayton. Clayton was a United States senator for the state of Delaware, a great orator, and a huge supporter of the railroad installation through his state. The Clayton House hotel opened for travelers on the railway, along with stores and other necessities. Homes, mostly for railroad workers, were built. The town was growing exponentially.

Richard Tibbitt's death only slightly complicated the growth of the town. Upon his father James's passing, Richard acquired a great deal of land that he then sold to the railroad, among others. However, after Richard's death in 1863 and with no direct heirs, his estate was contested by a cousin, James Whartenby, due to a clause in his father's will. James wrote his last will and testament to include an estate-tail, a British clause meant to keep property in the family. This wording left Richard to be the heir apparent, with no transferable interest in the property, meaning that Richard had no rights to sell or grant away any of said lands during his lifetime. He was merely holding the lands for his heirs to inherit. This proved problematic since he donated land used to create Smyrna Station along with selling other plots for business owners. In 1873, ten years after Richard's passing, the case made it to the Supreme Court of the United States (*Daniel v. Whartenby*, 1873), who sided with the old British law and turned over the entire property comprising the small town of Clayton to James Whartenby and Emma Harris, cousins and the only other living relatives as listed in the will of the deceased James Tibbitt. Whartenby paid his father and son attorney team, James A. Bayard and Thomas F. Bayard, with one quarter of the 173 acres of the town and then kindly resold each lot to those who had previously purchased land from Richard Tibbitt. This was a landmark case for the United States.

By the 1870s, the railroad town was bustling. In 1885, the Philadelphia, Wilmington and Baltimore Railroad Company officially moved their offices to Clayton and with it several railroad supervisors, express workers, laborers, and administrators. This meant the need for more hotels, lodging, new houses, and business for the town. The town of Clayton was officially incorporated and laid out in 1887. The community soon built several churches, a schoolhouse, and a town hall. Canneries and peach basket factories soon became major staples of the town. Clayton grew with many business owners working together to build the town. Many of the business owners in the early 1900s were also the men on the town council and school board and active members of local churches.

Later in the 20th century, the pace of the town slowed. The trains still went through town but the station was no longer an important stopping place. Trucking took over as a better transportation option. Houses and businesses on Main Street were torn down to create parking lots and expand other businesses. With an ever-growing population, the town has continued to retain its small-town feel.

Bombay Hook Island, located between the Duck Creek River and the Delaware Bay, held the best that central Delaware had to offer: great transportation abilities, marsh for crabbing, trapping, the bay for fishing, upland for hunting, and tillable ground for farming and orchard groves. Early Dutch settlers trapped, hunted, and cut the valuable salt hay that natively grew in the marsh as fodder for their cattle and livestock. In the center of rich Bombay Hook was Pearsons Cove Farm situated along the coast of the bay. That particular farm would eventually receive the name Woodland Beach, along with a flashy and spectacular story of both prosperity and hardship.

In 1675, Petrus Bayard was granted 600 acres of land on Bombay Hook Island by Governor Andros. This island lies along the eastern edge at the Delaware Bay. It was said that Bayard, overcome and grieved by the world around him, enjoyed his seclusion on Bombay Hook Island. In 1679, he formally purchased the entire Bombay Hook Island land rights from the Native Americans. Mechacksett, the sachem of the Kahansink, was the old Indian owner and proprietor of all that tract of land commonly called Bompies Hoeck (meaning little tree point in Dutch) by the settlers while the Native Americans called the same land Canaresse (meaning thicket). According to the *History of Delaware*, Bayard paid "one gunn, four handfulls of powder, three motts coats, and one anchor of liquor and one kettle" for this land. While Petrus eventually moved on, the Bombay Hook property remained in his family for generations.

From 1675 to 1812, the Bayard/Smith family held 5,000 acres of Bombay Hook Island, which included the Pearsons Cove Farm. After the death of Jonathan Bayard Smith, his lands fell into the Chancery Court, where the acres were divided and given to different Smith relatives. Those relatives in turn sold their lands to interested parties. Three men together purchased the majority of the parcels that made up the Bombay Hook property from the sheriff for $10,000 in 1860.

There are no official records of any churches at Pearsons Cove; however, there was one between Green's Landing and Bombay Hook. Started in 1783 on the road to Pearsons Cove, James Severson granted land for a Methodist Church. First called Carrolton and later Severson's Church, it continued to serve the Methodists living in the rural area. It was claimed that Francis Asbury even preached there in the 1700s, along with other circuit pastors. By the 1920s, the church was no longer used, and very little remains of it today.

Pearsons Cove sat on 540 acres of tillable land and beachfront property. This tract had several owners over the years, each with exciting plans for the beach town and personal connections to other thriving businesses. Becoming the famed Woodland Beach resort, it expanded from simple grain farming and hunting to railroads, steamships, hotels, and amusements. Still heavily agricultural, the lands around the resort continued to be farmed, hold livestock, and provide rich soil for apple and peach orchards.

As with any coastal community, the effects of large storms, rising coastal tides, and erosion took its toll on Woodland Beach. The hurricane of 1878 was truly of monstrous proportions. There were accounts of not only the roads washing out, but homes being moved off their foundations, livestock scrambling to stay atop shed roofs, and the destruction of large quantities of agricultural grain. The most lasting effect of this hurricane, however, is the impression that it made on the landscape.

Many people have tried to determine the exact downfall of the resort. Some blame the introduction of the automobile coupled with the natural causes and changes in the landscape that haunted nearby Collin's Beach to the north, while others still might just blame those mosquitoes and biting horse flies. The fact remains that after another large storm in 1914, Woodland Beach would never again enjoy the type of popularity it had once reveled in. Amid the weather and drastic environmental factors, the community could not continue the prosperity it once held, and the village returned to a peaceful location for seclusion and deep thought.

There was a renewed interest in the beach area from the 1930s into the 1960s for watermen. Today, the sleepy Woodland Beach community still attracts a small number of fisherman to the pier, owned and maintained by the State of Delaware.

One

Duck Creek Crossroads

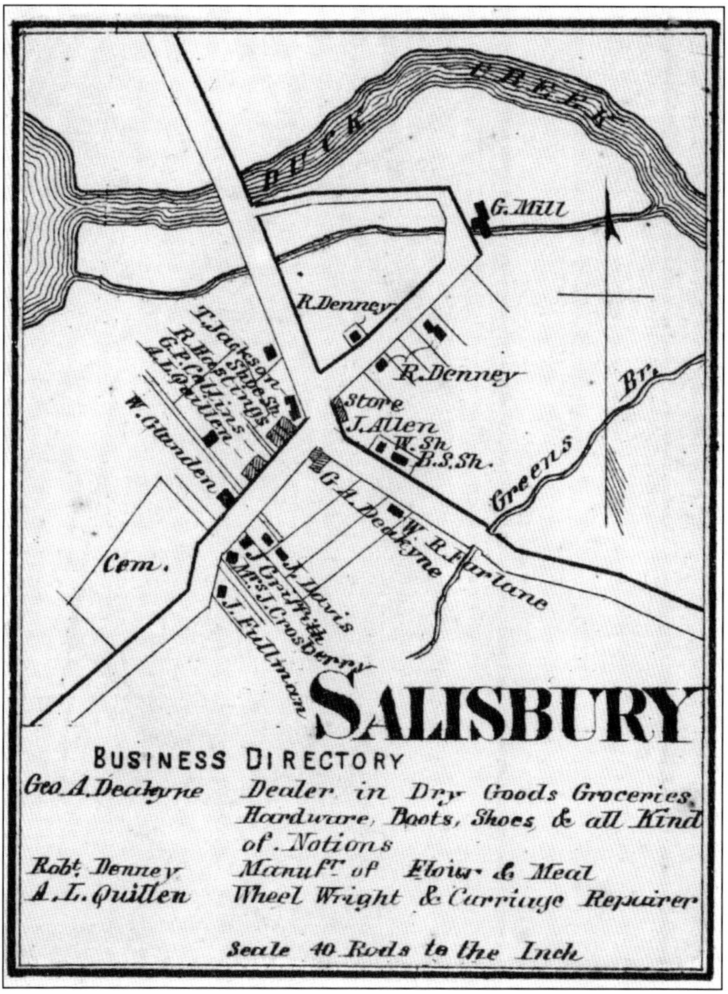

Salisbury was the first town settled in Duck Creek Hundred in Kent County. Benjamin Shurmer, who owned part of the tract called Gravesend, laid out the community prior to 1718. He saw the early potential for living along the Duck Creek and sold property to interested parties. The little village boasted two churches, several stores, a gristmill, and a blacksmith shop.

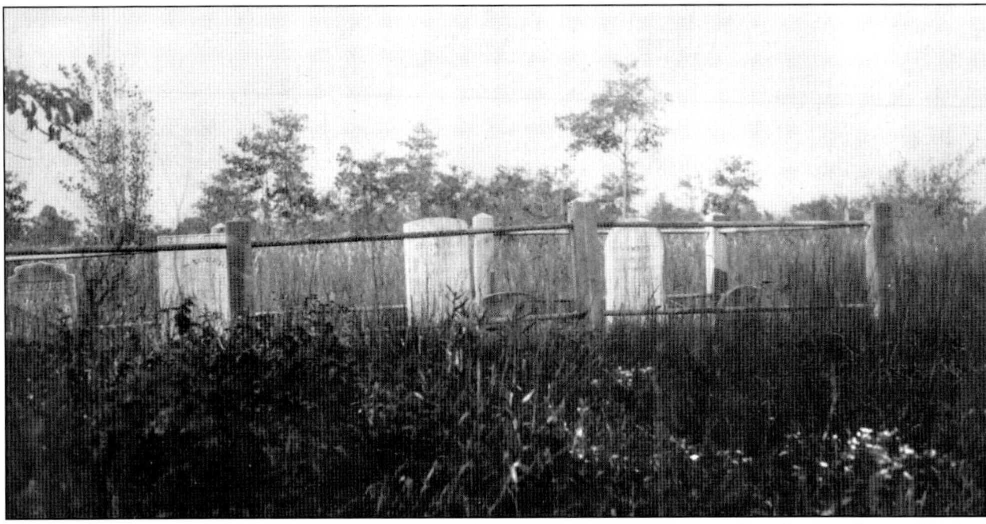

The Friends, Quakers from Pennsylvania, began congregating on Duck Creek in 1705. A meetinghouse and cemetery were soon built; the earliest grave was that of Elizabeth England, who passed away at only 17 years of age on March 18, 1708. In 1800, the Friends moved to the newly popular Duck Creek Crossroads community, where they remained until 1848. Afterwards, they moved to Camden, Delaware. The graveyard still remains in old Duck Creek Village.

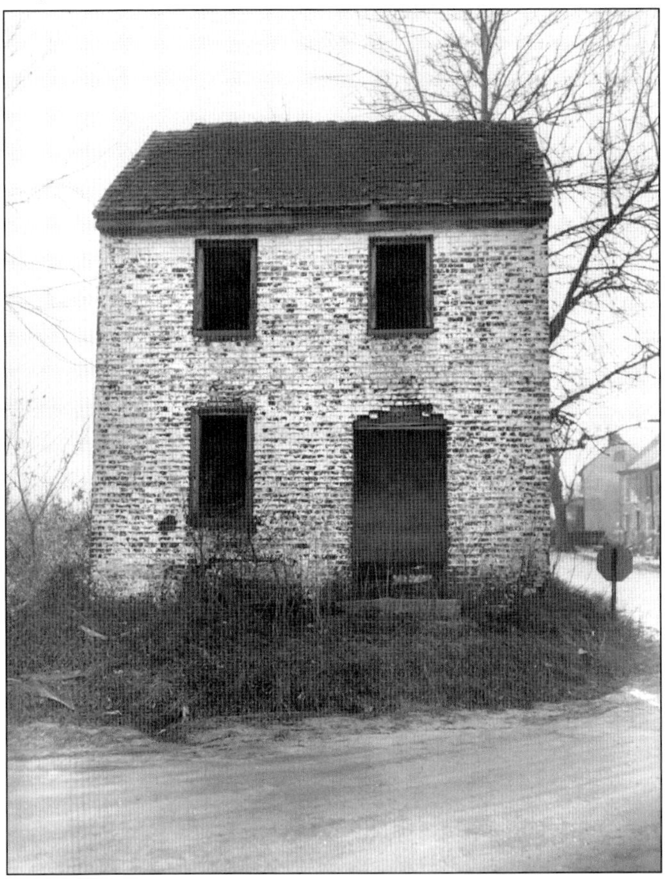

The first brick store in the village of Salisbury was built by Silas Spearman, presumably in or around the town layout prior to 1718. His store was on the southwest corner of the village crossroads. Spearman held the business for more than a generation. At left is a similar store that was located in the village of Duck Creek Crossroads. The photograph was taken in 1952, before the demolition of this structure.

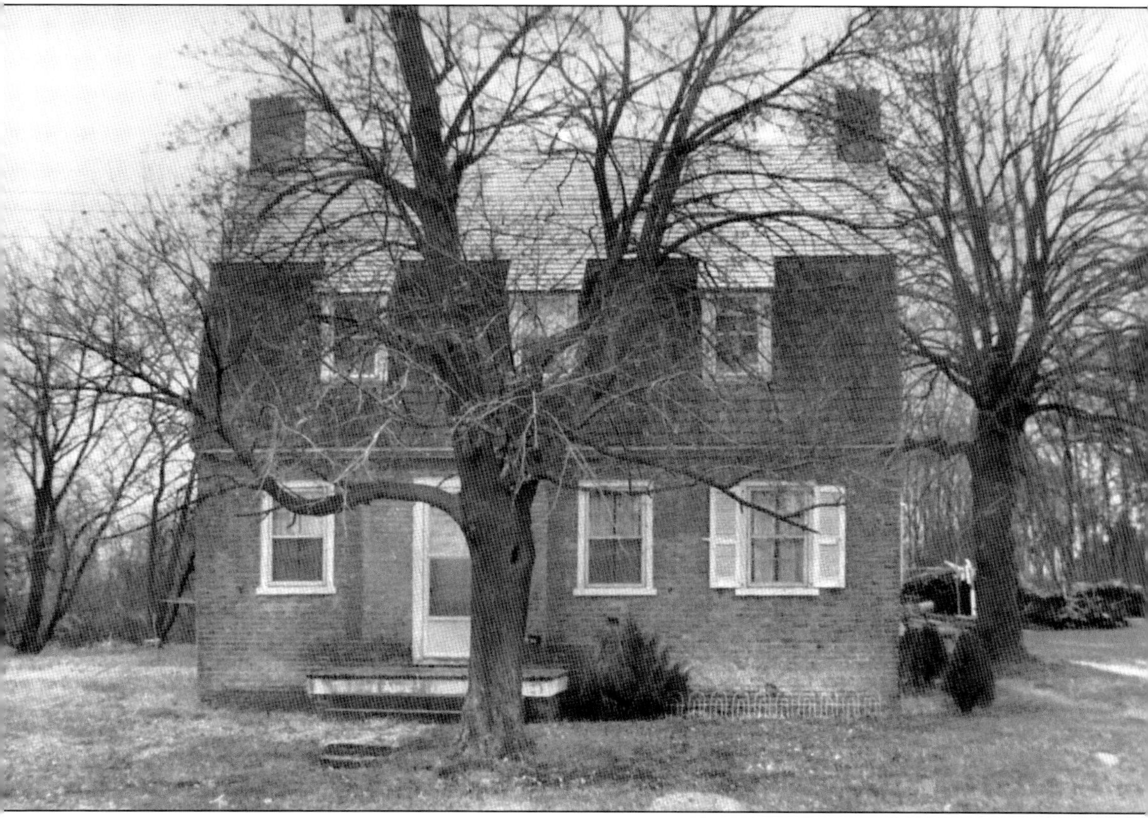

The Lindens is the only surviving dwelling of the original Duck Creek Village. The current structure, built sometime between 1725 and 1765, was constructed by John Swift of Philadelphia, who sold his home located near the head of "Ducke Creeke" in 1727. In 1840, the rear wing was replaced with an updated addition. The property contained a house as well as a water gristmill farther back on the property along the creek. Although it has gone by many names, it was best known as Denny's Mill. The miller lived in the Lindens and the date of the mill's use went back to 1717. The house was planned to be demolished in 1960 before the Duck Creek Historical Society stepped in and convinced the State of Delaware to allow the property to be preserved. The historic house is still in use.

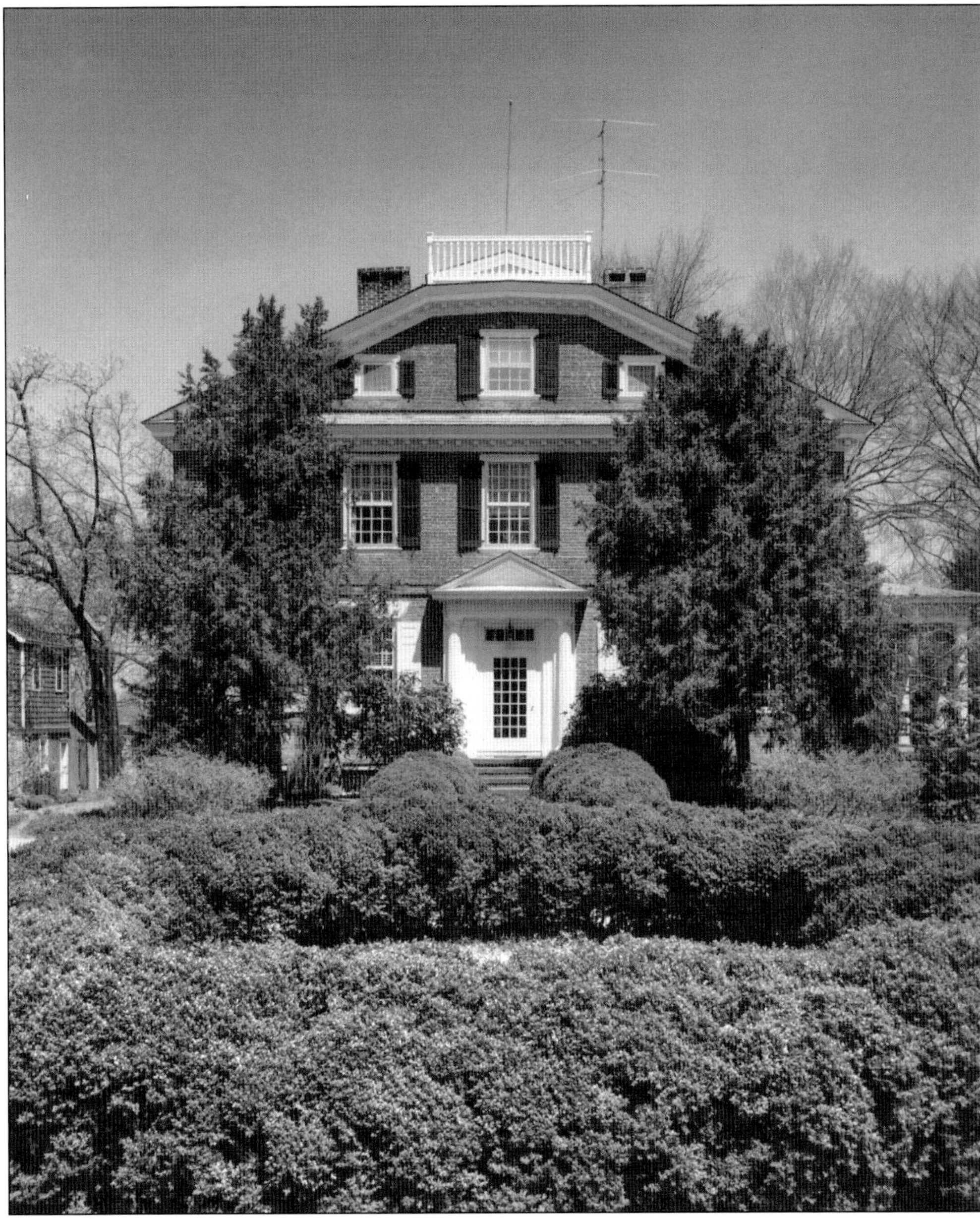

The original portion of Belmont Hall was built in 1686 as a two-story brick home on 600 acres of land situated on the Pearman's Choice tract. This land was granted to Henry Pearman by William Penn in 1684. By 1772, the property and grounds were owned by Thomas Collins, who renovated the house extensively. The name was officially changed to Belmont Hall in 1773. Collins, a lieutenant colonel in Caesar Rodney's militia, was promoted to brigadier general by Gen. George Washington and fought with General Washington in New Jersey in 1777. From 1772 until the official ratification of the federal Constitution in 1787, Belmont Hall was the location of many patriotic meetings, including the first meeting of the Delaware General Assembly in 1776, as Collins sat as the governor of Delaware from 1786 until his death in 1789. The property stayed in the Collins family, eventually being inherited by Caroline Speakman, who installed 20 acres of gardens and strongly encouraged residents to enjoy picnics at the "Belmont Park and Gardens."

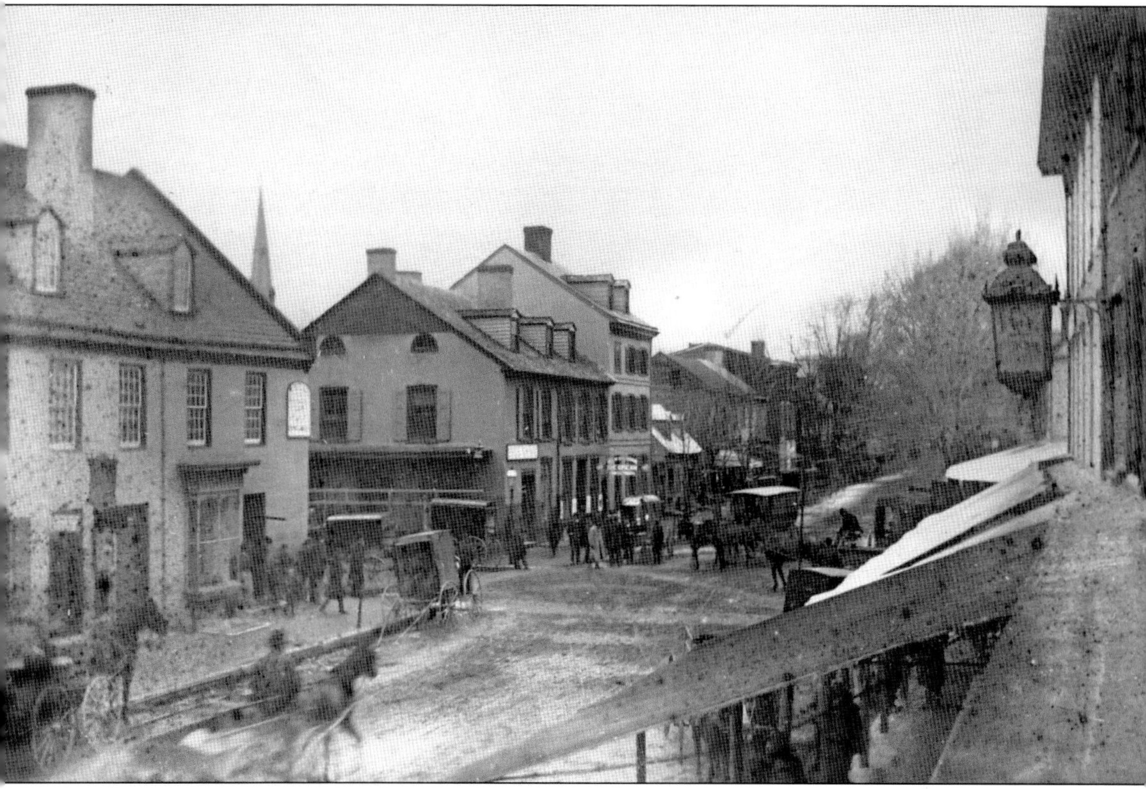

When Samuel Ball purchased the wooded southwest corner property on the boundary of the Gravesend tract (marked by the intersection of Maryland Road and the Kings Highway) from James Green in 1768, he sparked the central shift from Duck Creek Village to Duck Creek Crossroads. While the villages of Salisbury and Duck Creek remained in existence at that time, the hub of the activity was now at the Crossroads. Ball, a merchant from Philadelphia, built a store on the corner lot. The building shown to the lower left was constructed over the old original store when the Kings Highway was shifted to High Street. The intersection proved to be an ideal location for travelers to stop off for supplies, food, and wares. Soon, other businesses were started in and around the crossroads. The town of Smyrna was born. This photograph was taken c. 1900. (Courtesy of the Duck Creek Historical Society.)

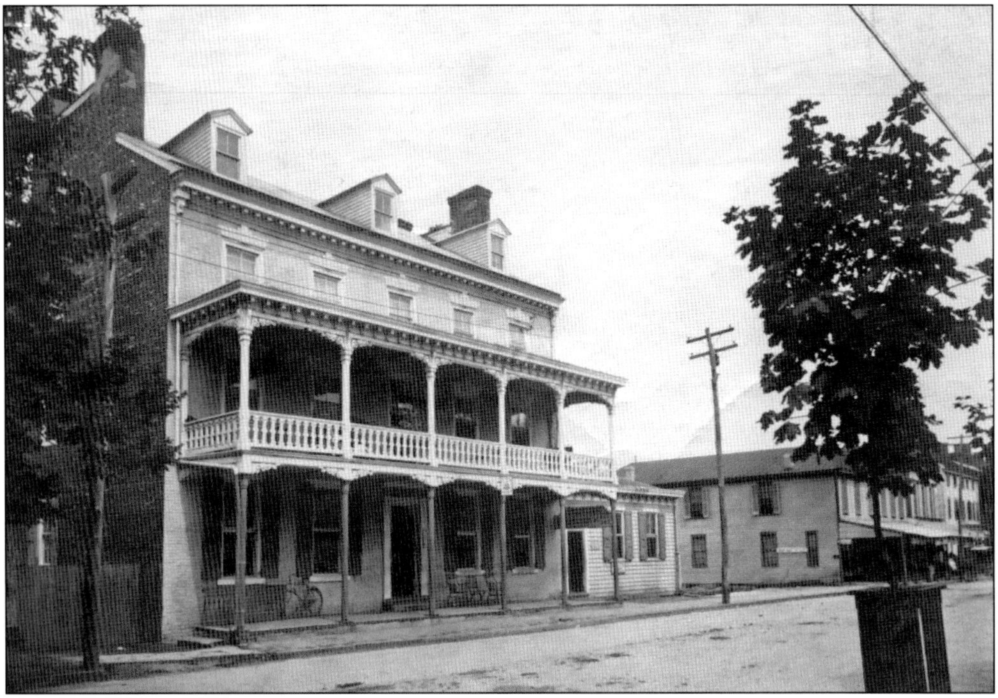

The Smyrna House hotel was built in 1787, just south of the Duck Creek Crossroads intersection. Originally the Indian King Hotel, it accommodated traveling merchants and steamboat pilots. The hotel was first owned by Thomas Hale and had a succession of proprietors before its demolition. The icehouse and stables were located next door behind the building. (Courtesy of the Duck Creek Historical Society.)

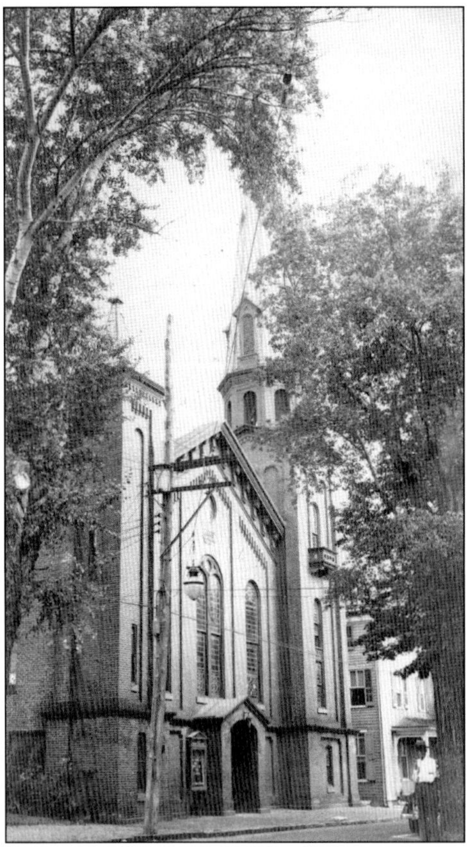

The Reverend Francis Asbury gave a sermon in an orchard near Duck Creek Village in 1780. By 1786, the Asbury Methodist Episcopal Church was built on the corner of Church Street in Duck Creek Crossroads on land donated by Allan McLane. The congregation moved to Mount Vernon Street in 1844, where they met until a fire devastated the building in 1869. They have continued services ever since their reopening in 1872.

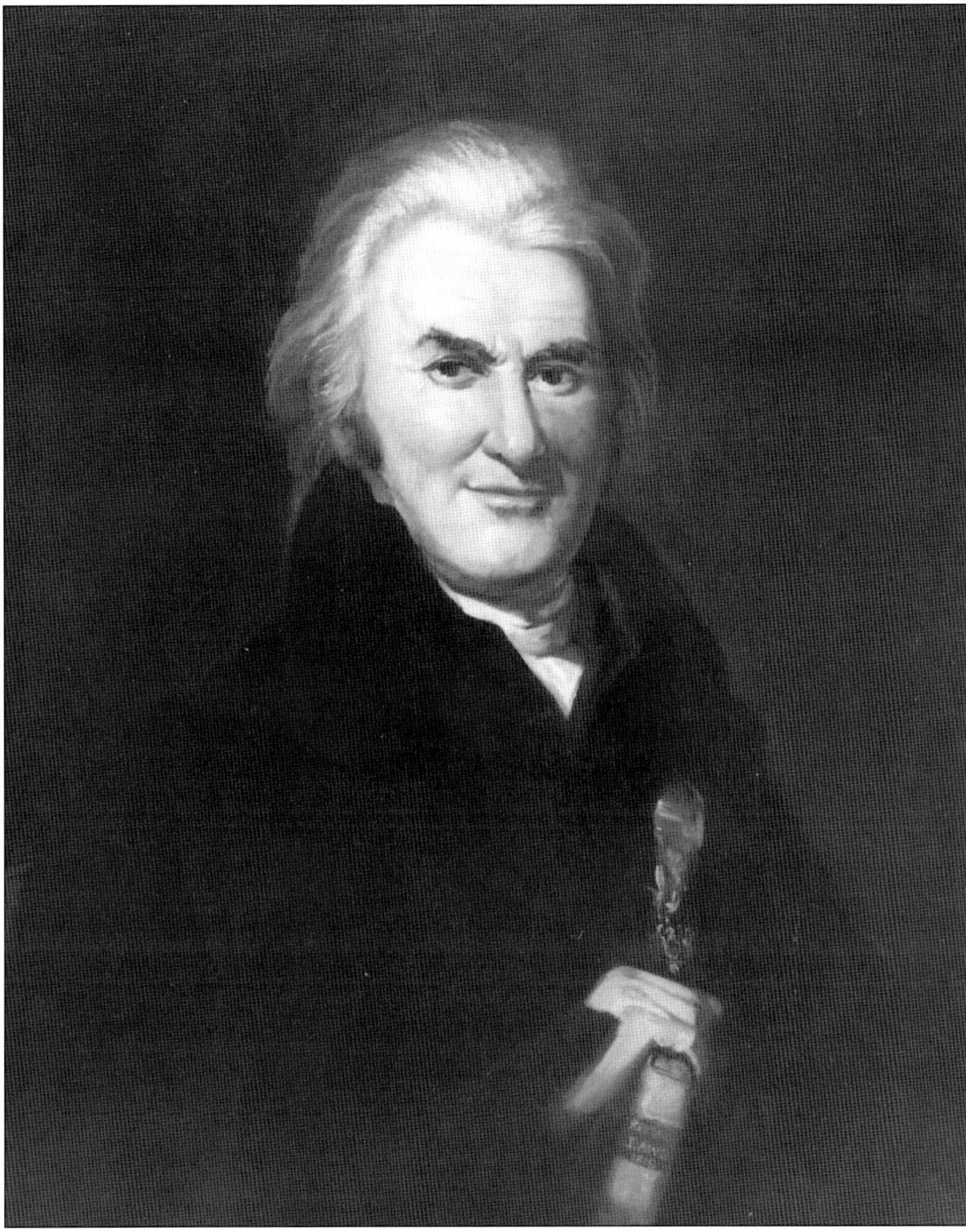

Allen McLane was born in Philadelphia in August 1746. As a young man, he relocated to Duck Creek Crossroads, where he enlisted as a lieutenant in the Delaware militia under Caesar Rodney in 1775. Lieutenant McLane went on to fight for Gen. George Washington, who had McLane dress as a spy (which sometimes included dressing as a woman) for the Continental Army to learn British secrets. The intelligence gathered helped General Washington avoid battles, and as a result, McLane was made a captain in 1777. While away at war, his wife moved out of Duck Creek Crossroads, only to return after his fighting finished. They rented a home on the corner of Mount Vernon and Market Streets. Captain McLane served as a delegate to ratify the federal Constitution for Delaware in 1787, as speaker of the house for the Delaware Assembly, and then as appointed tax collector for the City of Wilmington, where he resided until his death.

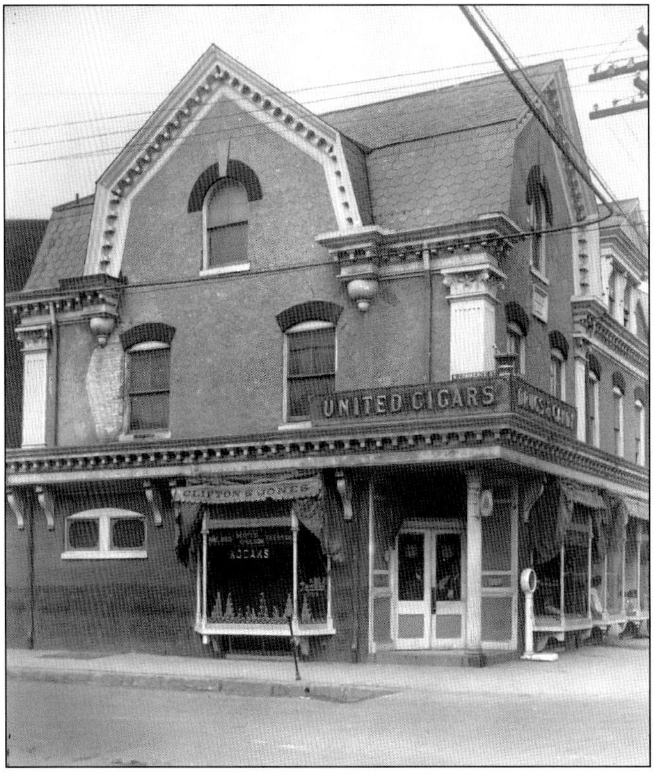

Ebenezer Blackson and Richard and Susan Holding owned the store on the northwest corner of the crossroads in 1810. The property went to Jacob Raymond in 1824, who demolished and rebuilt the business, following Federal-style architecture. Raymond, with John Clifton, ran an apothecary, complete with a marble soda fountain counter in the corner spot. Later, this became the Clifton and Jones Drugstore and was drastically remodeled.

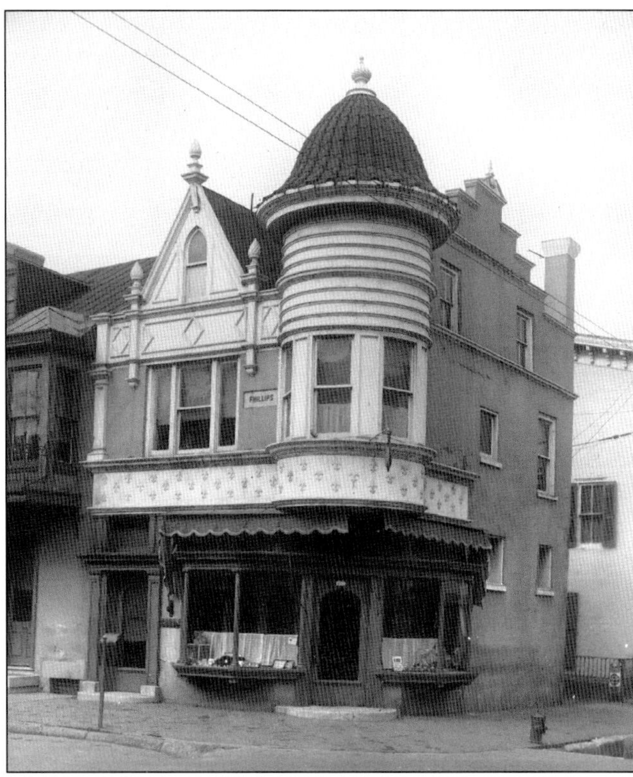

Robert Patterson originally owned this building, along with a string of others next to it on the northeast corner of the crossroads. In 1890, new owner Linwood Phillips completely renovated the outside. Phillips kept a jewelry store on the bottom floor and office space and living quarters upstairs. The building next door was a rumored tavern that faced Kings Highway, which today would be the alley behind the Phillips Building.

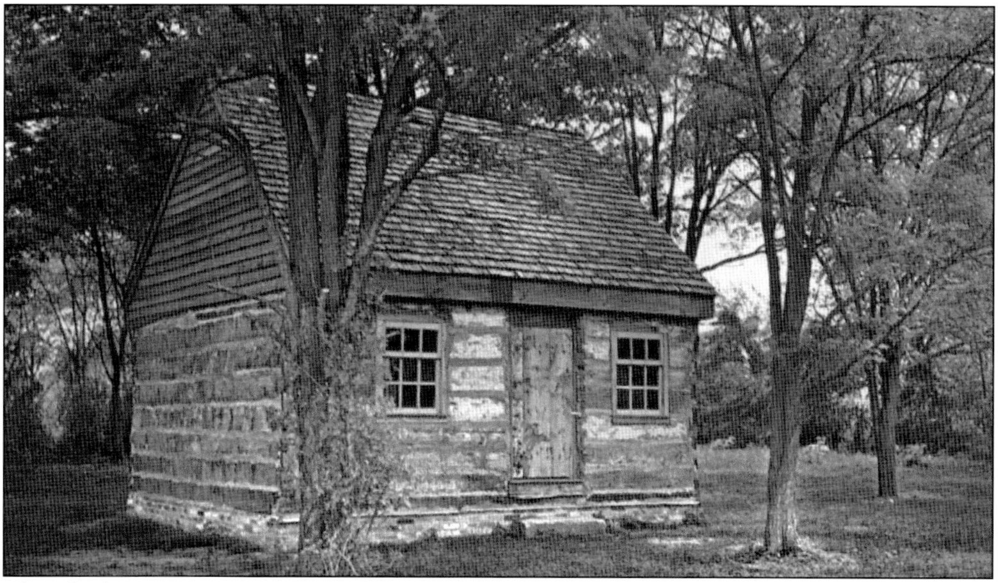

The Plank House was constructed around 1790 and sat just north of Duck Creek Crossroads. The home, possibly of a merchant or artisan, consists of a one-room layout and upstairs loft for sleeping. A wonderful example of early architecture, the house was constructed of wide plank beams with dovetail corners. This rare example of early construction was well preserved and hidden from view until it was discovered inside another structure on the east side of North Main Street during demolition in 1962. The Plank House was taken apart and moved to the Lindens property in Duck Creek Village, where it was reassembled. Over the years, environmental elements took their toll on the historic home. In 1999, it was again taken apart and moved. It now rests behind the Barracks on the grounds of the Smyrna Museum, where it has been restored and is available to tour.

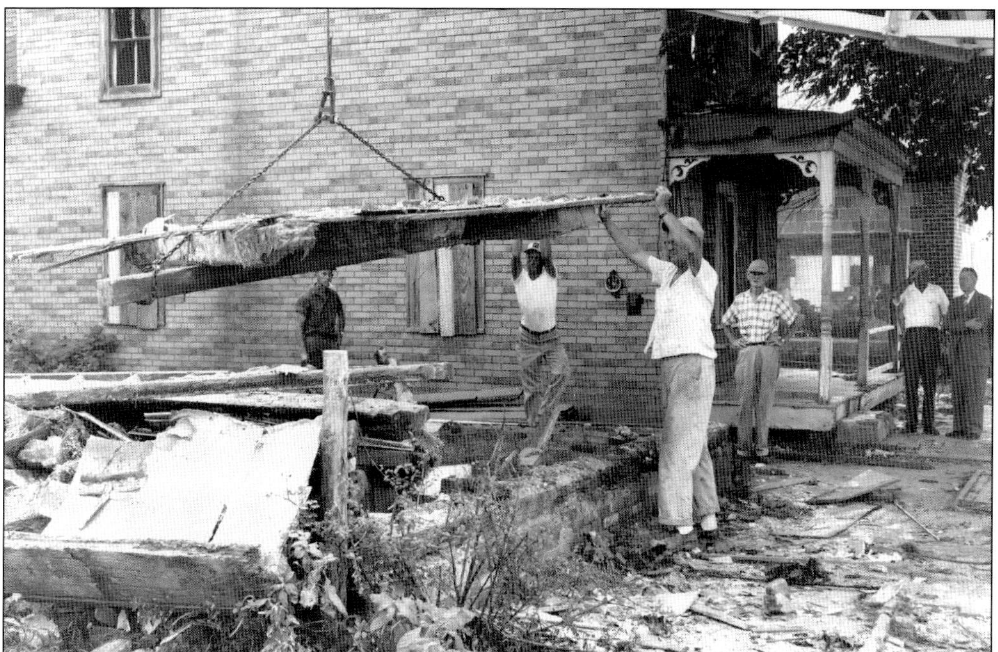

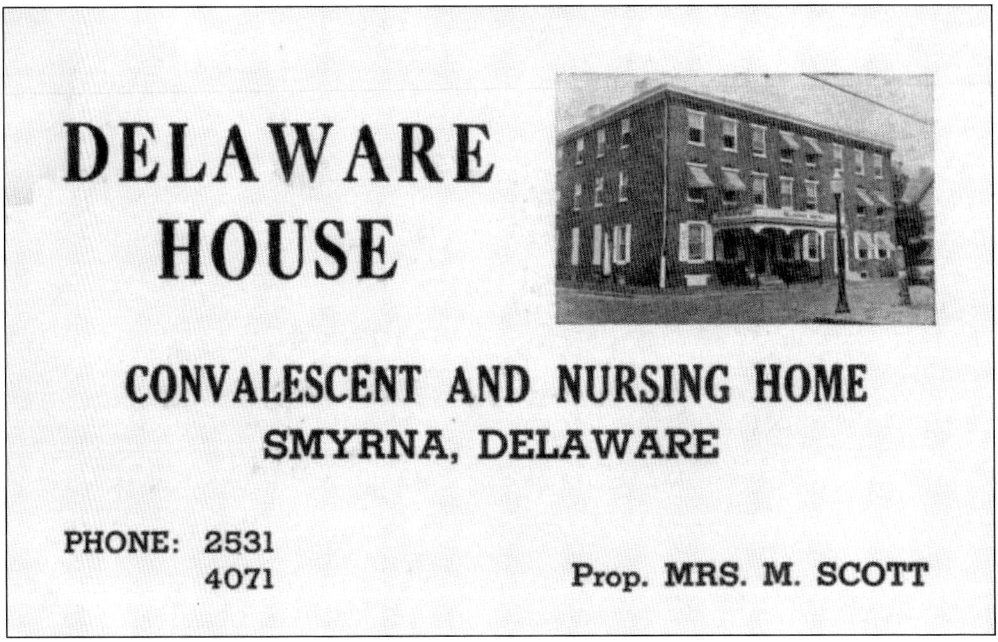

The Delaware House was built in 1817 by Robert Patterson as his personal home on the northern end of High Street (Main Street). In 1837, the very large double home was opened as the Steamboat Hotel by Thomas Jackson, for steamboat operators coming into Smyrna Landing. It was not known as the Delaware House until 1856, when it was extensively renovated by Dr. Samuel Fisher. According to legend, the Delaware House served as a rallying place for Confederate sympathizers during the Civil War. In 1944, the building was converted into a nursing home by Mary Scott. The building still stands and serves as private residences. (Above, courtesy of the Duck Creek Historical Society; below, courtesy of the Citizens' Hose Company No. 1, Inc.)

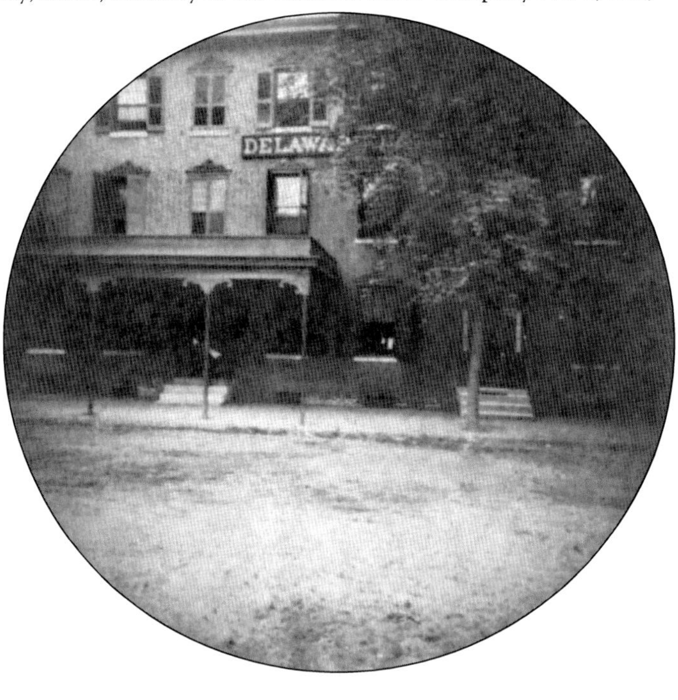

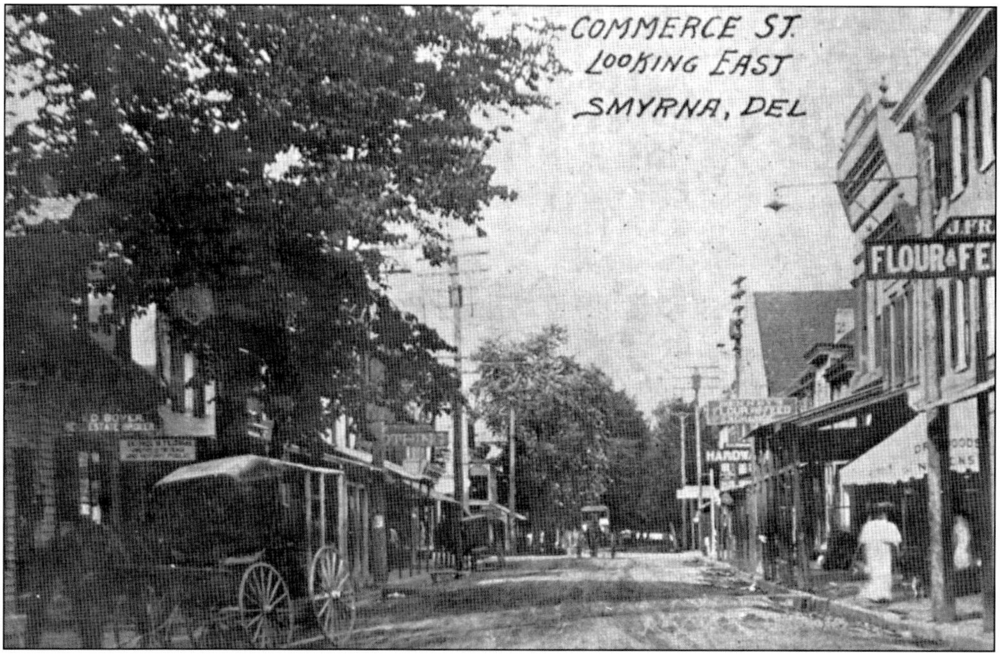

The popularity of the new official town of Smyrna, incorporated in 1817, grew by leaps and bounds. Soon, much of Commerce Street was lined roof to roof with much needed businesses, such as manufacturers, carriage makers, physicians, general stores, drugstores, and even real estate agents. During this time, it was customary for shops to be kept on the bottom floor while the business owners lived on the upper floors with their family.

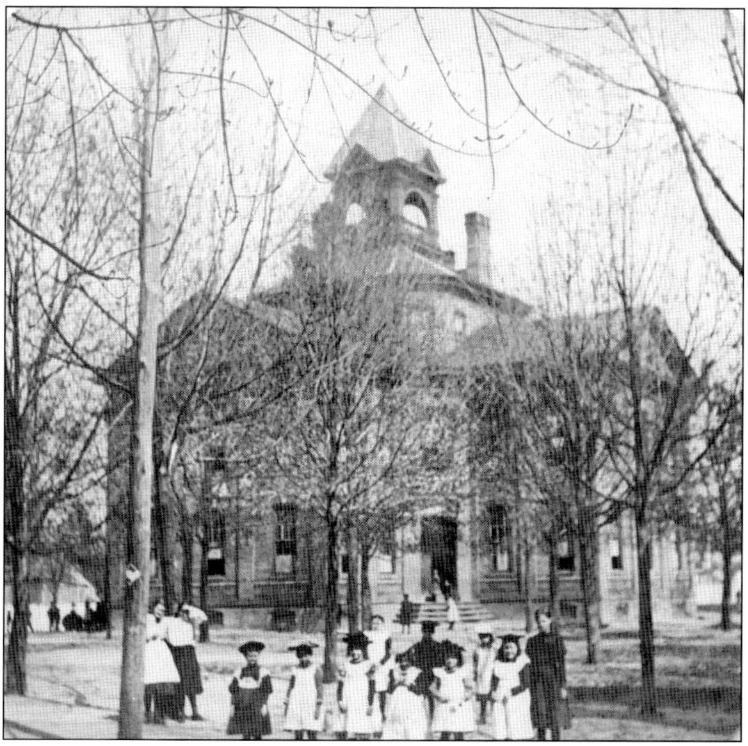

The first free school in the newly named Smyrna was started in 1818 on Commerce Street by Anne Spruance, Mary Patterson, and Ann Patterson. A succession of schools followed the first, and eventually, in 1884, the first centralized school was built in a field on South Street. This school, as shown here, cost $14,980 to construct. The South Street school celebrated the first class graduation with five students in 1885. (Courtesy of the Duck Creek Historical Society.)

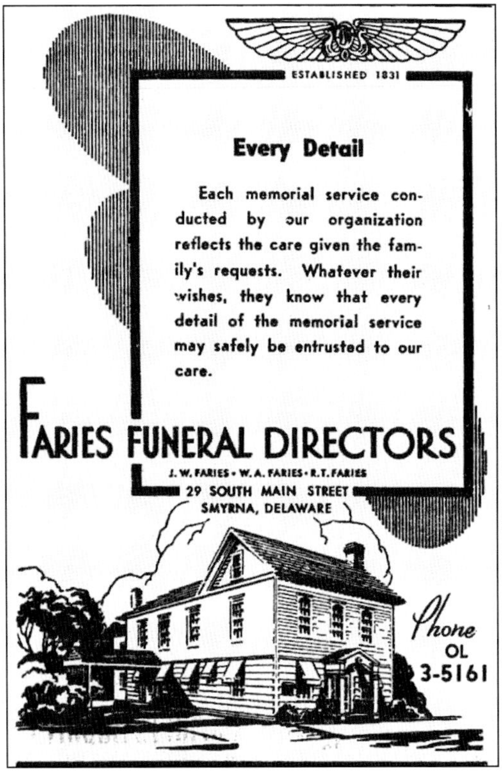

Faries Funeral Home is the oldest funeral business in Delaware. Started in 1831 as a furniture and undertaking business, it was run by William A. Faries and his brother. Although they were known for selling high-quality furniture, they shifted their focus to coffins, offering embalmment and other funeral services as the demand rose and their reputation as capable gentleman proceeded them. The company has continued through the years in the same building on Main Street. The structure has been renovated, updated, and enlarged.

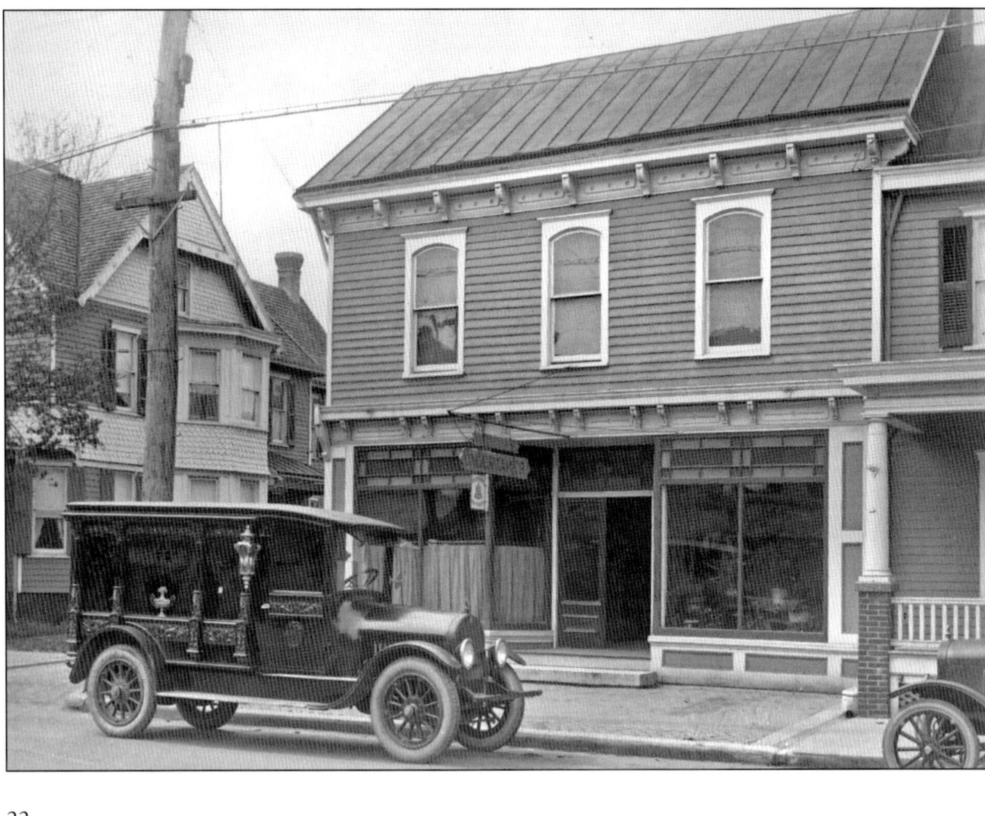

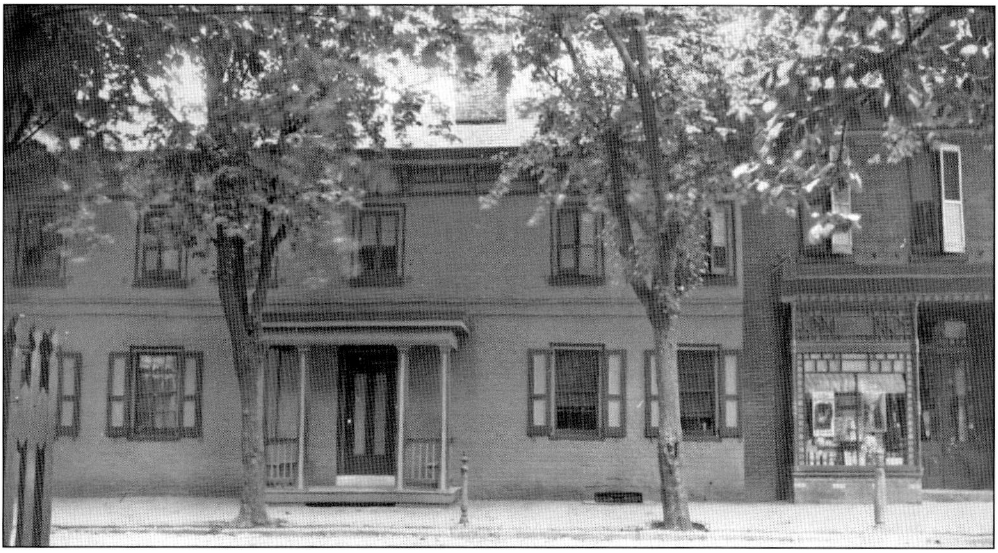

The Barracks was built by George Wilson around 1790 on High Street (Main Street), just south of the Four Corners. Here, in August 1863, Col. Edwin Wilmer conducted the Civil War Lottery. At the turn of the 20th century, the building was owned by James P. Hoffecker, a pharmacist who ran a drugstore adjacent to the historic house. The pharmacy wing was demolished in the 1970s. (Courtesy of the Duck Creek Historical Society.)

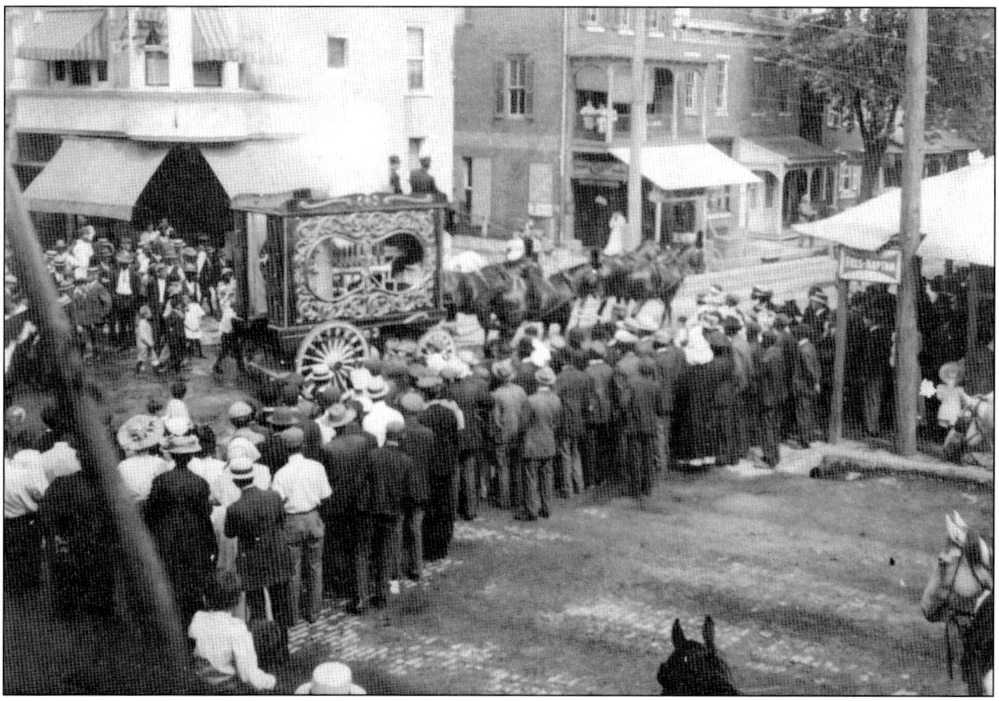

Residents of the town of Smyrna rallied to watch a parade go through town. This photograph shows the Four Corners looking east on Commerce Street. The Phillips Building is evident, along with a portion of the overhang attached to the lesser photographed J.B. Cooper Building on the opposite corner. John Cooper ran a general store in the crossroads. An advertisement for Fels-Naptha soap is visible on their canopy.

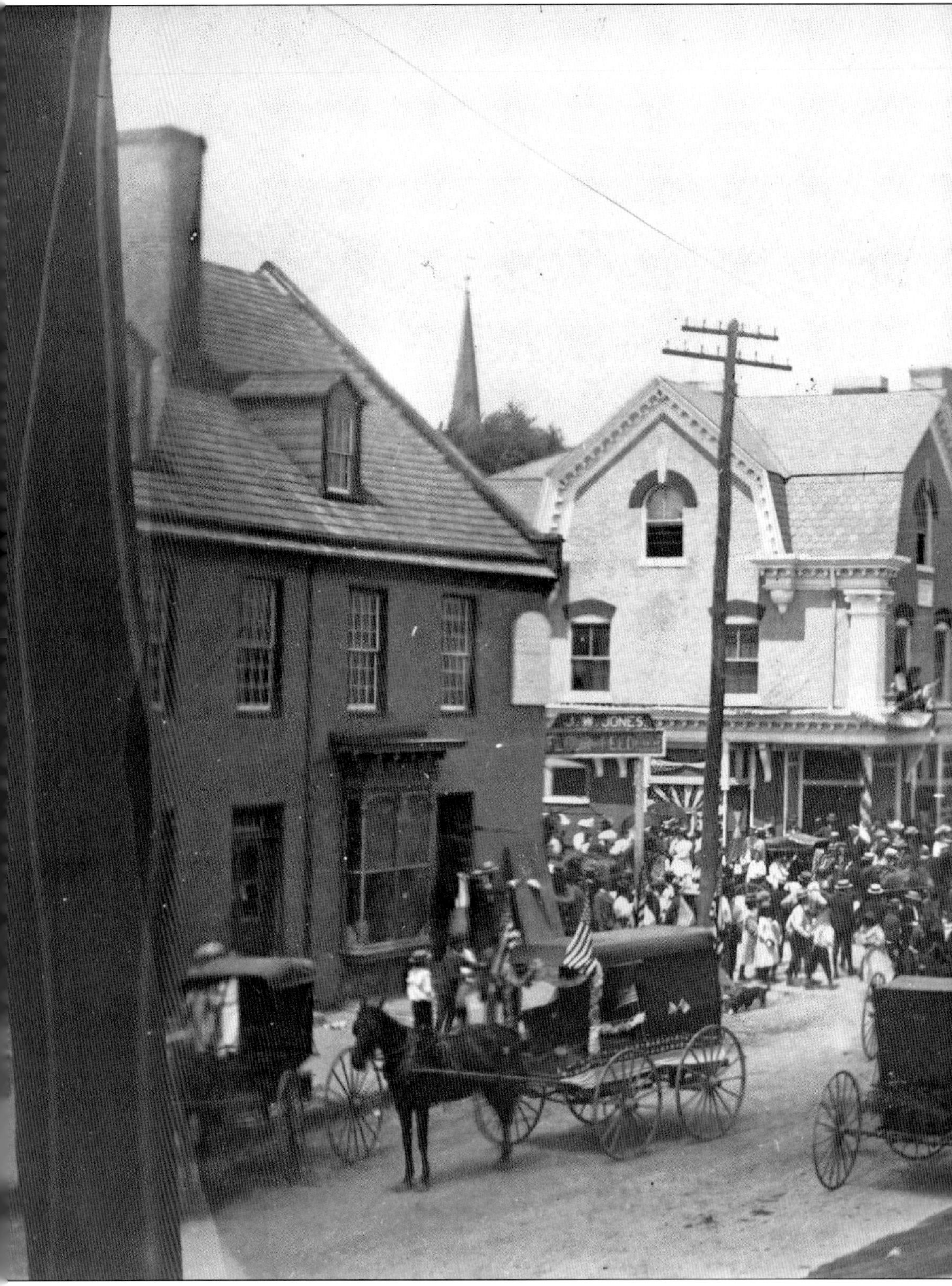
J. W. JONES

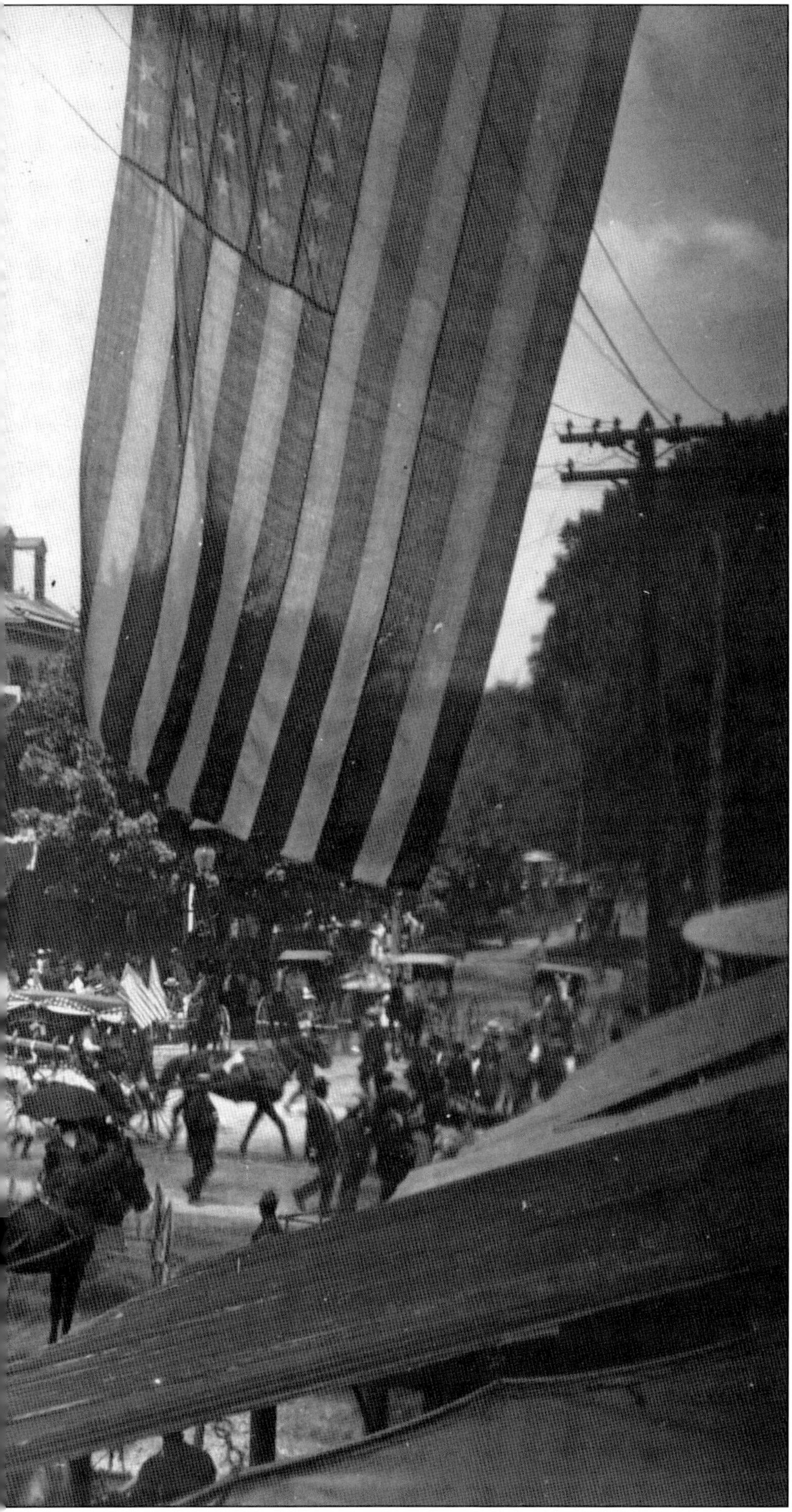

Smyrna's Four Corners provided a perfect hub between Smyrna Landing and the Maryland state border. Travelers could rest from their trek east to the landing, while other travelers and businessmen coming from Philadelphia could come into town from their docking point on the landing for much needed supplies and relaxation. The town grew to be quite self-sufficient, with merchants selling anything under the sun. Pictured here is a Fourth of July celebration and parade in the crossroads. Ball's Corner is to the left, while the Clifton and Jones Drugstore is straight in the middle of this photograph, taken in 1900. (Courtesy of the Duck Creek Historical Society.)

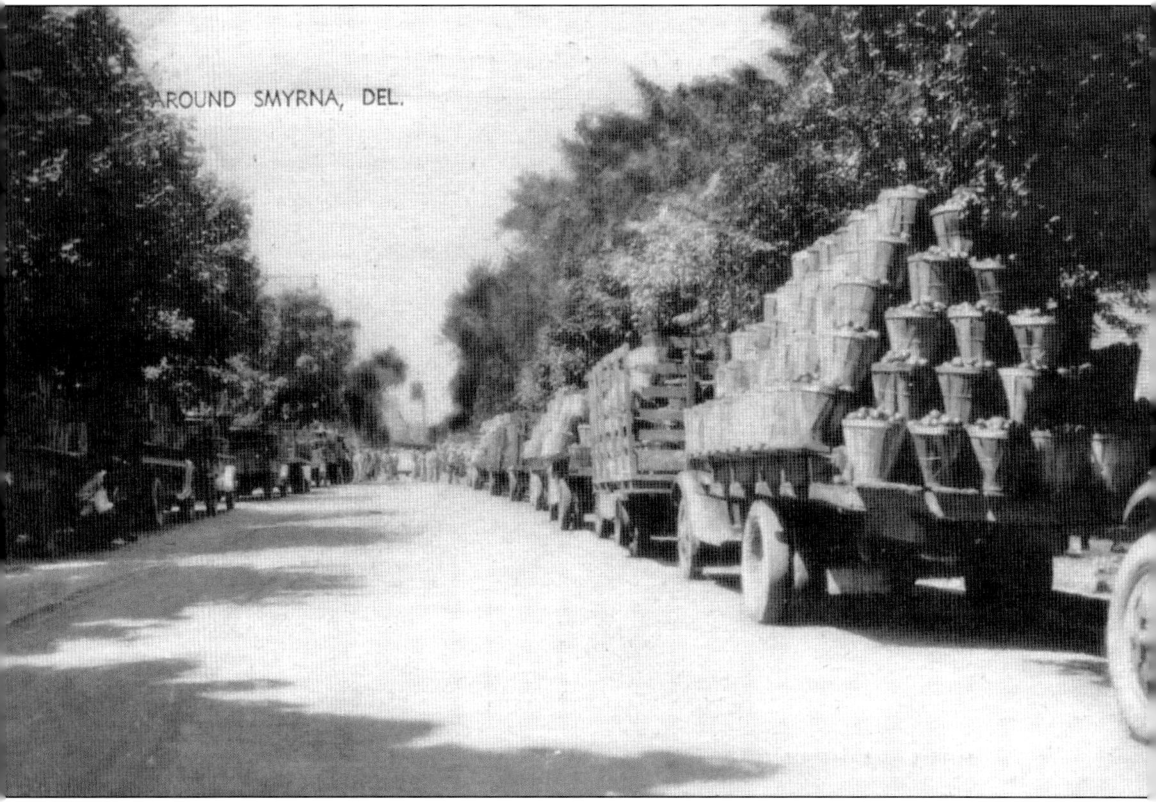

Peaches were first brought to Delaware in the 1600s by Spanish settlers. The trees grew well in Kent County's fertile soil. In 1840, Simon Spearman, renting a farm near Kenton, shipped the first harvest of peaches off to be sold at market. The demand for peaches rose so high that subsequent farmers in Kenton and Duck Creek Hundred planted large orchards of the fruit for profit. Spearman, son of shop owner Silas Spearman in the village of Salisbury, kicked off a booming industry for the area. Growing peaches, making baskets for peaches, hauling peaches, transporting the crop, canning them, and then finally selling them gave jobs for many Duck Creek Hundred residents over the next 60 years. In fact, Delaware became the number one peach exporter in the country, with Duck Creek Hundred producing the most in the state. In 1900, however, a disease called yellow blight attacked most of the peach crops and the local industry never recovered. (Courtesy of Brooks Keen.)

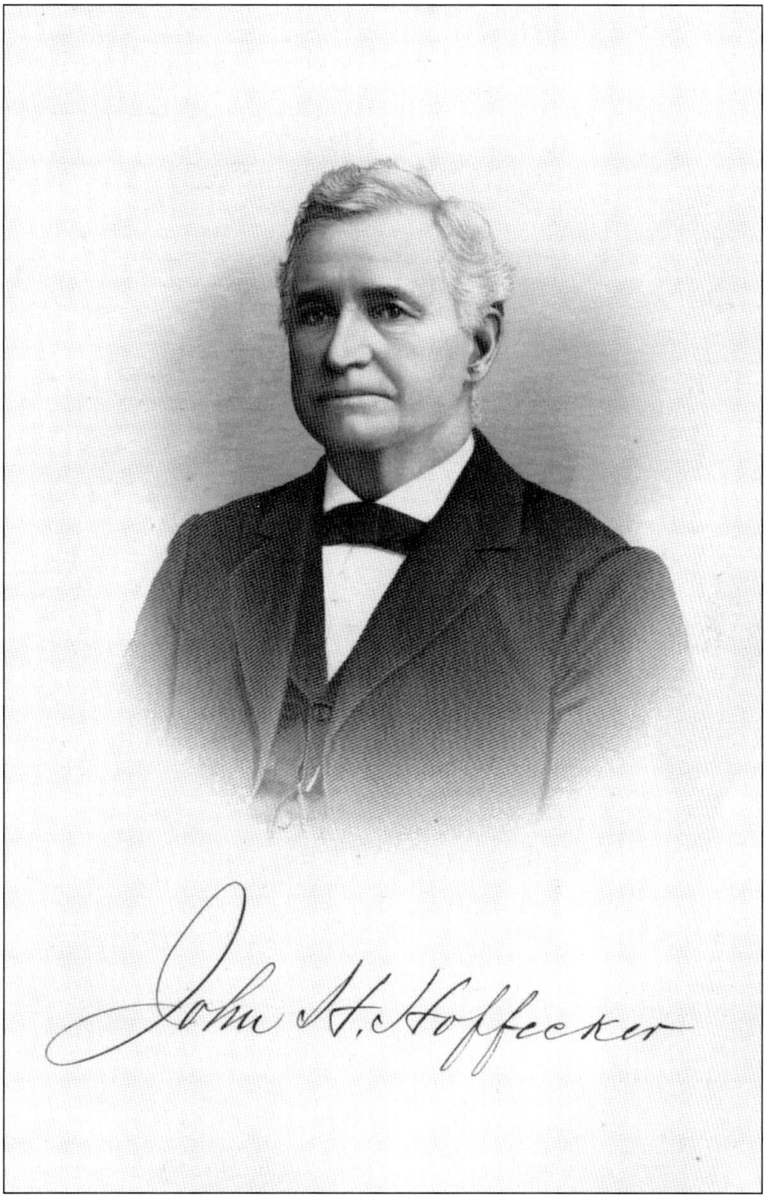

John H. Hoffecker was born the oldest son of Joseph Hoffecker and Rachel VanGasken in September 1827. John's grandfather, Henry Hoffecker, immigrated to Duck Creek from Germany sometime before 1800 and settled into farming. John started out on the farm he inherited from his father, turning it into a fruit orchard. He soon expanded into the business world of Smyrna, joining his brother Joseph in the first canning business in Smyrna. John became president of the Fruit Growers National Bank, president of the Philadelphia and Smyrna Transportation Company, director of the Delaware Railroad Company, president of the school board, and director of the Kent County Mutual Fire Insurance Company as well as director of the Smyrna Building and Loan Association. Speaking to the Delaware General Assembly after John Hoffecker's passing, a senator from Georgia stated that "He [Hoffecker] showed a disposition to build up and benefit his community." There may have never been a single Smyrna citizen that contributed more to his town than John H. Hoffecker.

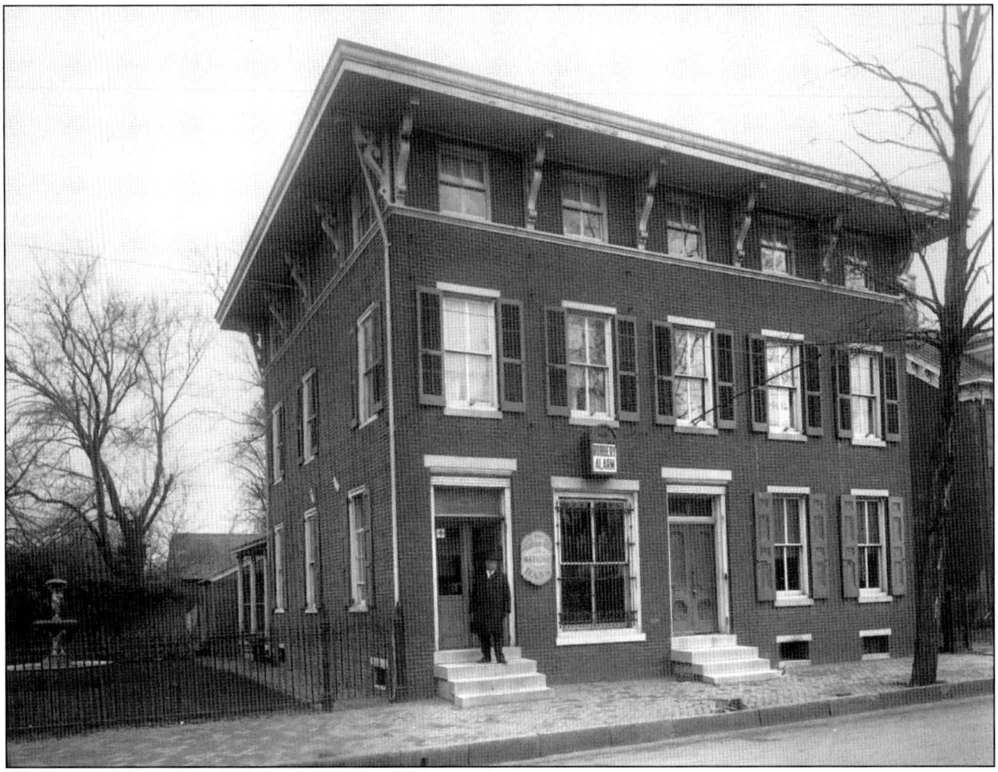

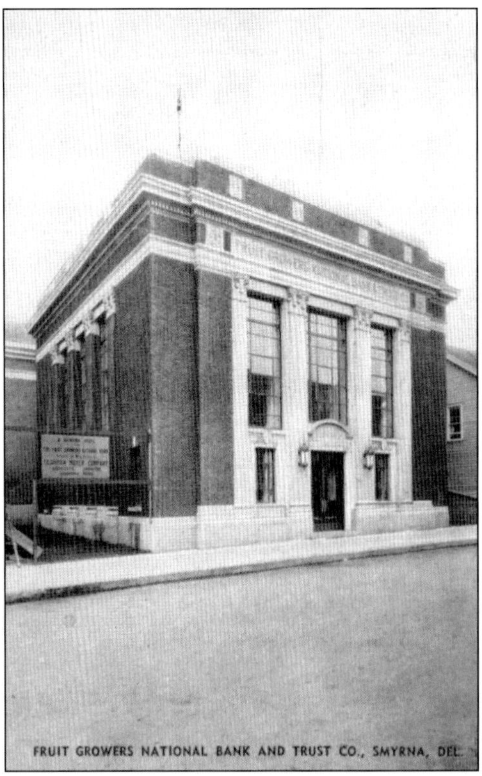

The Fruit Growers National Bank and Trust Company was officially incorporated in June 1876, initially operating out of a portion of John H. Hoffecker's residence in Smyrna until the home was completely converted for business use in 1880. Hoffecker surely had personal interest in the financial institution, being a farm and cannery owner himself. Walter O. Hoffecker (John's son) sat as president of the Fruit Growers National Bank and Trust Company for 30 years. In 1926, the bank moved to a brand new large building on Commerce Street, near the crossroads intersection on the side of Ball's Corner. This building now houses Citizens Bank.

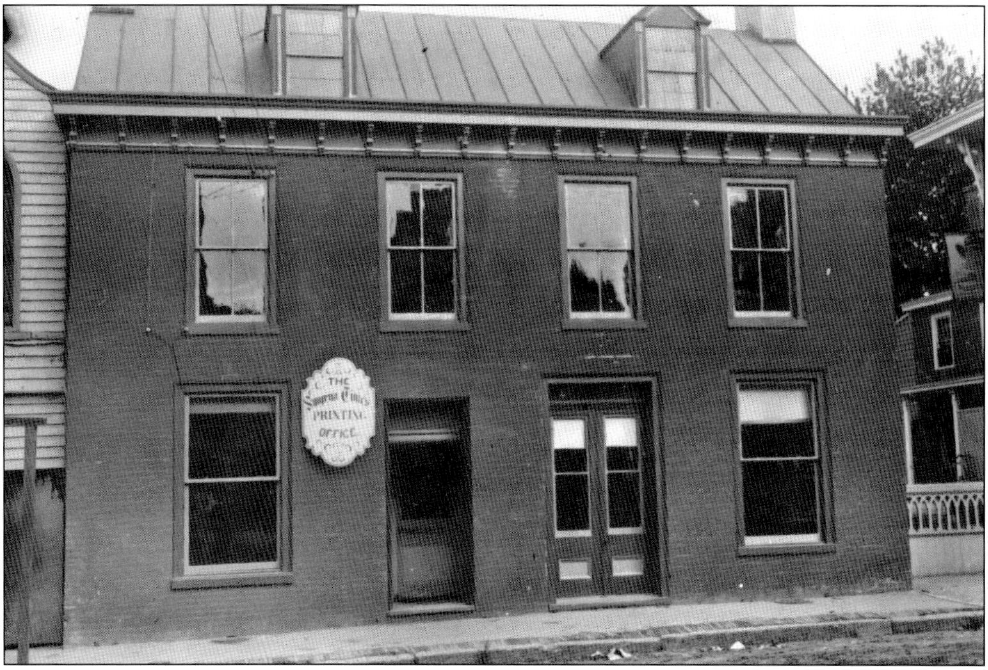

The first Smyrna printed newspaper debuted in 1832 as the *Delaware Star*. In 1839, Samuel Jones created the *Smyrna Telegraph* before falling into debt and being jailed in 1847. The paper was taken over by a few temperance men advocating for prohibition and was published by Abraham Poulson. Eventually, Poulson took over the paper and changed the name to the *Delaware Herald and Peninsula Advocate*. His son Thomas purchased his father's company, and partnered with Robert D. Hoffecker in 1854. Later that year, Hoffecker officially changed the name of the publication to the *Smyrna Times*. He purchased the above building, originally the home of Judge Isaac Davis, in 1896. Between Robert, his brother Joseph, and his son Robert Jr., the Hoffeckers ran the *Smyrna Times* for 92 years before selling it to a longtime employee in 1946. (Above, courtesy of the Duck Creek Historical Society.)

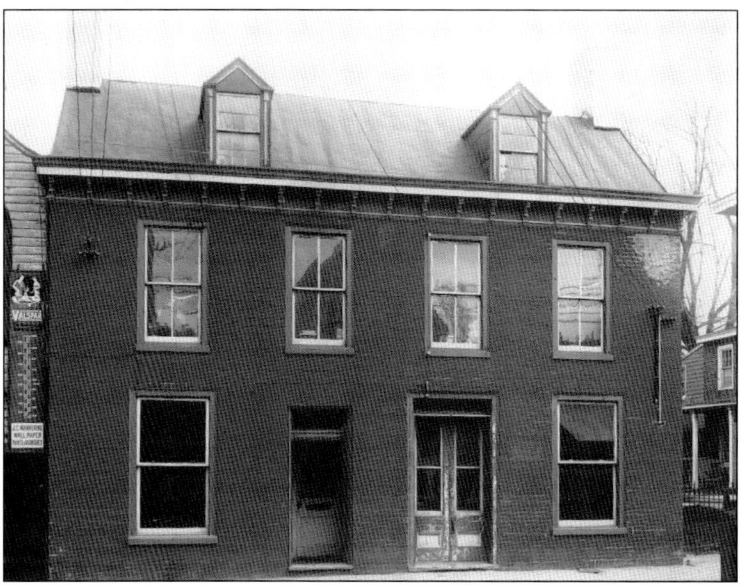

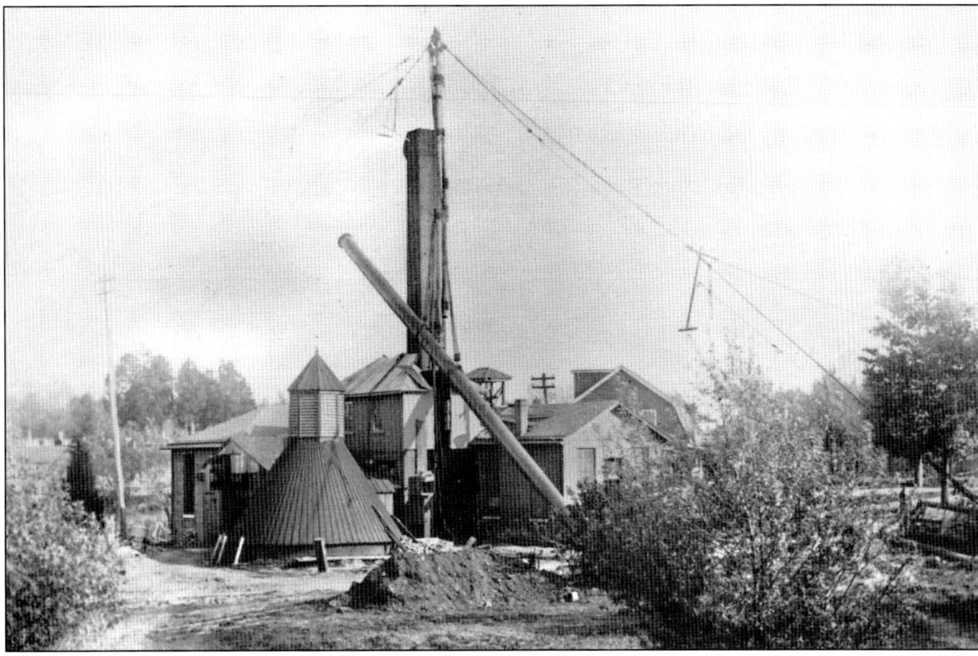

The Smyrna Coal, Coke, and Gas Company was started to help light up the busy town 40 years after the town was officially incorporated. Their process included turning rosin, and later coal, into gas to be used as fuel. Beginning in 1860, gaslights were installed in the town, and by 1880, there were 47 gas lamps illuminated by almost three miles of gas lines. The water works building was located near the gristmill, along the millrace to Lake Como. The standpipe erected there used two Gordon and Maxwell duplex compound steam force pumps, and it was thought that the natural well the pipe fed from was inexhaustible. John H. Hoffecker was among those instrumental in the water, electric, and gas works installation for the town of Smyrna. (Above, courtesy of the Duck Creek Historical Society; below, courtesy of Brooks Keen.)

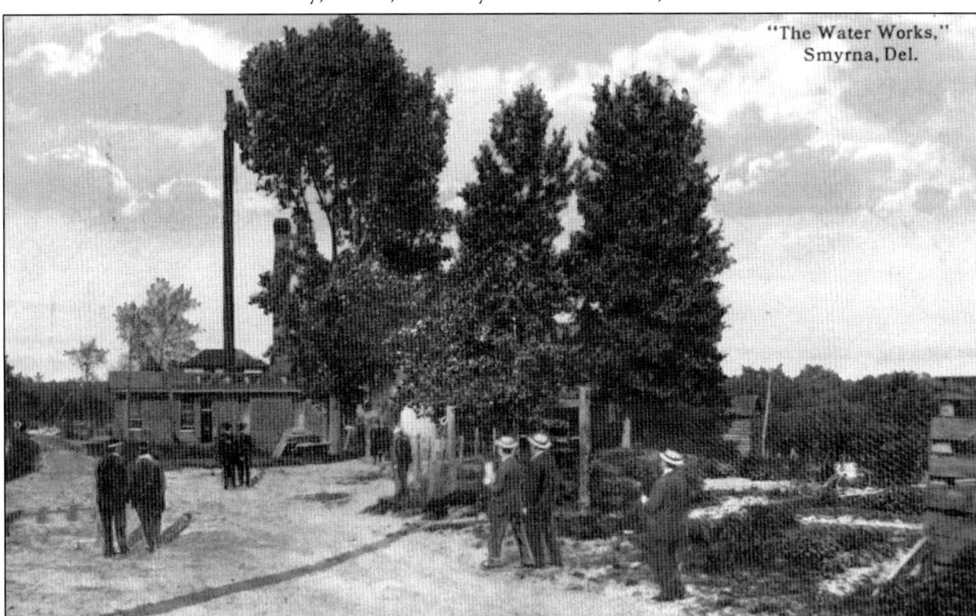

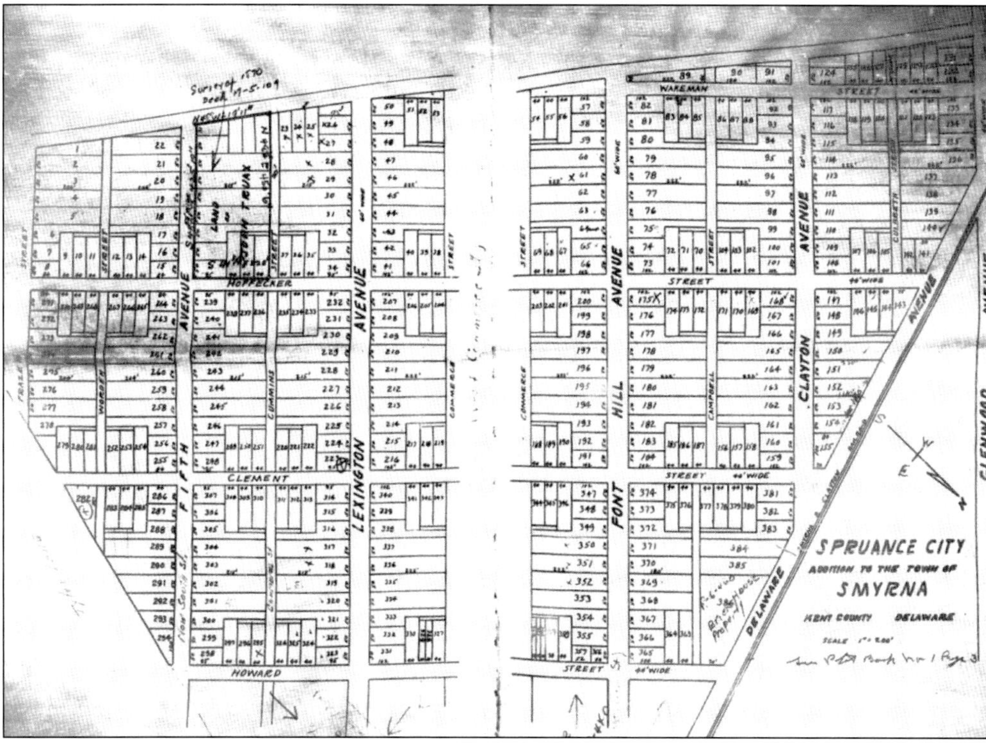

The Font Hill mansion, located just west of Smyrna, was originally built by the VanGaskens. James W. Spruance, an eventual owner, surveyed the estate grounds and organized a subdivision in 1869. He called it Spruance City and devised to sell the lots at auction. Each parcel, including the mansion itself, were up for lottery. The cost was only $100. He sold 140 tickets. Spruance City still exists today.

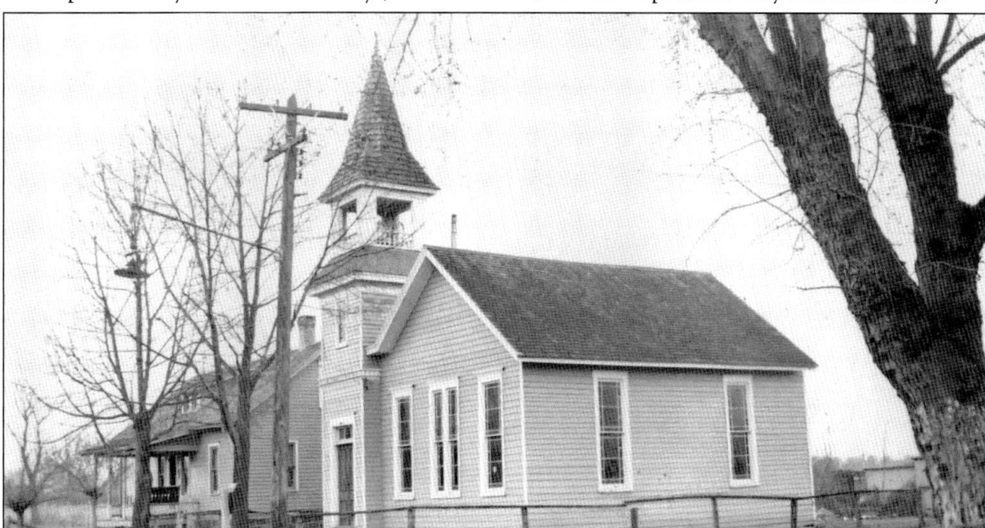

Joshua Jerman and his wife, members of Asbury Methodist Episcopal Church, opened a church of their own in 1880 to appeal to disenfranchised members of the community not attending regular services. Meetings took place in a store building in Smyrna before moving to a lot purchased by Asbury Methodist Episcopal Church in Spruance City. The church was called Jerman's Methodist Episcopal Church. By the mid-1930s, the congregation dwindled and the church closed.

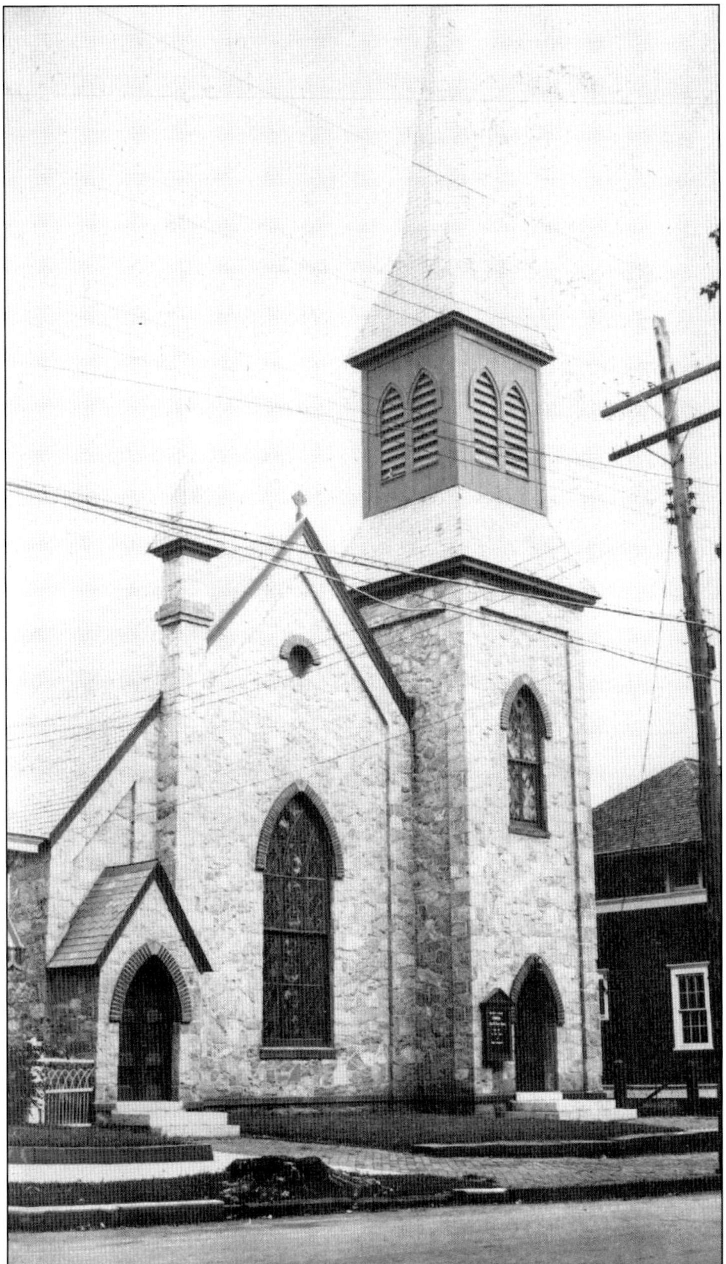

The First Presbyterian Church first met in 1748 at a spot called "Holy Hill" on the shore of Lake Como, just south of present-day Smyrna. A burial ground was laid out with the oldest marker belonging to Jacob Peterson, who died November 11, 1782. Historical writings recall Holy Hill as being the prettiest spot in and around the town of Smyrna and a peaceful resting location. The church moved in 1846, after the congregation dwindled, before finally building the church at the present site on Commerce Street. The cornerstone for the current building was laid in 1883. The original structure on Holy Hill was demolished, but the cemetery is still maintained by the First Presbyterian Church of Smyrna. Stone blocks from the original church were used to build a wall around some of the burial plots in the Holy Hill Cemetery.

Two

Smyrna Landing

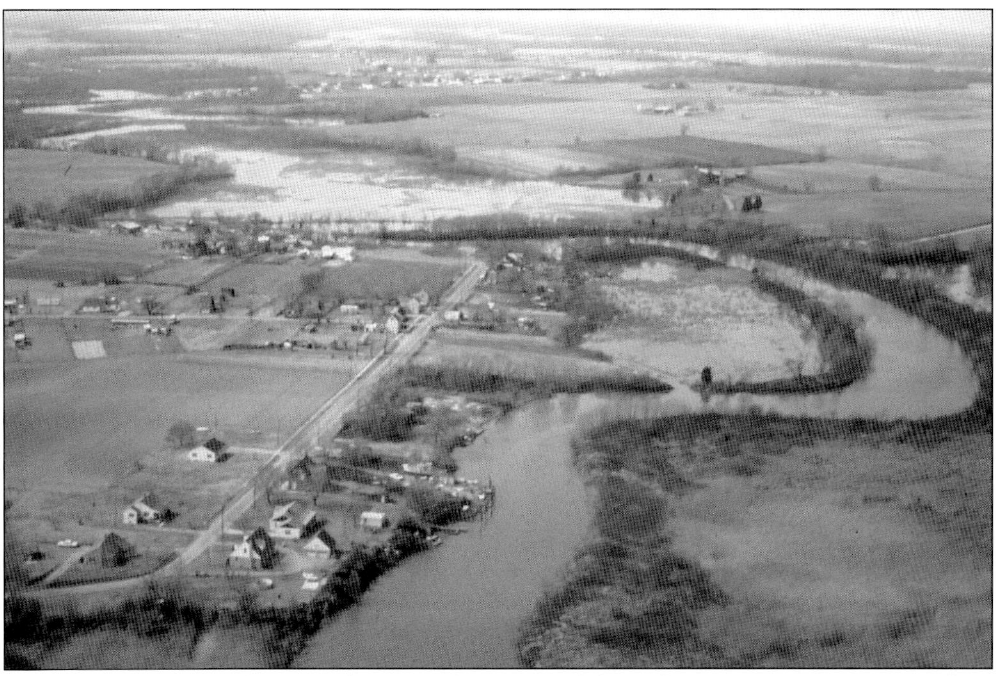

A vital shipping village between the town of Smyrna and the Delaware Bay was Smyrna Landing. Originally called Green's Landing, this land is situated on what was the eastern portion of the Gravesend Tract granted to William Green in 1680. The landing was located just two miles east of the town settlement.

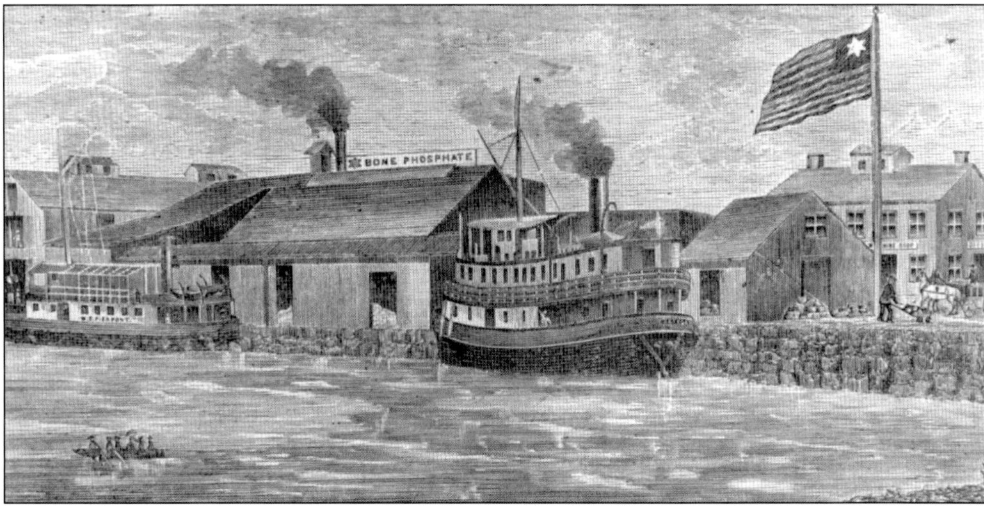

The Peninsula Bone Fertilizer Company and J.E. Tygert & Company were both companies run by John E. Tygert of New York. Tygert, having offices in Philadelphia, operated a phosphate manufacturing company from Smyrna Landing with is brother Herman Tygert. Initially starting their fertilizer business in Harrington, John moved to Smyrna Landing with his wife, Mary, to take advantage of the easy shipping opportunities. In that same year, the company employed 50 workers in their plant, which manufactured 100 tons of phosphate every day. They manufactured Star Bone Phosphate, made of animal bones and other ingredients for the best possible mix of fertilizer available. The company owned several steamboats, including the Pierrepont, for moving both fertilizer and passengers from Smyrna Landing to Philadelphia on a daily schedule.

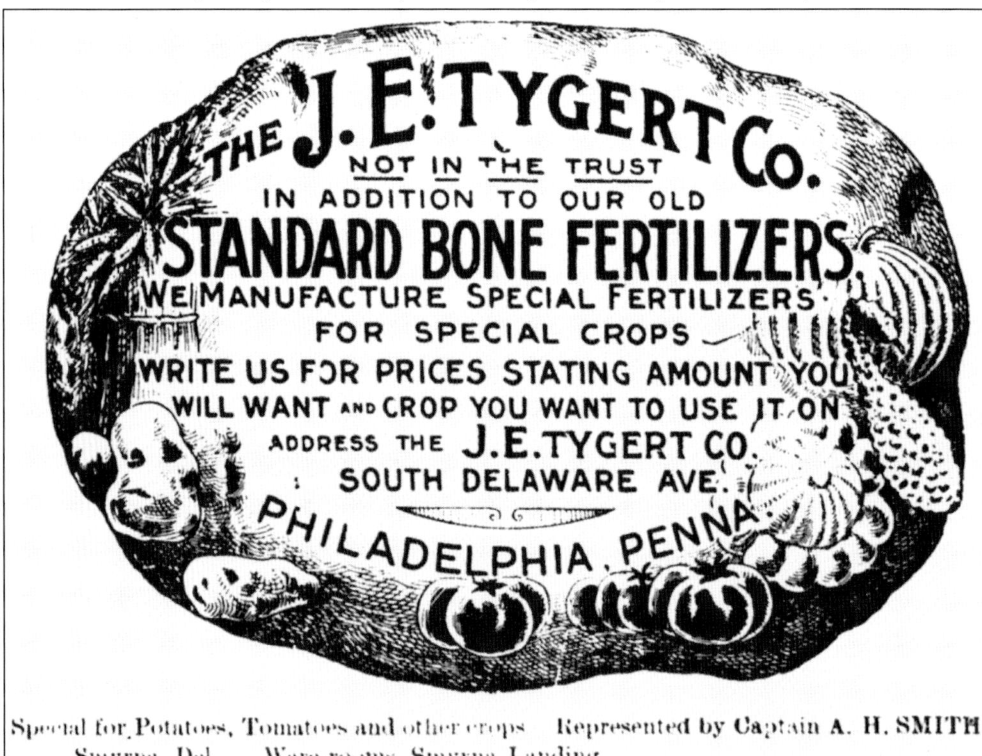

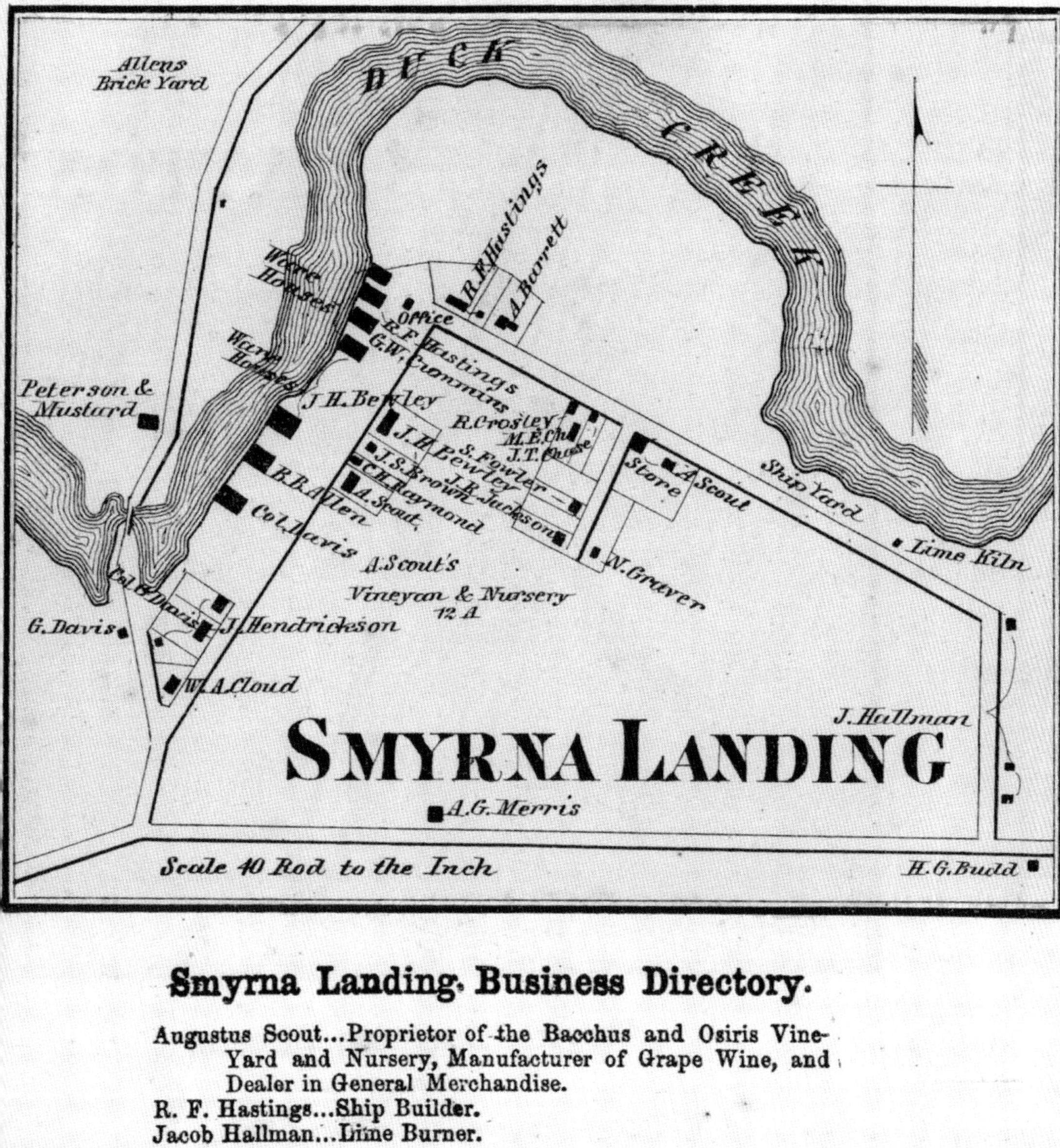

Smyrna Landing. Business Directory.

Augustus Scout...Proprietor of the Bacchus and Osiris Vine-Yard and Nursery, Manufacturer of Grape Wine, and Dealer in General Merchandise.
R. F. Hastings...Ship Builder.
Jacob Hallman...Lime Burner.

The layout of Smyrna Landing, as shown in 1885, portrays the importance of the now quiet water community. Shipyards; a lime and fertilizer factory; warehouses for grains, produce, and other goods; stores; and offices lined the creek edge. Ships were built, repaired, and docked along the river. Augustus Scout, a business owner in this little village, was born in Smyrna around 1817. Scout started out as a cabin boy and then cook out of a Philadelphia port at the age of 17. He went on to make many voyages to far away lands. France, Germany, England, Cuba, and the West Indies were a few of his stops before retiring and returning to his home port of Smyrna. Finally, in 1850, he settled into land life. He opened a store, a shipyard, a nursery, and a vineyard in Smyrna Landing.

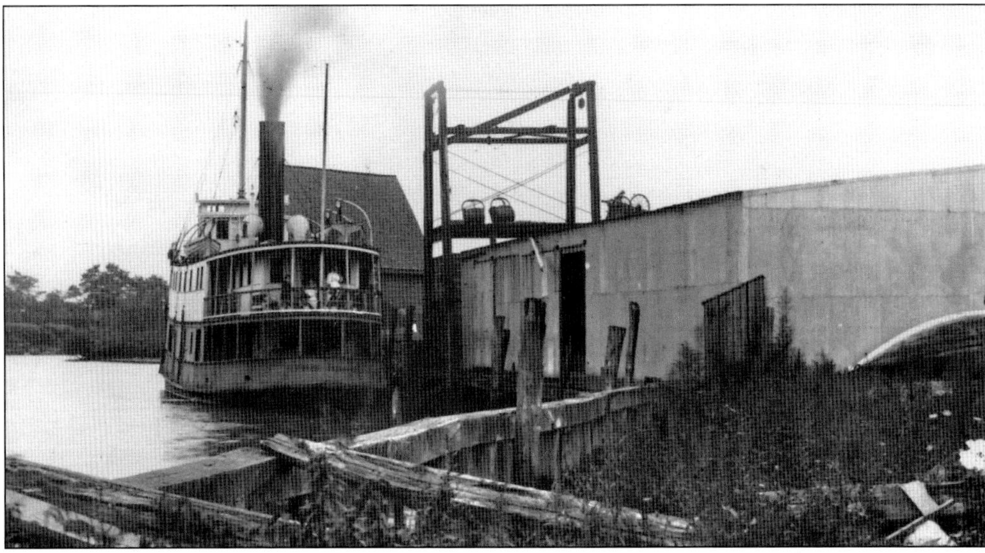

Large steamboats similar to the *GF Brady* came into dock at Smyrna Landing. Here, crops of peaches, apples, strawberries, and other fruits, as well as grains and livestock, were exported to Philadelphia to be sold. Boats like the *Brady* also boasted of first-class passenger accommodations. Owned by the Philadelphia and Smyrna Transportation Company, the *GF Brady* ran three times a week from Philadelphia to Smyrna Landing. The transportation company, under the direction of Walter O. Hoffecker, sold the *GF Brady* in 1911 to the Morton Line in New York. In 1926, after being overturned by gale-force hurricane winds on the Hudson River, the ship sunk, killing the cook and fireman that were on board. (Above, courtesy of the Duck Creek Historical Society; below, courtesy of the Delaware Agricultural Museum.)

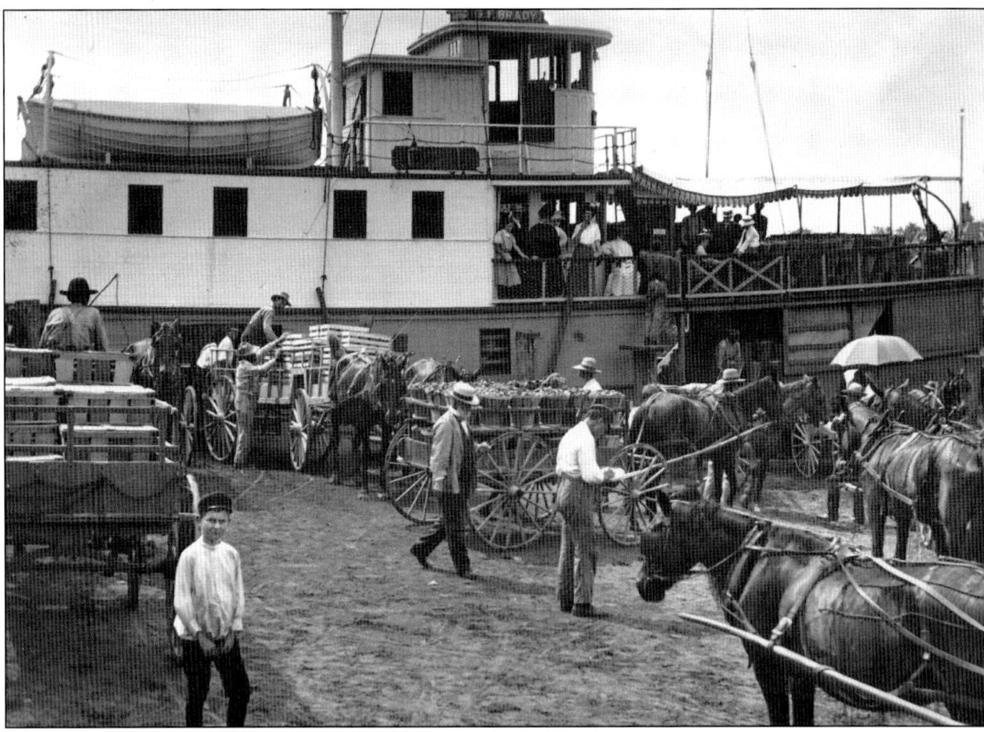

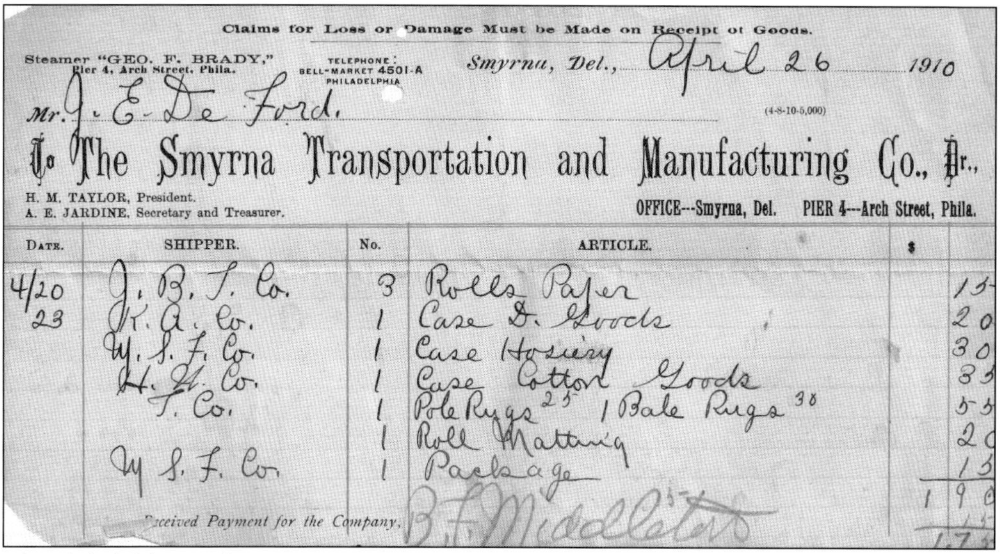
Claims for Loss or Damage Must be Made on Receipt of Goods.

Steamer "GEO. F. BRADY," Pier 4, Arch Street, Phila. TELEPHONE: BELL-MARKET 4501-A PHILADELPHIA

Smyrna, Del., April 26 1910

Mr. J. E. De Ford.

(4-8-10-5,000)

To The Smyrna Transportation and Manufacturing Co., Dr.,

H. M. TAYLOR, President.
A. E. JARDINE, Secretary and Treasurer.

OFFICE---Smyrna, Del. PIER 4---Arch Street, Phila.

DATE.	SHIPPER.	No.	ARTICLE.	$	
4/20	J. B. T. Co.	3	Rolls Paper		[illegible]
23	K. A. Co.	1	Case D. Goods		[illegible]
	W. S. F. Co.	1	Case Hosiery		[illegible]
	H. A. Co.	1	Case Cotton Goods		[illegible]
	T. Co.	1	Pole Rugs 25 1 Bale Rugs 30		[illegible]
		1	Roll Matting		[illegible]
	W. S. F. Co.	1	Package		[illegible]
				1	[illegible]

Received Payment for the Company, B. F. Middleton

The Philadelphia and Smyrna Transportation Company was incorporated in Delaware in 1893. The company held offices in Philadelphia and Smyrna. Other than the *GF Brady*, they owned the steamships *Ella* and *Elizabeth VanSciver* for their shipping needs. The company, originally headed by John H. Hoffecker, manufactured and sold fertilizer along with their shipping services. Fertilizer was big business in the late 1800s, as towns like Smyrna were still based in agriculture. Special formulated mixes were created for different plants to ensure the most plentiful crop. For a transportation company, this was a great second part of the business. The more the farmers could grow, the more they could ship. Companies such as this one made money from the sale of the fertilizer, then again for the shipping cost of the produce. (Above, courtesy of the Duck Creek Historical Society.)

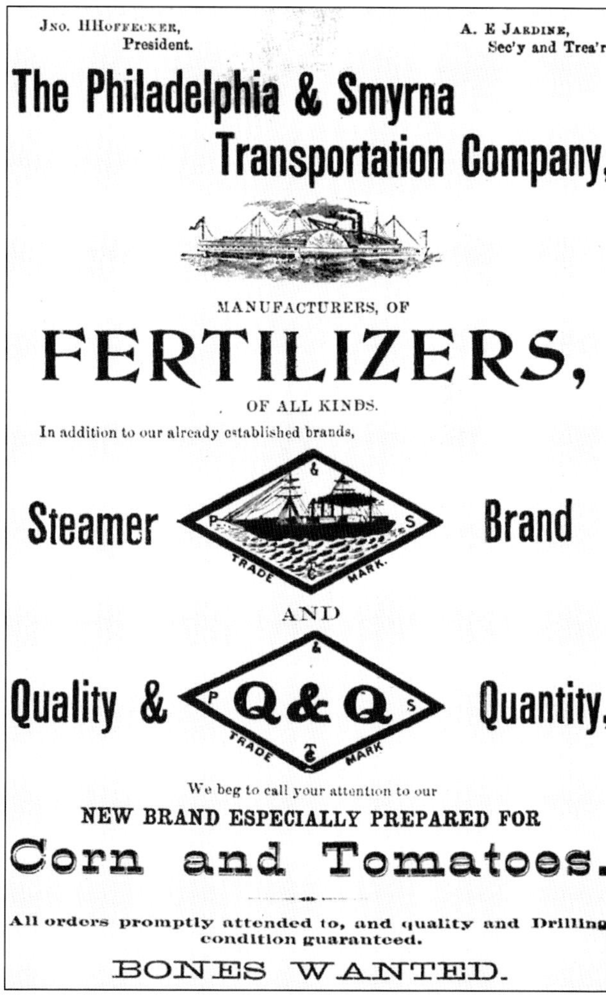

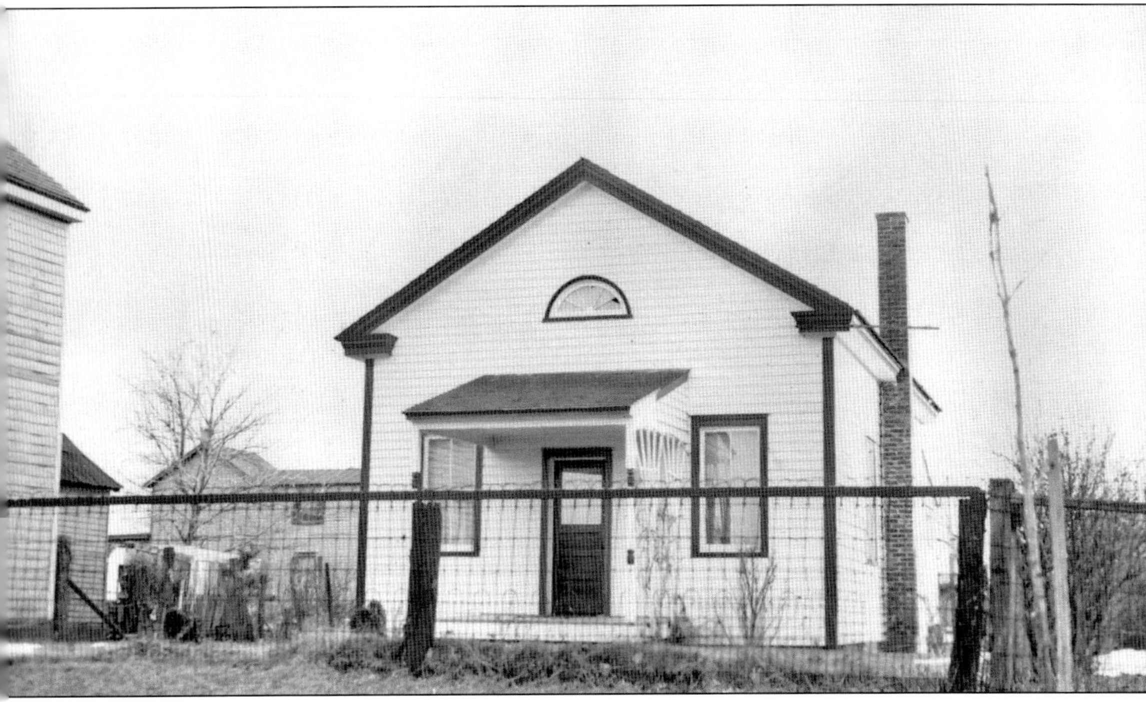

Although only two miles from the town of Smyrna, the community in Smyrna Landing built its own church in 1860. The Smyrna Landing Methodist Episcopal Church was erected on a portion of property purchased for $60 in April 1860 from Thomas Chase. The church was located along the back road of the landing village, opposite of the creek next to Chase's property. The services were led by Rev. C. Hill and then Rev. W. Brisbane. In 1928, the congregation attendance dipped low enough to close the doors. In the 1930s, the building was converted into a home.

Three

SMYRNA

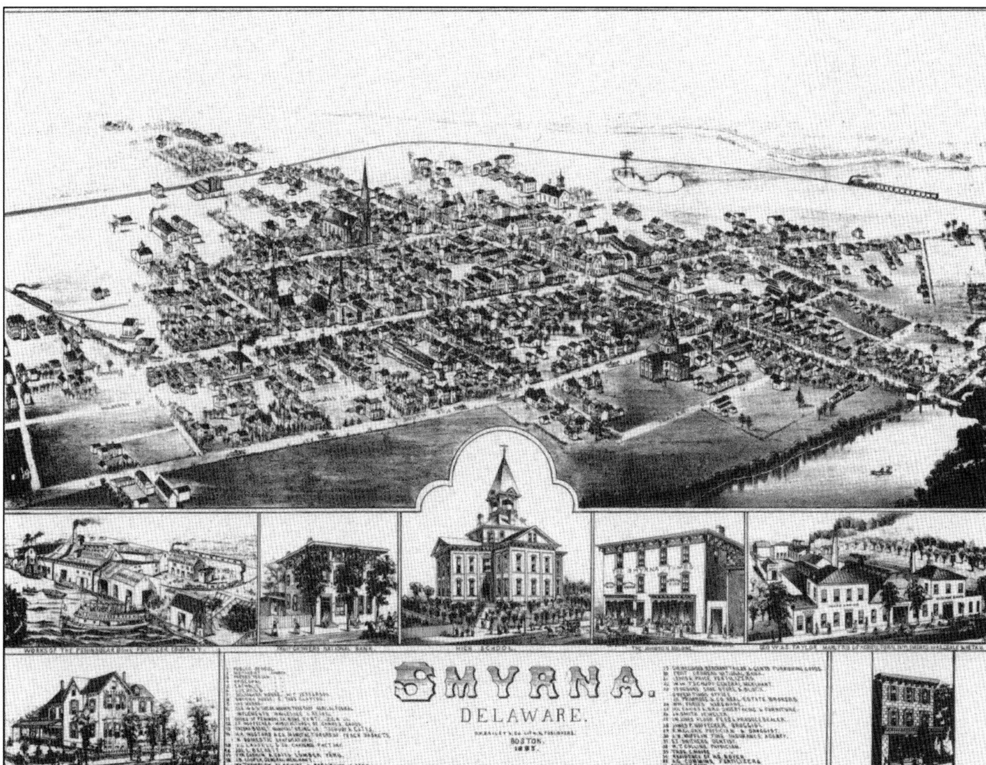

By 1885, the town of Smyrna had truly exploded since its inception with Samuel Ball's purchase in the Four Corners. The town's population was 2,423 persons on the 1880 census, and that number continued to climb as Smyrna expanded farther beyond the main streets and businesses boomed. The railroad was connected from Clayton to Smyrna in the year after the Philadelphia, Wilmington and Baltimore Railroad Company moved their offices to nearby Clayton. This gave Smyrna the best of all transportation and shipping abilities. Still heavily using Smyrna Landing for boat shipments, business owners could now easily connect to the train system in Clayton.

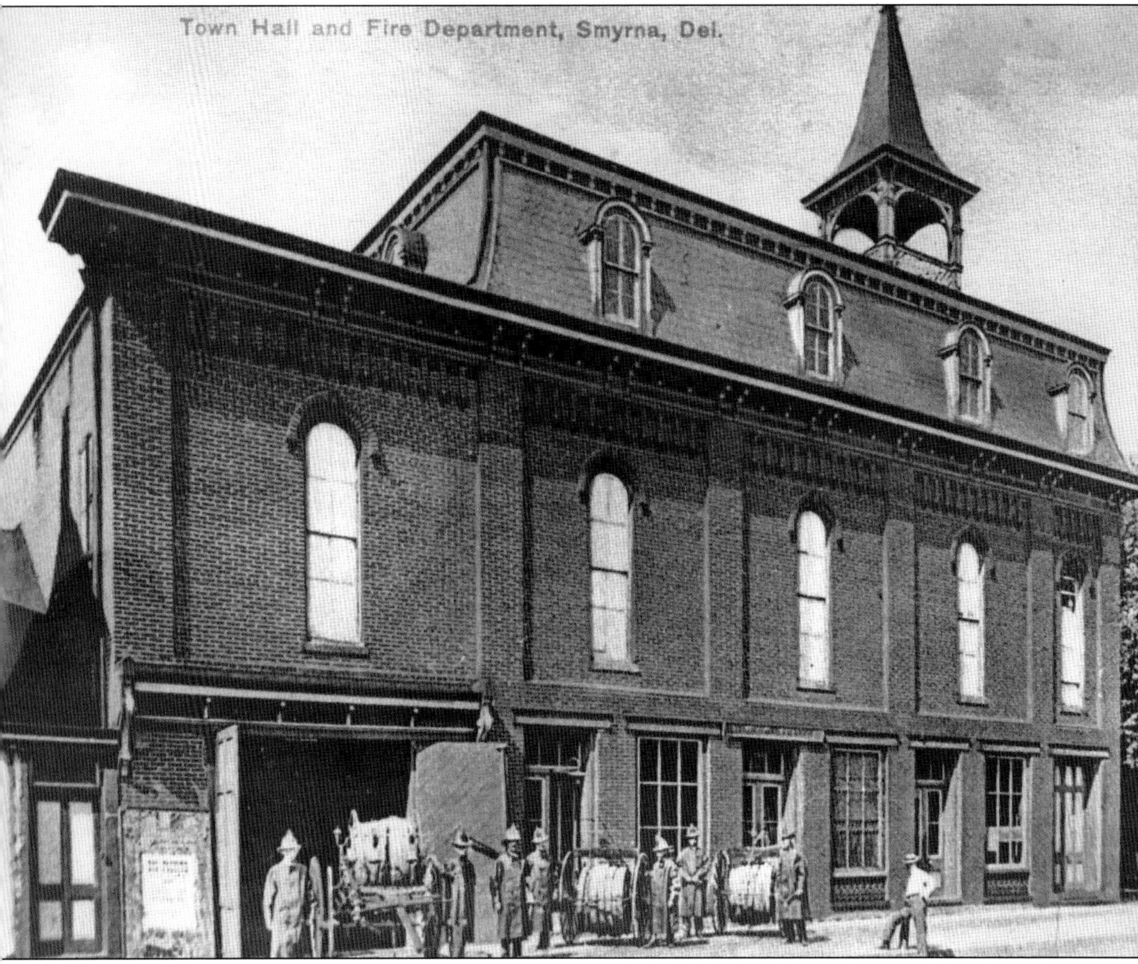

The old town hall was erected in 1869 on the corner of what is now Main and South Streets. This building served many purposes for the town of Smyrna over the years. Early on, it held the volunteer fire department, as seen above in 1885, before it built its own station on Commerce Street. The building also housed the post office, police department, town jail, public library, an opera house for stage shows upstairs, and then a movie theater called the Roxy that showed all of the newest films and offered weekend matinees at 2:00 p.m., in addition to their evening shows. Many social events were held in the historic building. On Christmas day 1948, the building suffered a devastating fire caused by holiday lighting decorations. The tower and top floor of the building were destroyed. Events were still held on the lower floors of the facility until 2003, when the hall was finally restored to its former glory.

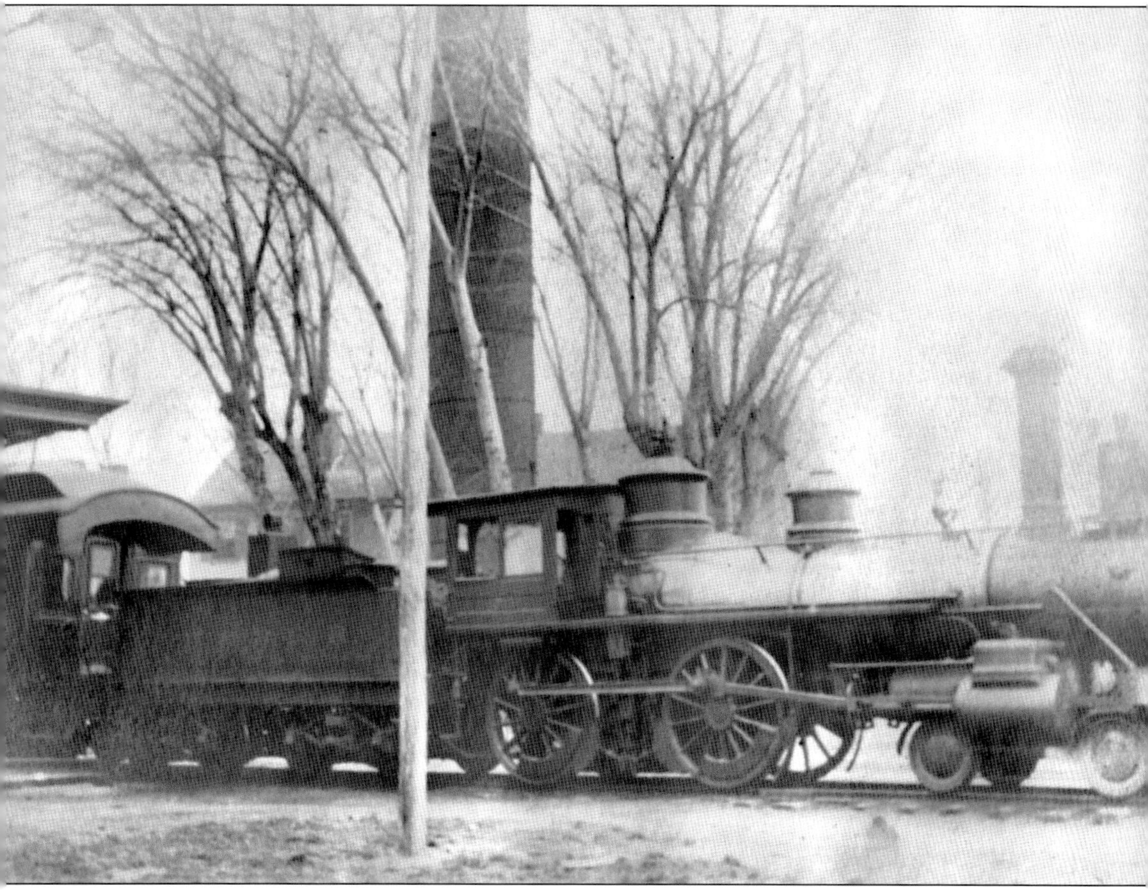

While the Delaware Railroad Company did not have any luck convincing Smyrna to allow for a large installation within town, there was a need to run tracks to somehow connect Smyrna to the new town of Clayton to the west. Originally, the Smyrna rail line traveled along Commerce Street to a small depot across from the Presbyterian church in the mid-1800s. This connection allowed for new transportation options for the exportation of Smyrna-made goods and opened new possibilities for local residents to travel. In 1885, a new depot was built by the Philadelphia Railroad Company on the western edge of the town of Smyrna. The water standpipe can be seen in the background. (Courtesy of the Citizens' Hose Company No. 1, Inc.)

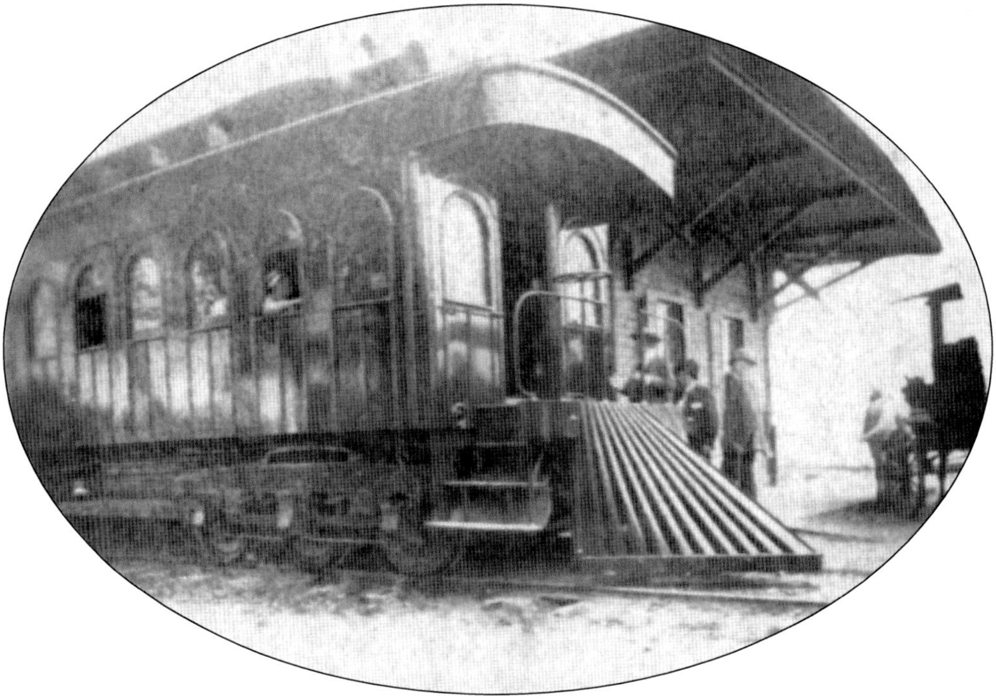

The Philadelphia Railroad Company operated out of the town of Clayton, which was west of the town of Smyrna. They shuttled passengers from the small depot just outside the town of Smyrna to the Clayton train station and back with the "Dummy Train." Locals referred to the small train as the "dummy" because it could not turn around. The engine, instead had to back all the way home to the Smyrna depot. Here are two views of railcars for the Philadelphia, Wilmington and Baltimore Railroad Company. (Both, courtesy of the Citizens' Hose Company No. 1, Inc.)

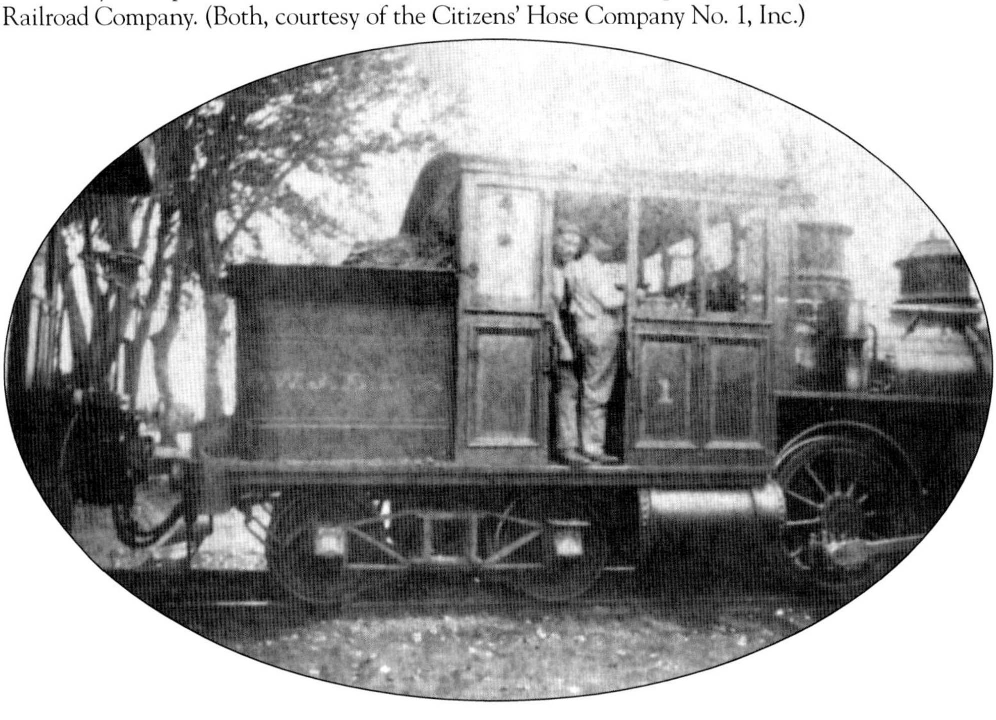

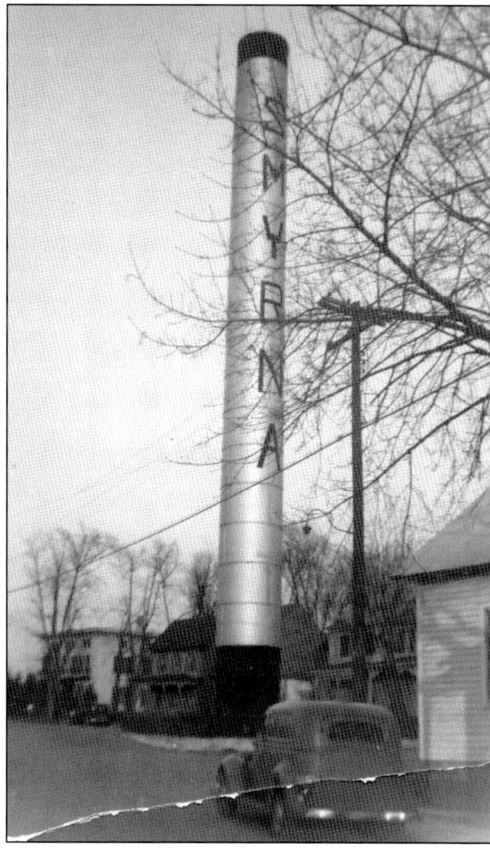

Across the street from the small Smyrna train depot stood the newly installed water standpipe. Situated at the intersection of West Commerce Street, High Street, and Clayton Road, this tall structure provided water for the town of Smyrna. Constructed in 1885, it was built by A.H. Coon and S.L. King of Kingston, Pennsylvania, for $18,971. The structure was replaced by a more modern water tower in 1946. In 1967, as the population in town continued to grow, the water supply system was updated to a 400,000-gallon elevated water tank. (Right, courtesy of the Duck Creek Historical Society; below, courtesy of Brooks Keen.)

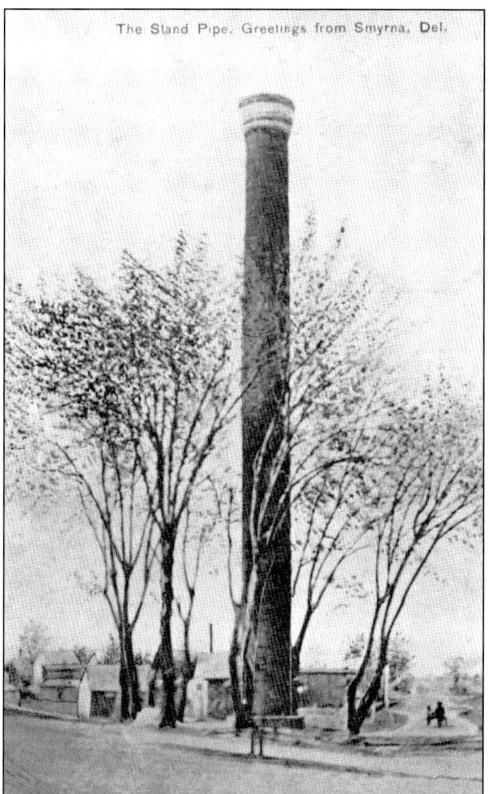

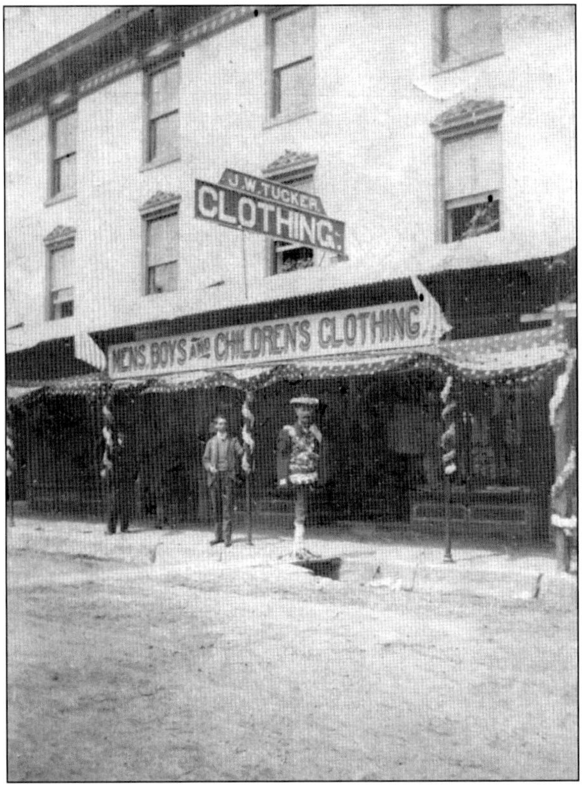

The John Tucker store was located on Commerce Street in Smyrna next to the corner Clifton and Jones Drugstore and directly across from the Farmers National Bank and Trust Company. The building, shown here in 1901, was a location to buy "ready-made clothes." The second photograph, taken around 1925, shows J.W. Tucker Clothier Company. The enormous store took over the large W.W. Tschudy store, opened on Commerce Street in 1870. Tucker's store remained a staple on Commerce Street before becoming Wooten's Store. George Wooten eventually purchased the corner Clifton and Jones building as well, giving him ownership of the entire block. He renovated the corner building to the way it looks today and renovated the top floors of the huge store building for apartments. In 1964, the store building was thoroughly destroyed in a devastating fire.

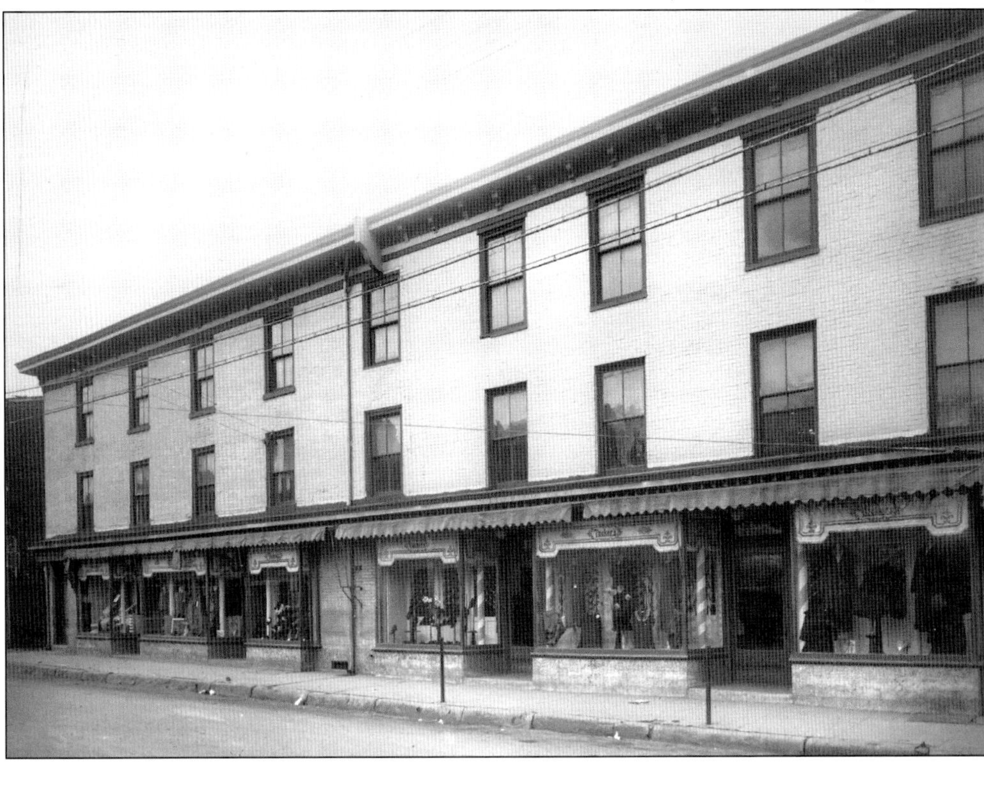

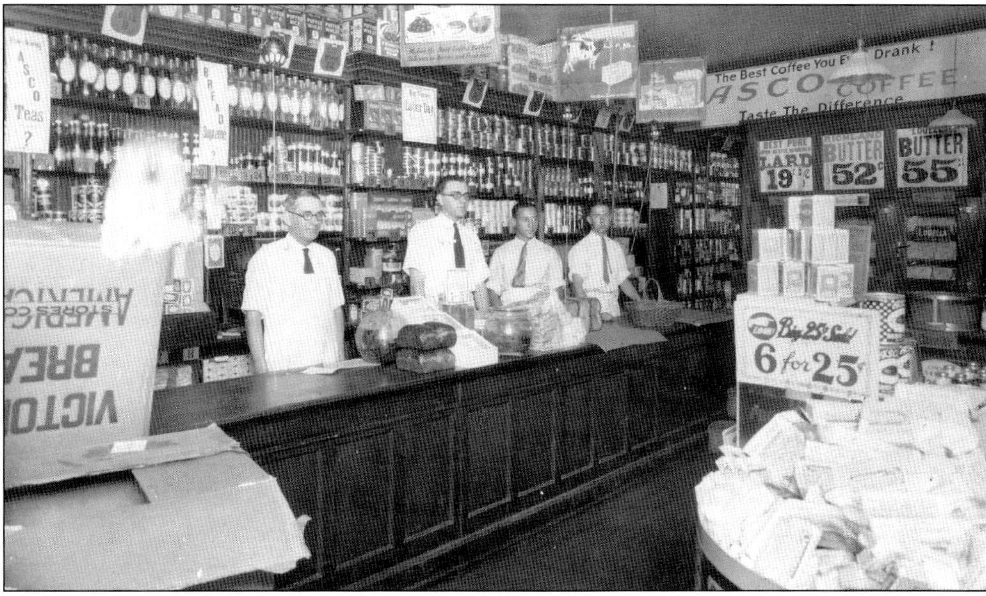

Located on the southeast corner of the Four Corners in Smyrna, previously the J.B. Cooper building, was an "American store." This store sold groceries, coffee, soap, and a number of other necessities. Pictured are, from left to right, H. Clifton, Vaughn Collins, George Smith, and Jack Robinson. (Courtesy of the Duck Creek Historical Society.)

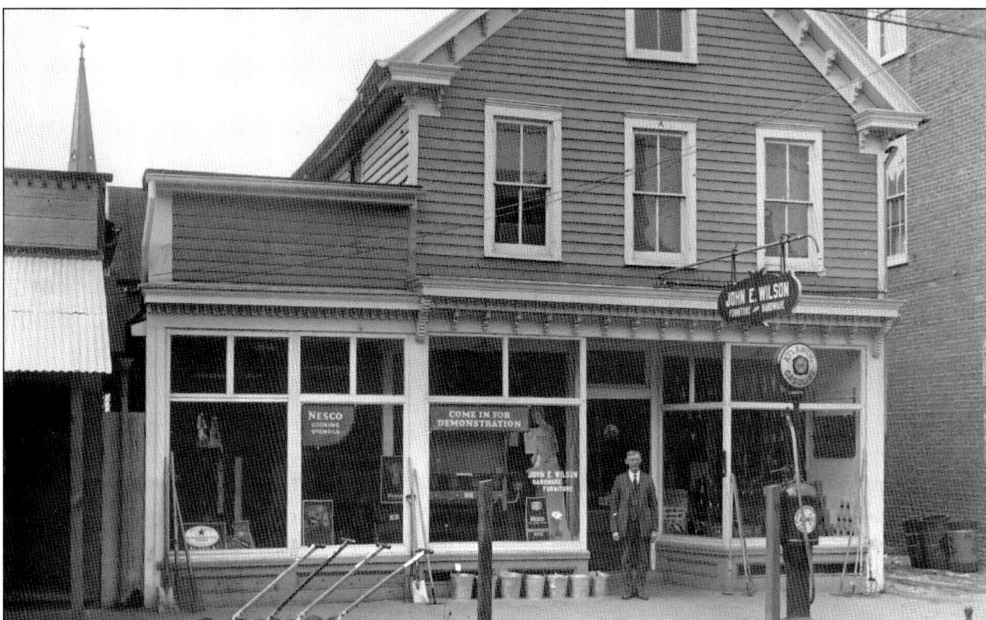

John E. Wilson sold furniture, cabinets, and hardware at his store on Commerce Street in Smyrna. This photograph shows Wilson in front of his store around 1925. This store was the beginning of a profitable family business. The Wilson family business grew to eventually become the Wilson Cabinet Company. The cabinet company made cabinets before branching out to refrigerators and the new concept of ice freezers. Their company employed many residents from the town of Smyrna.

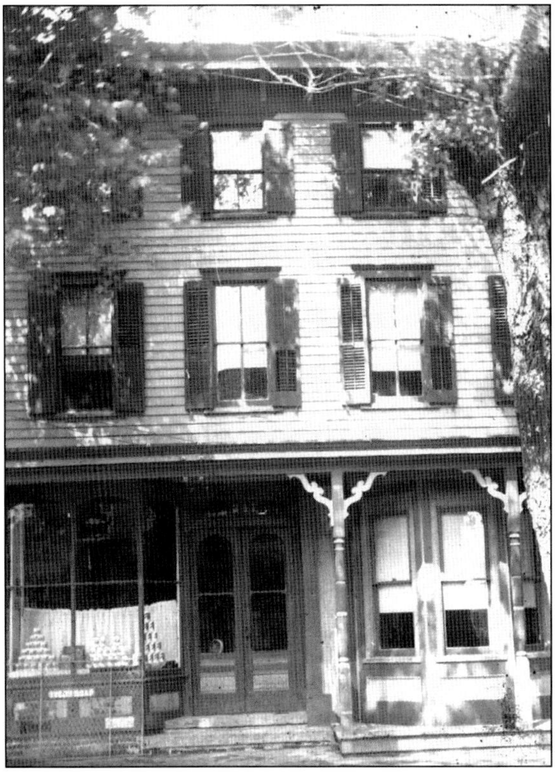

Charles and Eva Boehmler emigrated from Germany in 1879 to Smyrna. The Boehmlers had two children, George and Florence, and ran a confectionery out of the bottom floor of their home on South Main Street. This building has remained all of these years and has housed many popular businesses in Smyrna. George Boehmler (the young boy in the photograph below) grew up to hold the vice president position at the Citizens' Hose Fire Company No. 1 in Smyrna for two terms, once in 1919 and another in 1922, before marrying Hazel Carter in 1925 and settling in to a house on South Street. His sister Florence married Charles R. Vaughn of Clayton in 1950.

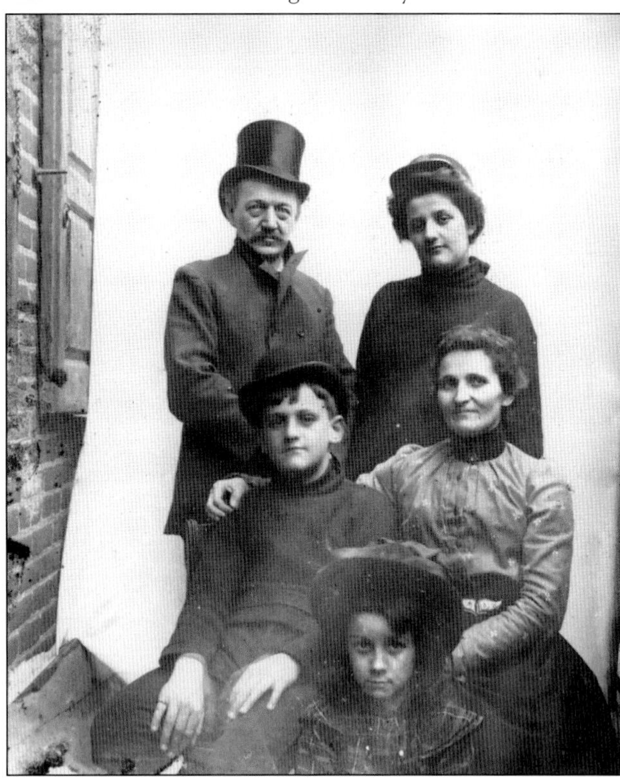

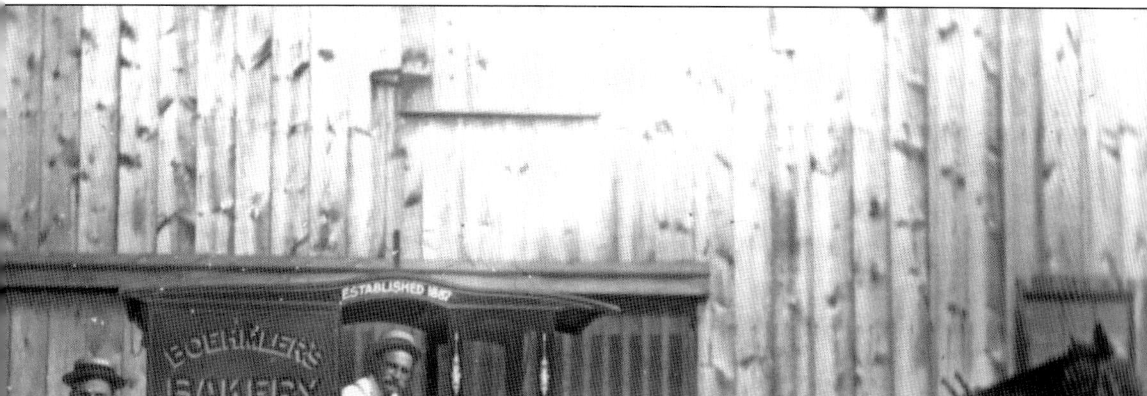

By 1900, Charles Boehmler was deceased, leaving Eva as mother, business owner, and baker. Their advertisements in the *Smyrna Times* site her as owner, with her brother Gotleib Schneider. Gotleib, who was living with the family as of the 1900 census, immigrated to the United States the same year as Eva. Eva, having the previous occupation as "wife" on all official documents, was suddenly in charge of running a successful business and a household after the death of her husband. By all accounts, this was a common practice during history. Wars, diseases, and other hardships often left housewives to take care of the family. Ultimately, they did this while having little to no experience running businesses. The Boehmler delivery cart, seen above, was also spotted in photographs of parades in the Four Corners. The company seemed to be very involved in the community and placed many advertisements in the local paper.

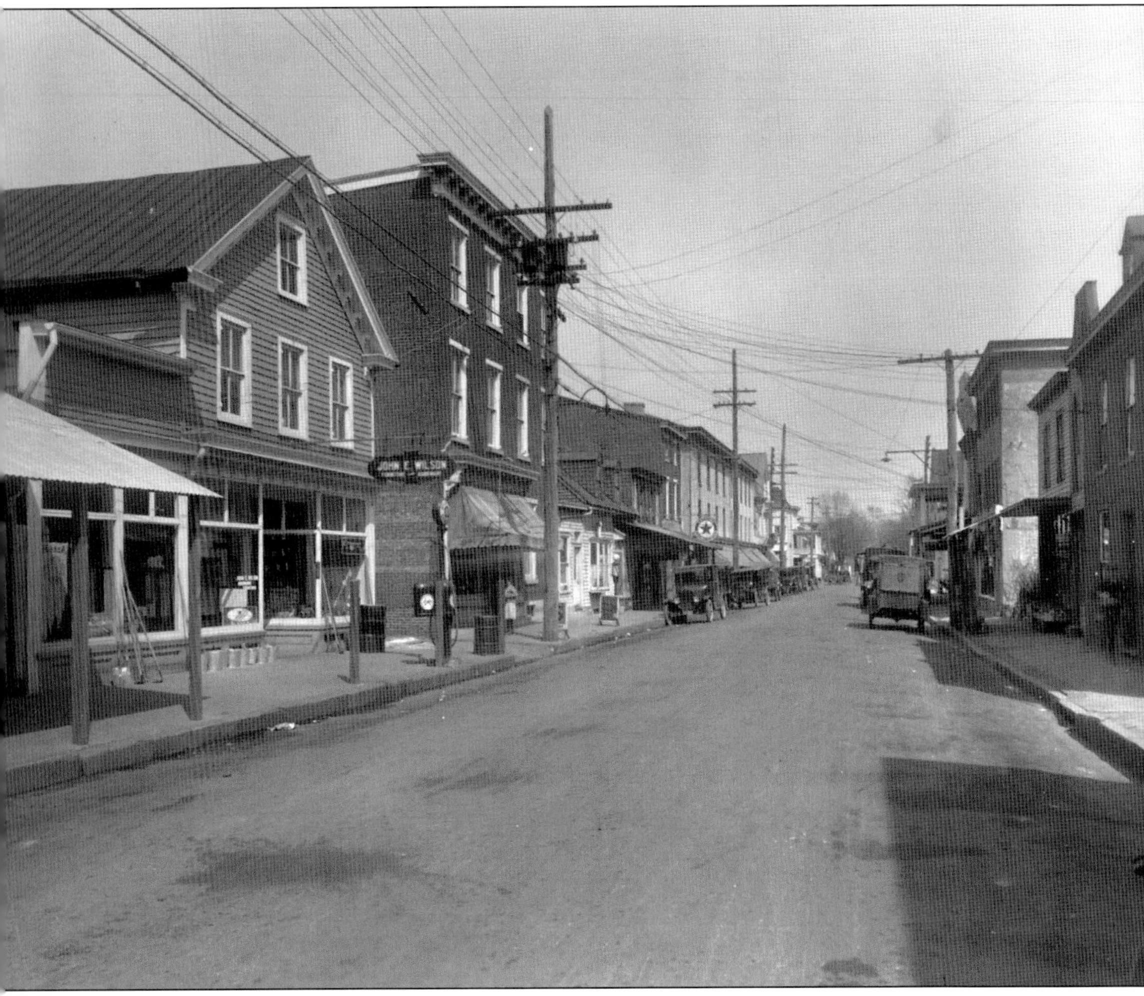

Swain's Pharmacy was located on the busy Commerce Street in Smyrna, nestled next to John E. Wilson's Furniture and Hardware store. Originally owned by Charles B. Swain of Smyrna, it was taken over by his wife, Lillian H. Swain, after he passed away during the horrible influenza epidemic of 1918 at the young age of 27. This epidemic hit in the fall of 1918, and some of the victims died within hours of symptoms appearing. Their lungs filled with so much fluid that they suffocated. This disastrous flu killed a confirmed 389 Delawareans just between October 4 and October 14 alone. As with other businesses at the time, the wife took up the profession of her husband and is shown as "Druggist" on the 1920 census record. Her son Charles Swain Jr., who was only five years old when his father fell ill, eventually took over work at the pharmacy.

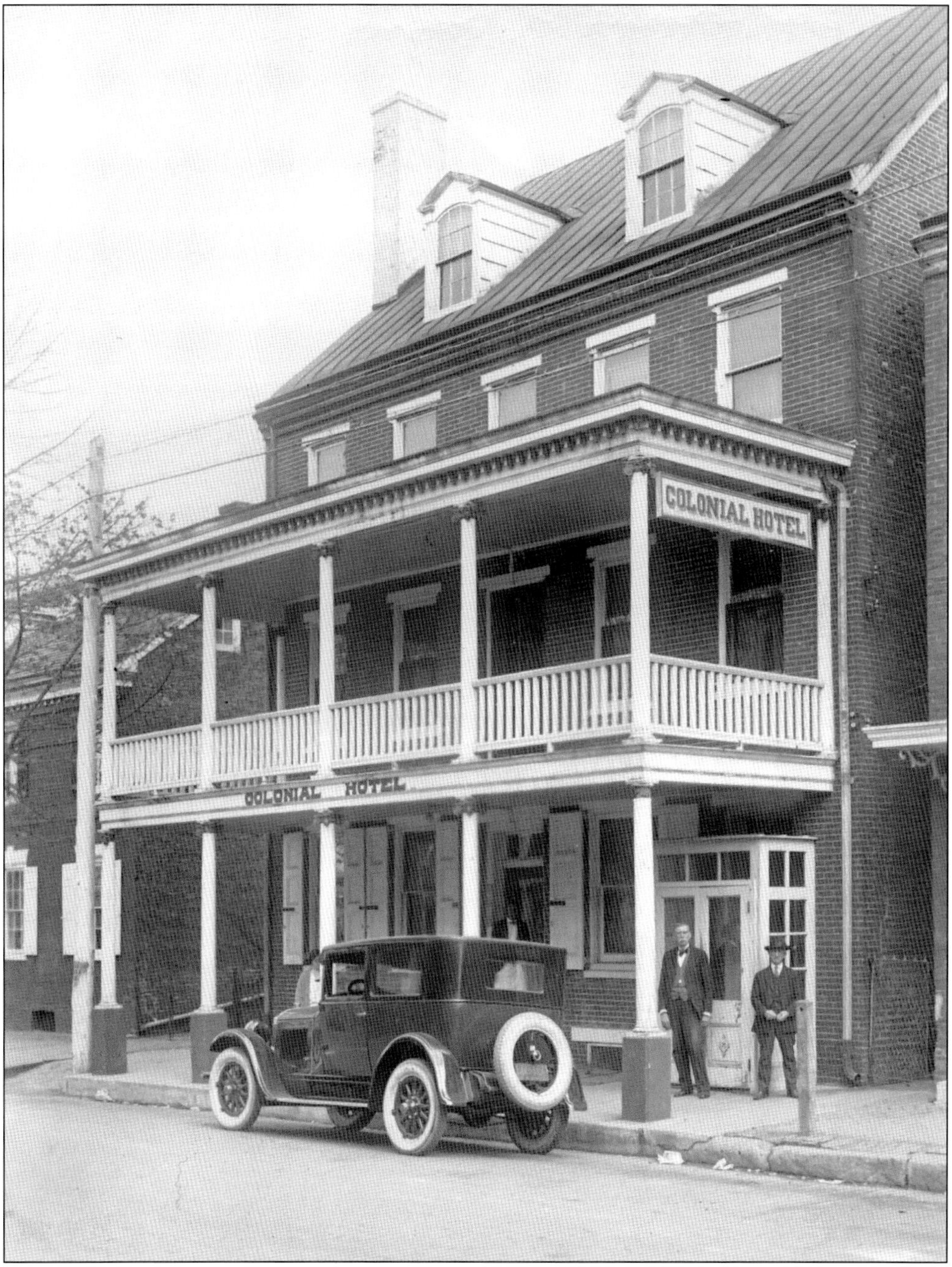

The Colonial Hotel was a home owned by Enoch Spruance. Spruance, a merchant in the town of Smyrna, owned property in and around the town. Prior to 1851, he owned a share in a shipyard and five other lots at Smyrna Landing and, in later years, property on Bombay Hook Island. The residence was transformed into a hotel by Linda Goldsborough and Anne Turner in 1912, who also gave it the name it continues to hold today. An addition was added from the rear wing of the Smyrna House and moved by rollers around the block to Commerce Street. The building immediately to the west of the hotel, called Ward's Hall, held the early post office, social halls, and, later, merchants.

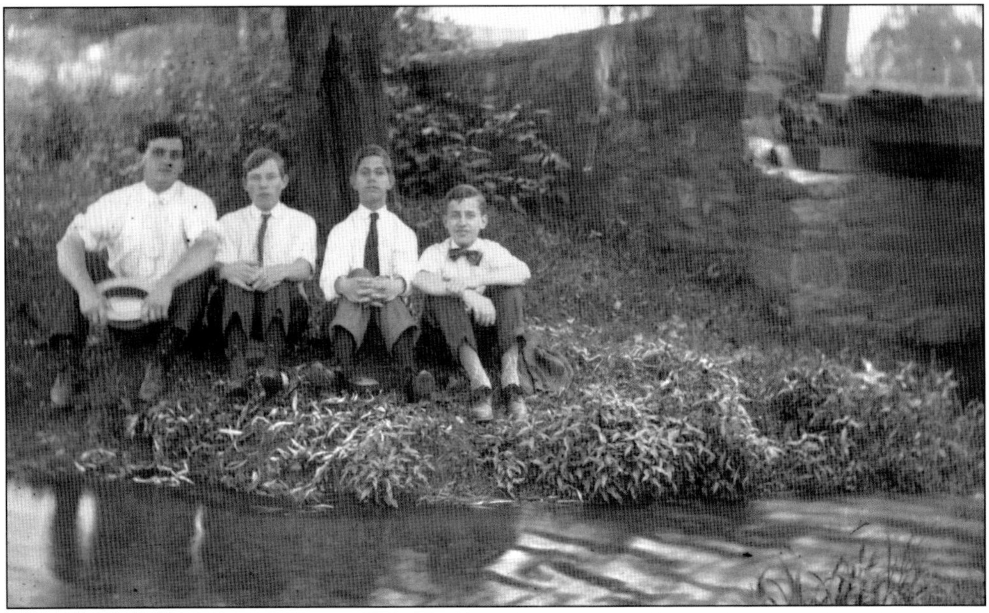

Lake Como was created prior to 1751 as a millpond for a gristmill called Gravely Run. The Kings Road ran immediately next to the mill, with the lake on the other side of the roadway. In later years, the lake proved to be a grand entertainment venue for local youth. Although used through all seasons for playground and sport, the lake causeway was the place to wander on pleasant summer evenings. Above, a group of boys sit next to the bank of the lake. Below, another group poses in front of the old mill fence. (Below, courtesy of the Duck Creek Historical Society.)

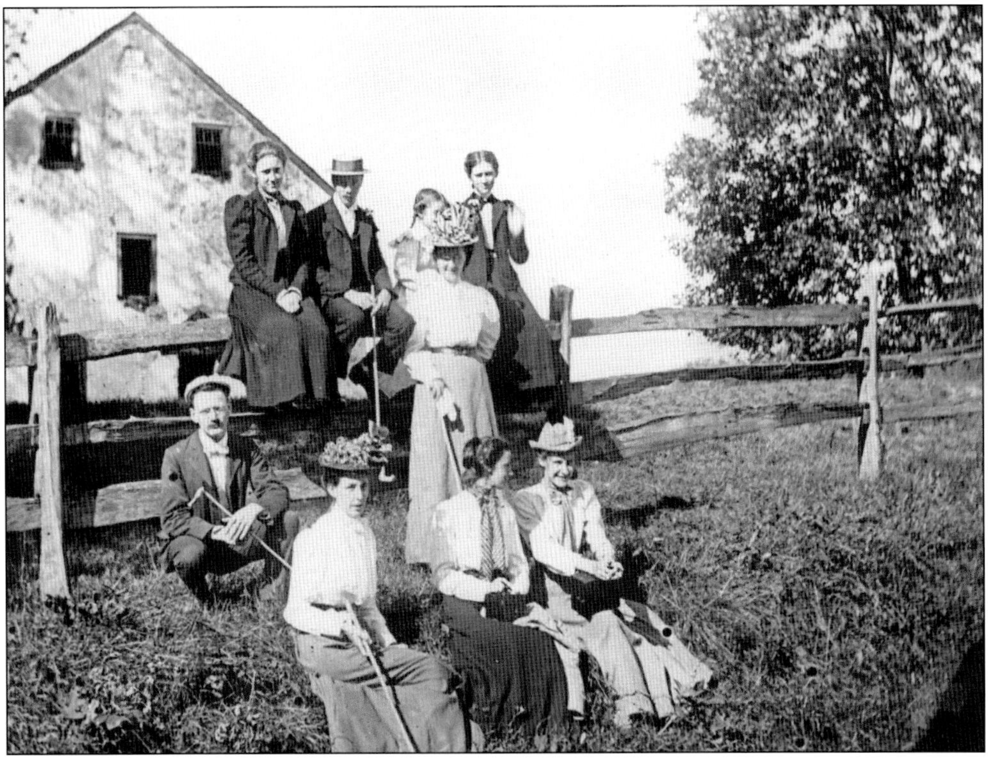

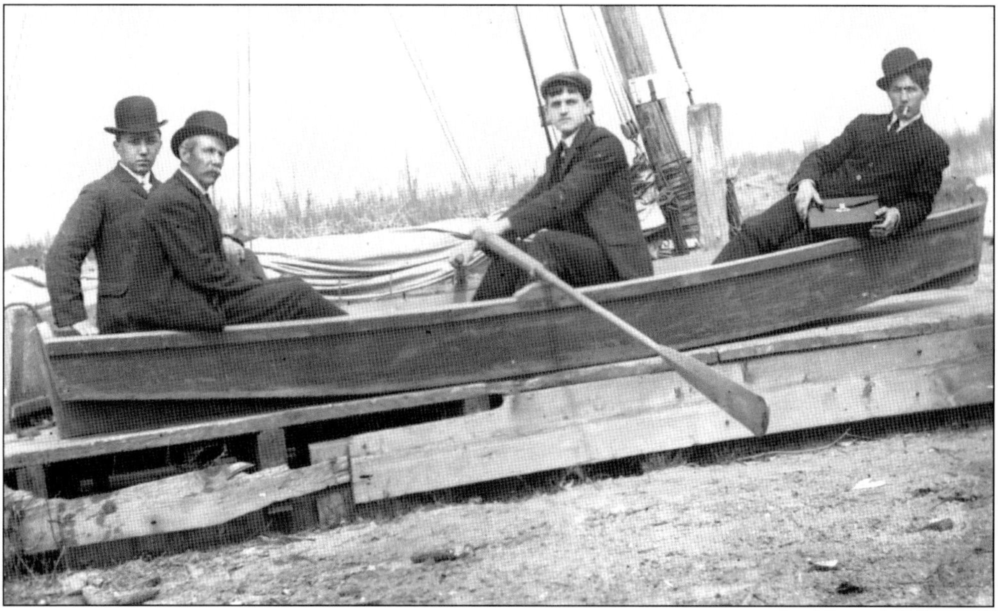

Meant simply to provide water for the mill, Lake Como offered so much more to the residents of Smyrna. Just past the end of South Main Street the lake sat, waiting for enjoyment. Youngsters had their choice of boating, fishing, and swimming opportunities in its waters, depending on the season. Many were known to ice skate over the lake or go gunning there in the colder winter months. While walks were nice, carriage rides in the open air were exciting along the back road at the other end of the lake. Eventually, the town of Smyrna took ownership of Lake Como, and it now serves as a beach and recreation area for the town.

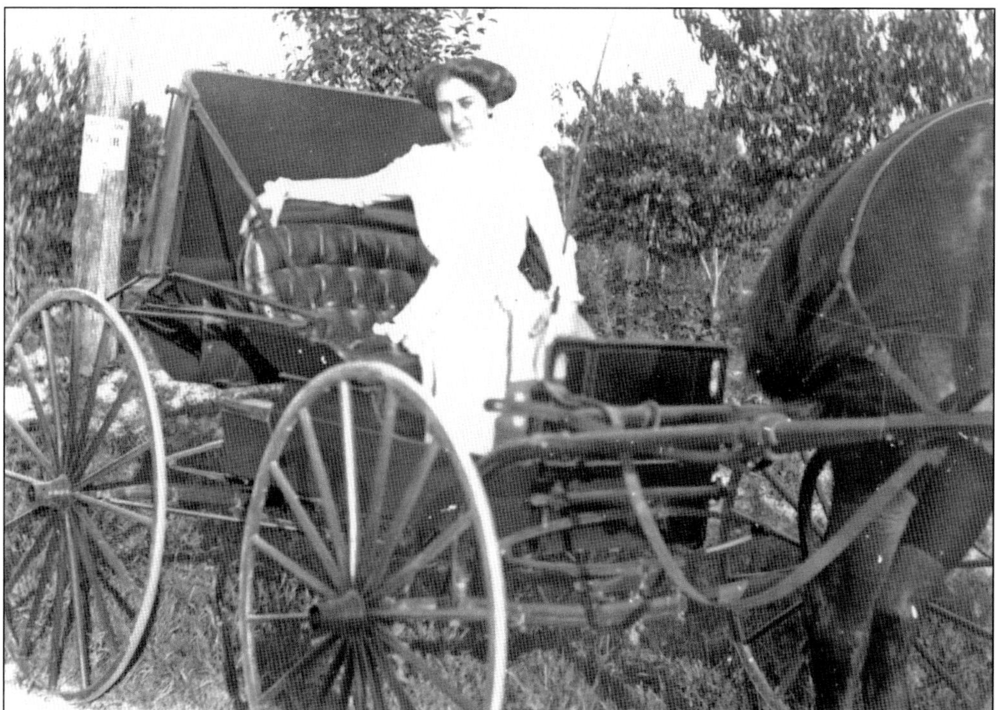

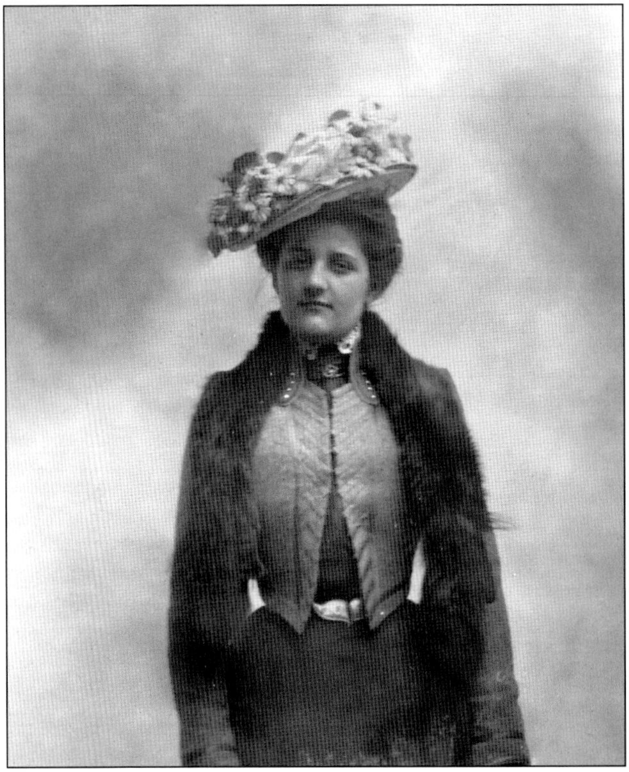

The young woman at left was presumably connected with the Boehmler family, as she was seen in their family photograph. Taken around 1900, she was modeling the high-Victorian fashion of Smyrna. Her Edwardian hairstyle was capped off with a lovely floral hat, perhaps manufactured at one of the many millinery shops in Smyrna, like that of Elva Jester near the Four Corners. The girl below, name unidentified, shows a more casual attire in a slightly earlier photograph. Still, with the popular hairstyle, the clothing choice was perhaps more indicative of what would normally be worn day to day in small-town life. Casual or high fashion, early women's dress in the 1900s included layers of underclothes and skirting.

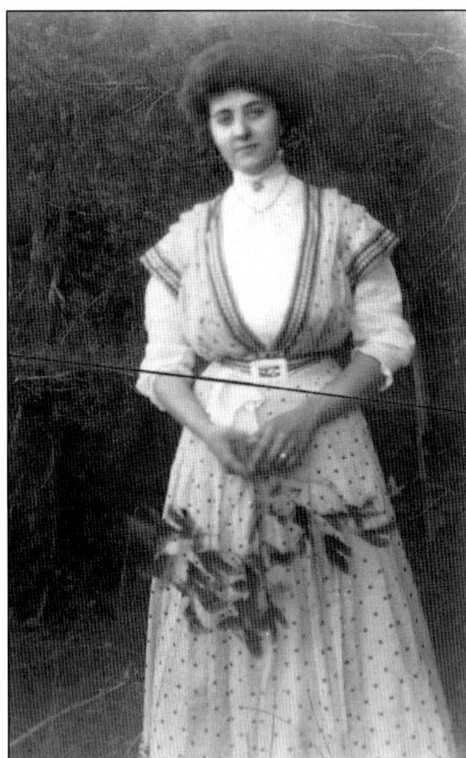

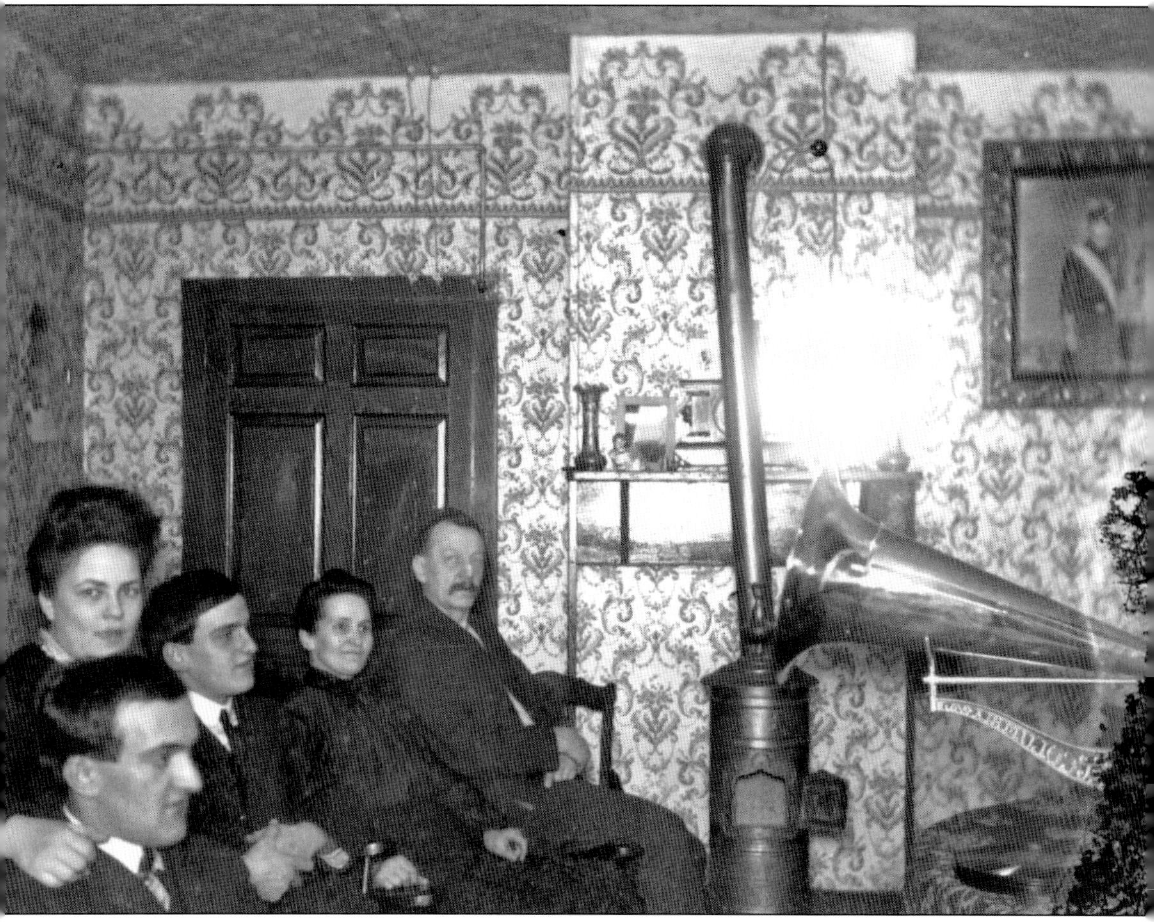

The above photograph depicts how downtime would be spent at home around the turn of the 20th century in Smyrna. This unidentified family sits in a very Victorian-style parlor together while they listen to a phonograph. The Columbia Phonograph Company was the original name for a local company in Washington, DC, selling and distributing the Edison phonographs throughout DC, Maryland, and Delaware. Ultimately, the Columbia Phonograph Company became Columbia Records. Also, note the framed photograph hanging on the right and the visible electric wiring on the left. This way of installing electricity in homes that predated the electric service was common. Most had plaster walls and drilling into them to run electric was not an option. The same was done with copper plumbing pipes. Some homes in historic Smyrna still have these tubes as reminders of innovation in the early 1900s.

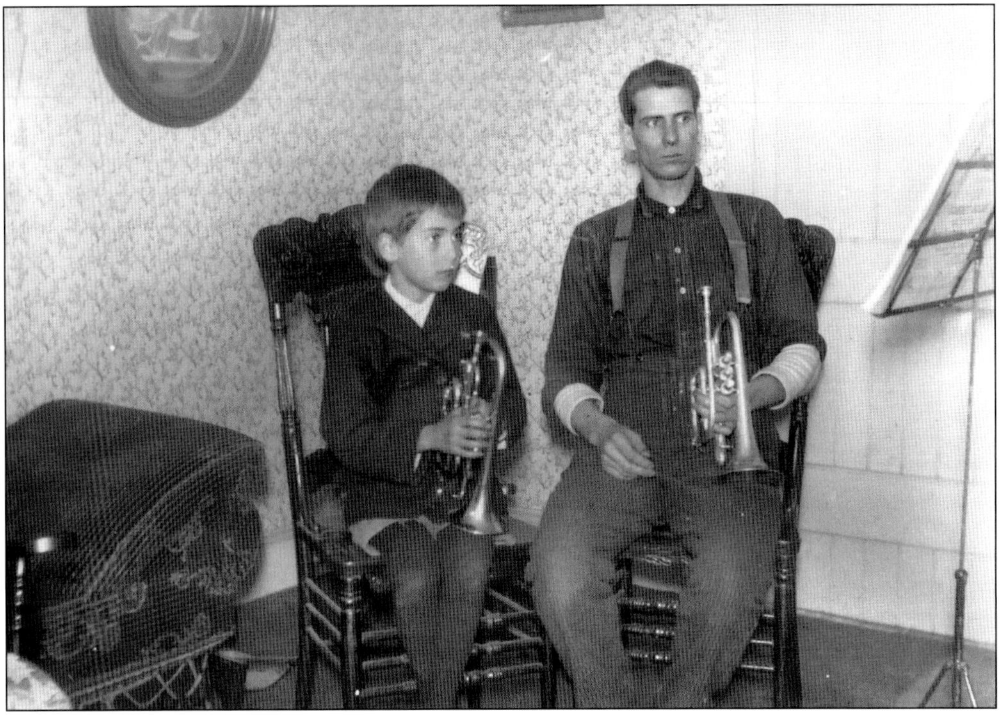

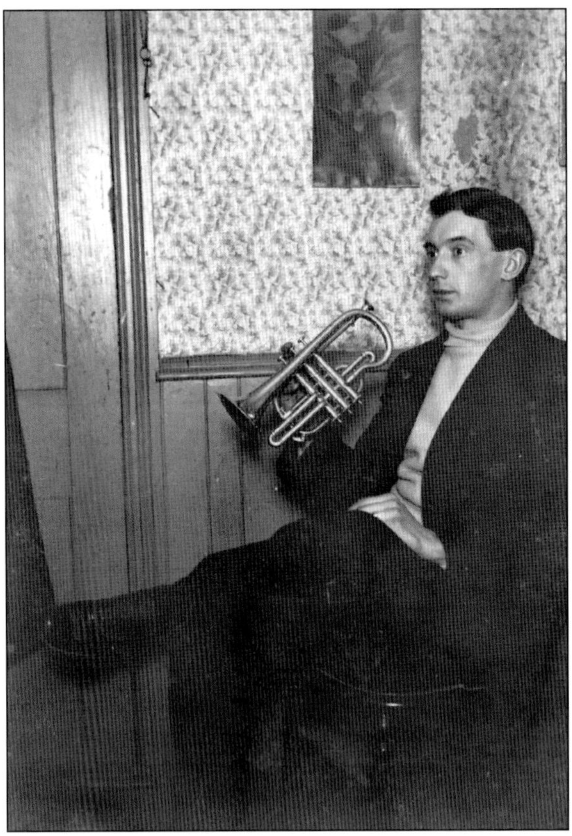

George Washington Sylvester, at left, was born in Tennessee in 1871. He moved to Smyrna, Delaware, where he married Margaret Price in 1893. They had two children, Earl and Mary, and lived in a home on South Street for part of their marriage. Sylvester worked as an engineer at a tomato cannery in the town of Smyrna. When home, he enjoyed playing music. George organized the Sylvester Cornet Band. Here, he is seen presumably teaching the cornet, a brass instrument similar to a trumpet but producing a more mellow tone, to another man and a young boy in a Victorian sitting room (above).

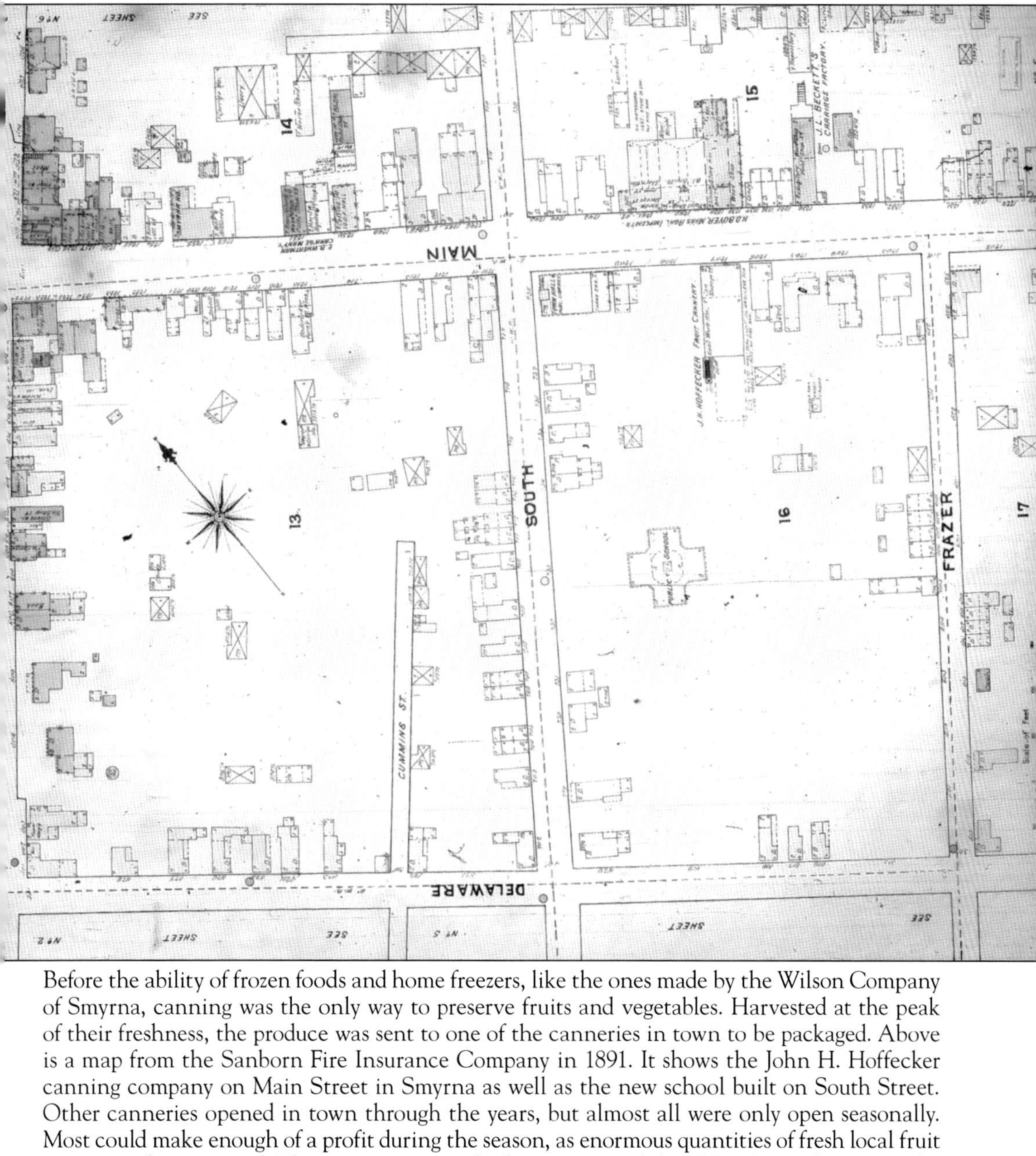

Before the ability of frozen foods and home freezers, like the ones made by the Wilson Company of Smyrna, canning was the only way to preserve fruits and vegetables. Harvested at the peak of their freshness, the produce was sent to one of the canneries in town to be packaged. Above is a map from the Sanborn Fire Insurance Company in 1891. It shows the John H. Hoffecker canning company on Main Street in Smyrna as well as the new school built on South Street. Other canneries opened in town through the years, but almost all were only open seasonally. Most could make enough of a profit during the season, as enormous quantities of fresh local fruit came in to be preserved. The cannery owners had contracts with local farmers and set prices for the produce. Each cannery had a brand name and their own labels to use in the sale of the goods. Peaches, corn, and tomatoes were very popular canned goods.

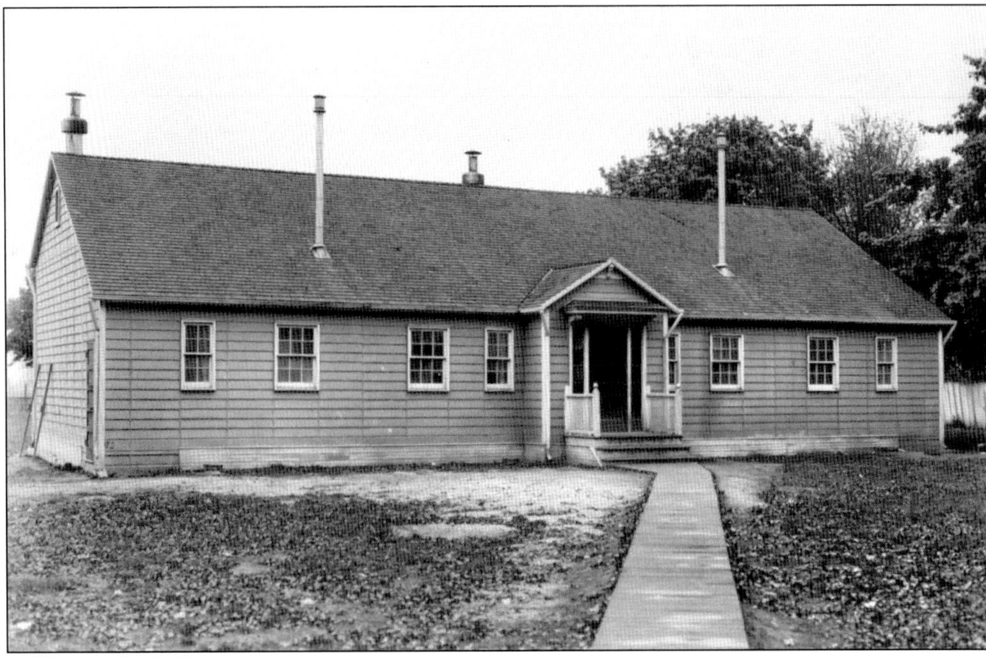

Between the railroad, businesses in town, out-of-town agriculture, and canning and fertilizer companies, the population soared in Smyrna. More schools were needed to house the increase in children. In September 1920, at a cost of $16,550, a two-room school was built to supplement the school on South Street. It was called the Smyrna White Portable School.

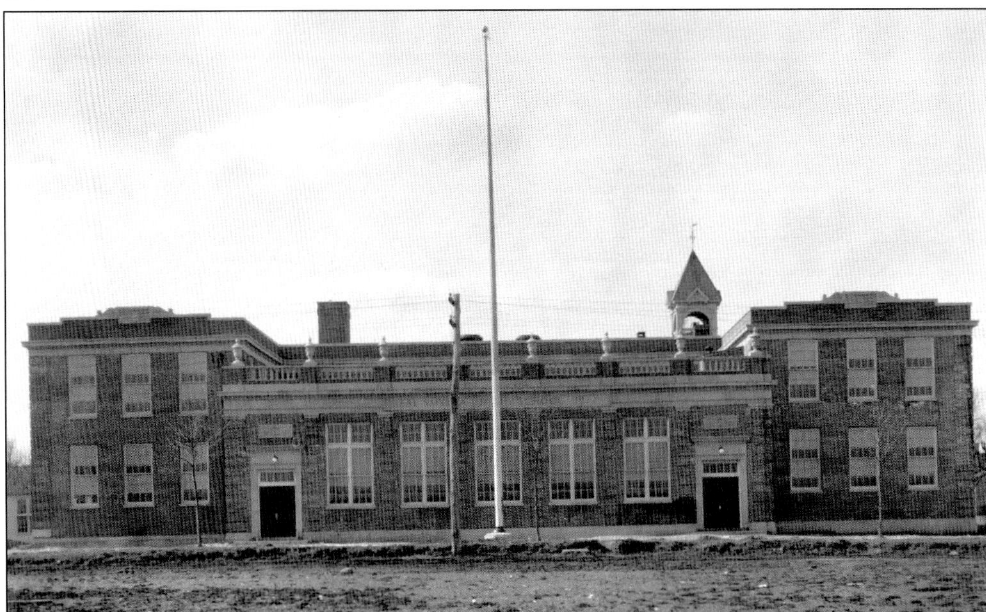

In 1922, the student population had outgrown their South Street building. A new school was completed in April 1924. The 12-room white school was constructed at a cost of $150,315. The old South Street school was demolished. By 1935, additions were needed to keep up with enrollment. Afterwards, a portion was named the John Bassett Moore High School in honor of Smyrna-born Judge J.B. Moore.

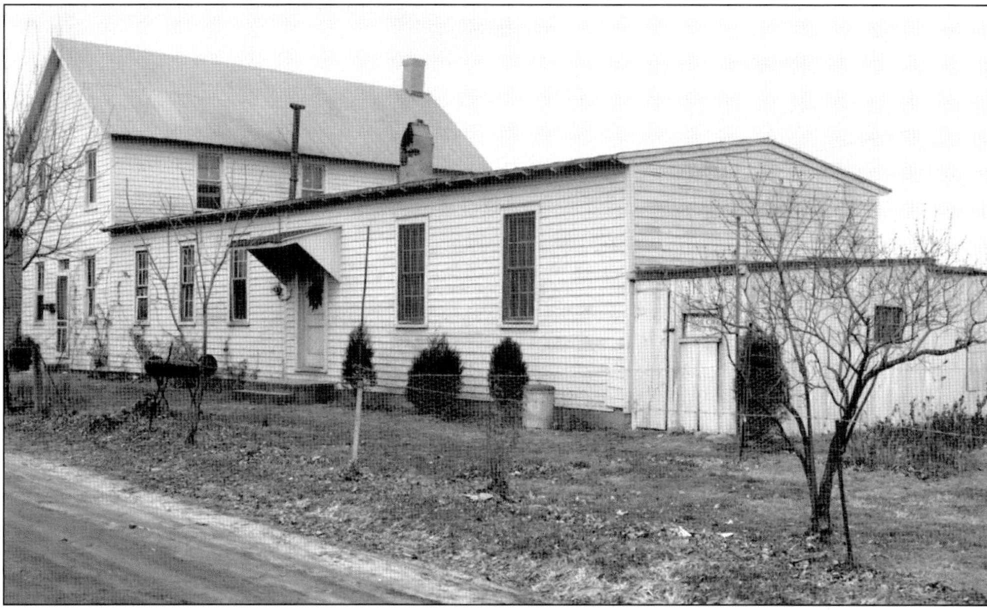

The Smyrna Colored School was built in 1921 through the Pierre S. DuPont initiative to replace dilapidated schools for minorities in the state. DuPont personally donated millions of dollars to the Department of Education to help finance these projects. The Smyrna Colored School was originally a five-room building. In 1940, after renovating a large indoor barn and chicken pen, the school was expanded to include a home economics room for girls' education. The girls participated in canning and sewing fairs with other minority schools to present their skills in the New Homemakers of America group.

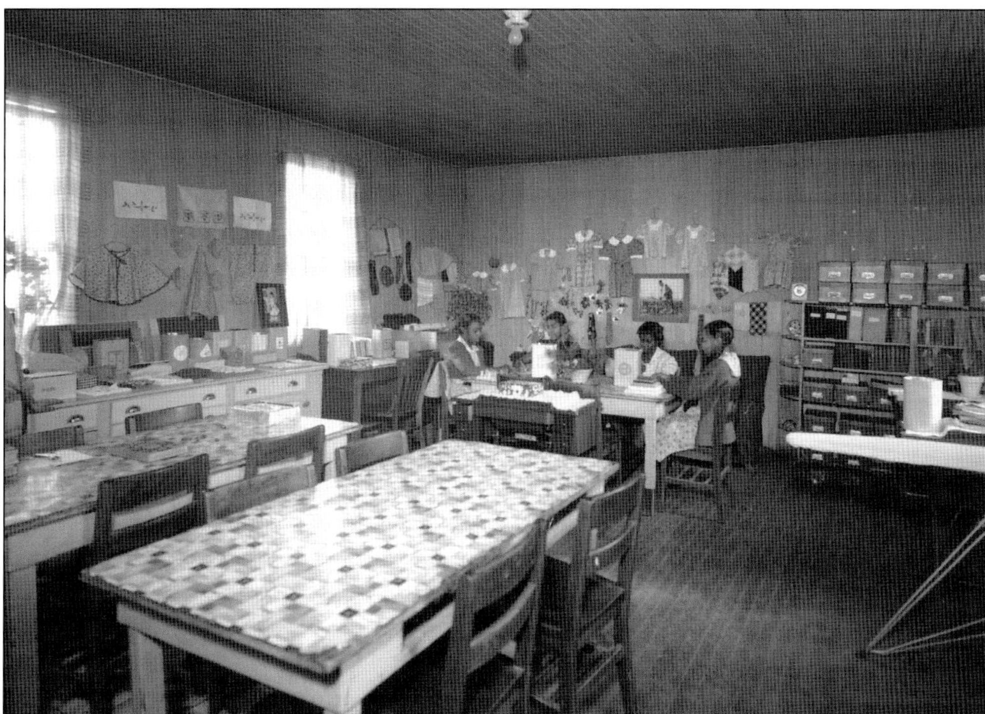

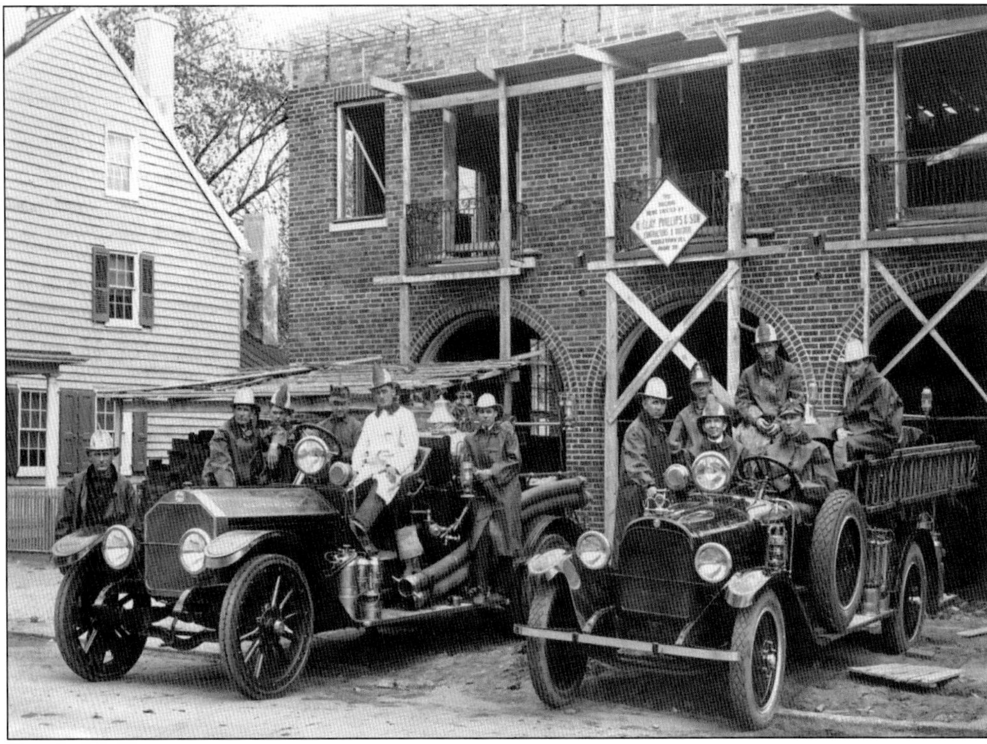

A far cry from the days of the bucket brigade, the Citizens' Hose Company No. 1 was officially formed in 1886 with 30 members while using space at the old town hall. In 1925, they finally moved into their own house, built on land purchased from McDowell on Commerce Street. In that year, the fire chief for the company was George W. Sylvester. He remained chief until 1930. The images on this page show Citizens' Hose Company No. 1 in 1925, just after the move (above), and again in 1929 (below). Other expansions and additions were made to the firehouse, but the company still resides at the same location on Commerce Street in Smyrna.

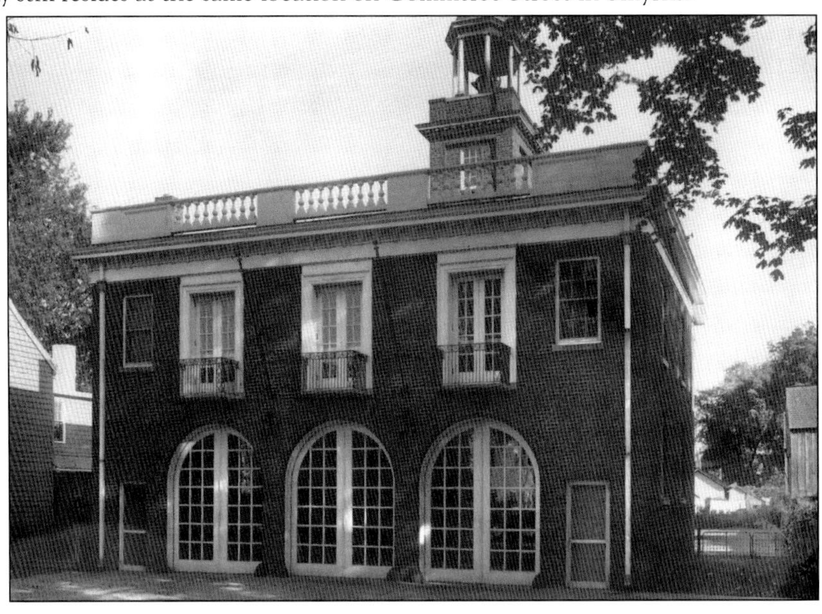

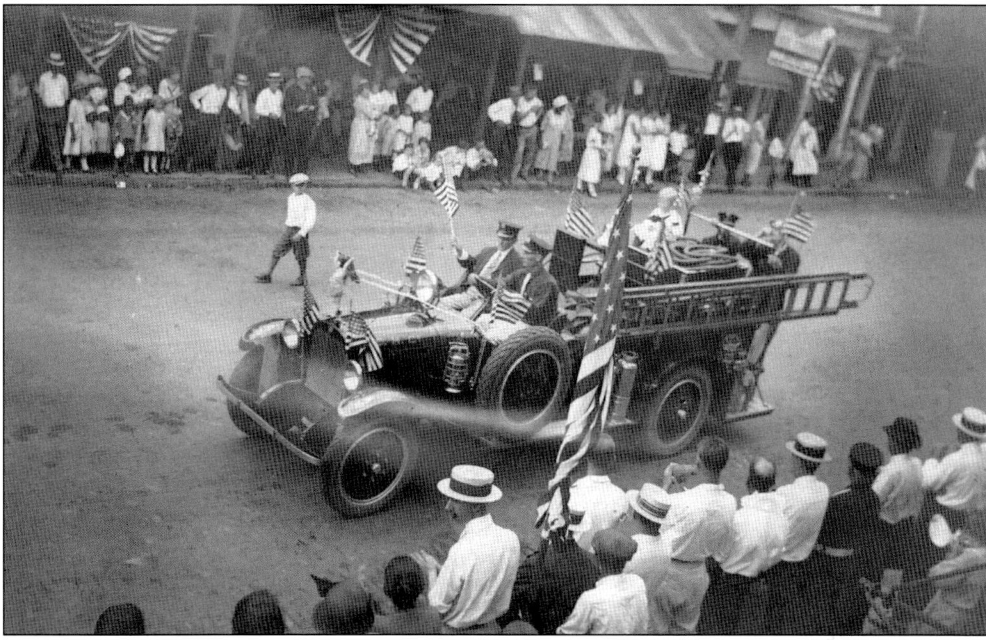

In July 1925, the Citizens' Hose Company No. 1 hosted the fifth annual convention of the Delaware Volunteer Firemen's Association. The hose company was a charter member in the association, which began in 1921. The cost of membership for the company was $5. The parades were meant to show the pride the firemen had in their trucks and their community commitment. (Courtesy of the Citizens' Hose Company No. 1, Inc.)

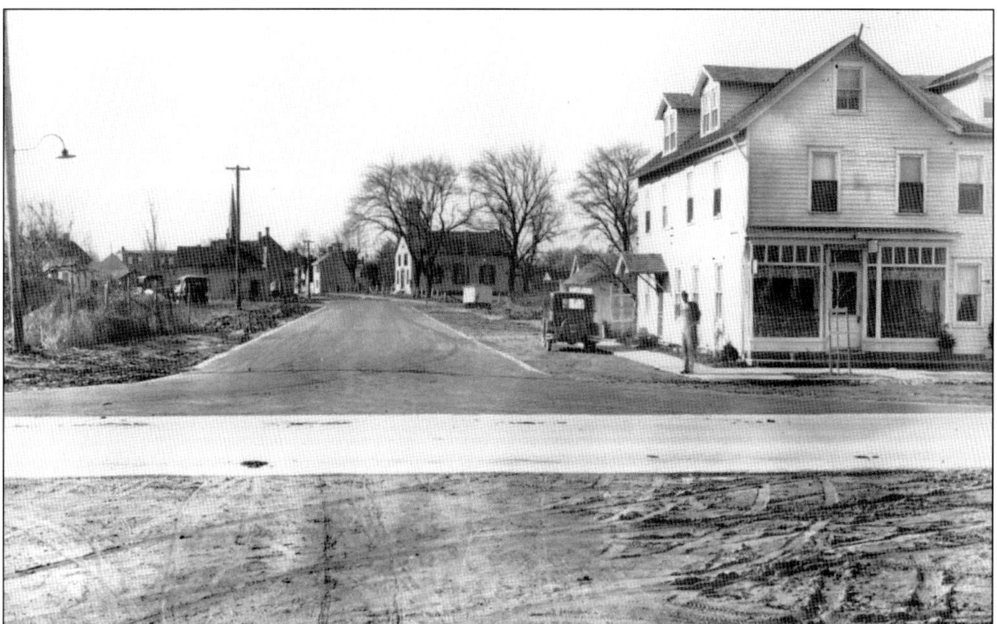

In Smyrna, like other towns at the time, roadways were not uniform and were well worn with large ruts from carts, horses, and new automobiles. Precipitation on the streets was not a driver's friend, as roads would get washed out, muddy, and mostly impassable. This photograph was taken on New Street in Smyrna in 1929.

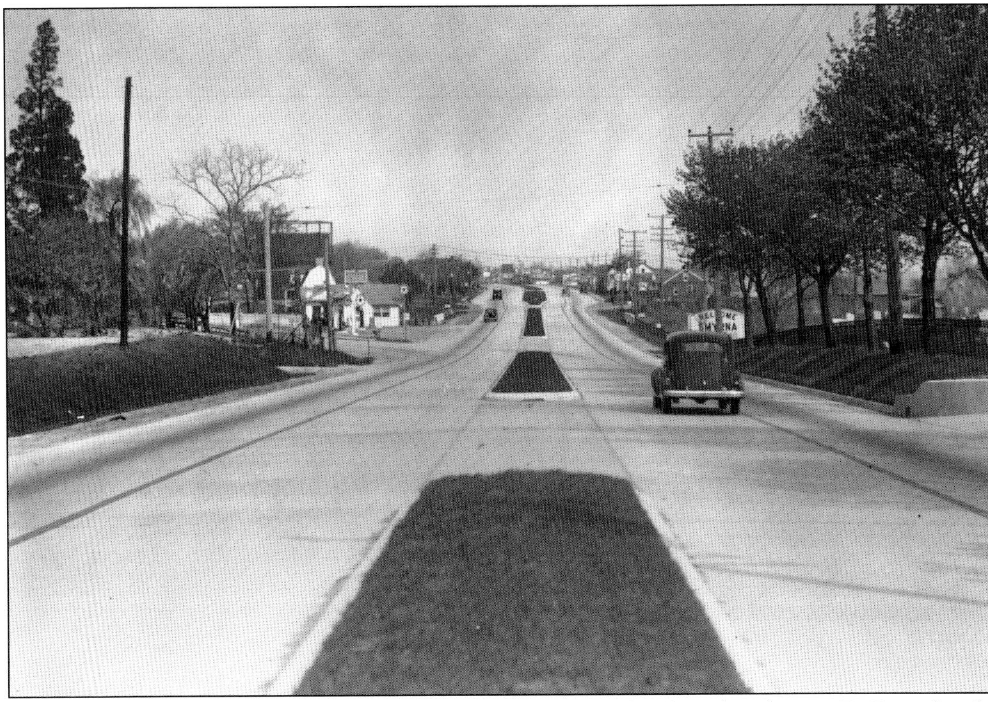

Thomas Coleman DuPont, an engineer from MIT and of the famed Delaware DuPont family, set out to build a "grand boulevard" the entire length of the state of Delaware. He financed and oversaw the entire project himself until 1917, when he turned the remainder of the project over to the newly formed Delaware Highway Department, under the watchful eye of his lead foreman, Douglas Buck. Even under the Delaware Highway Department, DuPont continued to fund the project in its entirety. The concept of the boulevard revolutionized transportation in Delaware and set the standard to which all other highways in the country would be created.

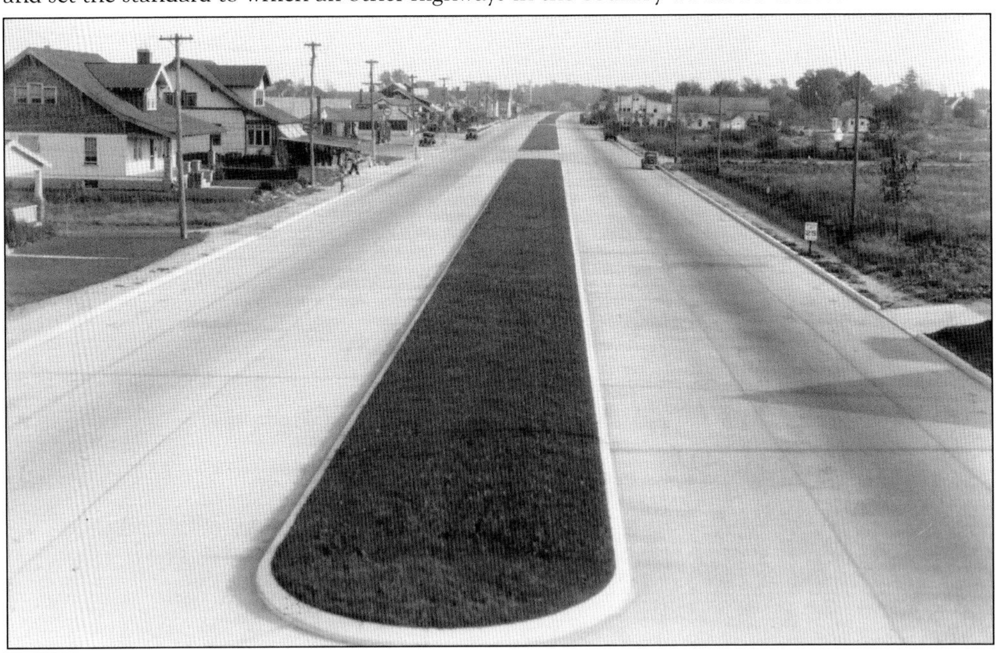

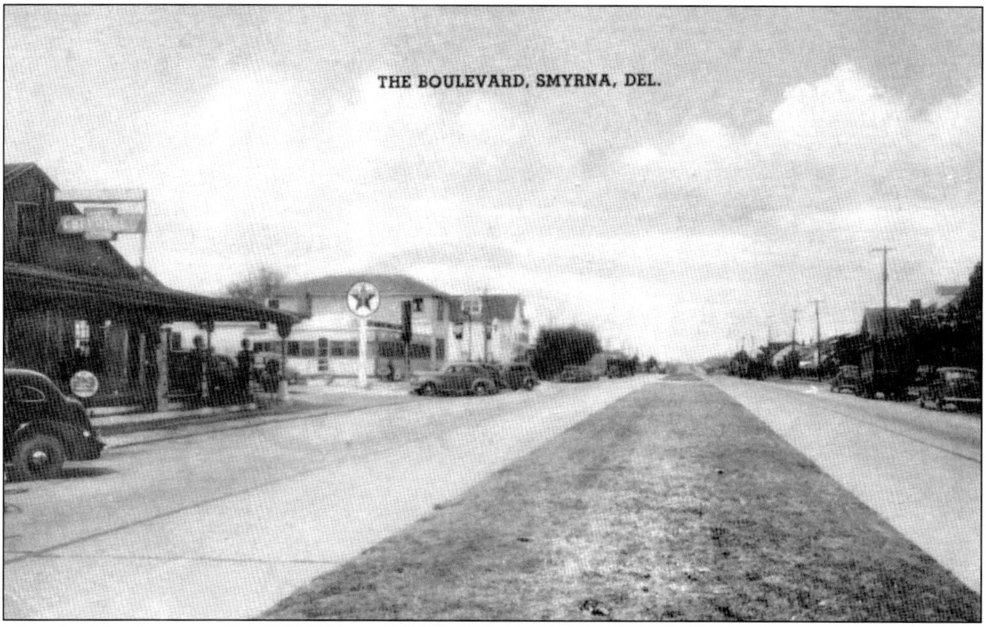

The dual highway, made of concrete, did not traverse through towns, but was laid near them, eliminating downtown traffic and creating an efficient travel time from point A to point B. Of course, the project had opposition from those with different political affiliations and from the landowners and farmers whose land the new road would pass through. The Thomas Coleman DuPont Boulevard led to a renewed surge in local businesses. Instead of being located in the downtown hub of Smyrna, they were now springing up all along the highway corridor. Gas stations, diners, and roadside stands popped up all along the boulevard in Smyrna for the hungry traveler.

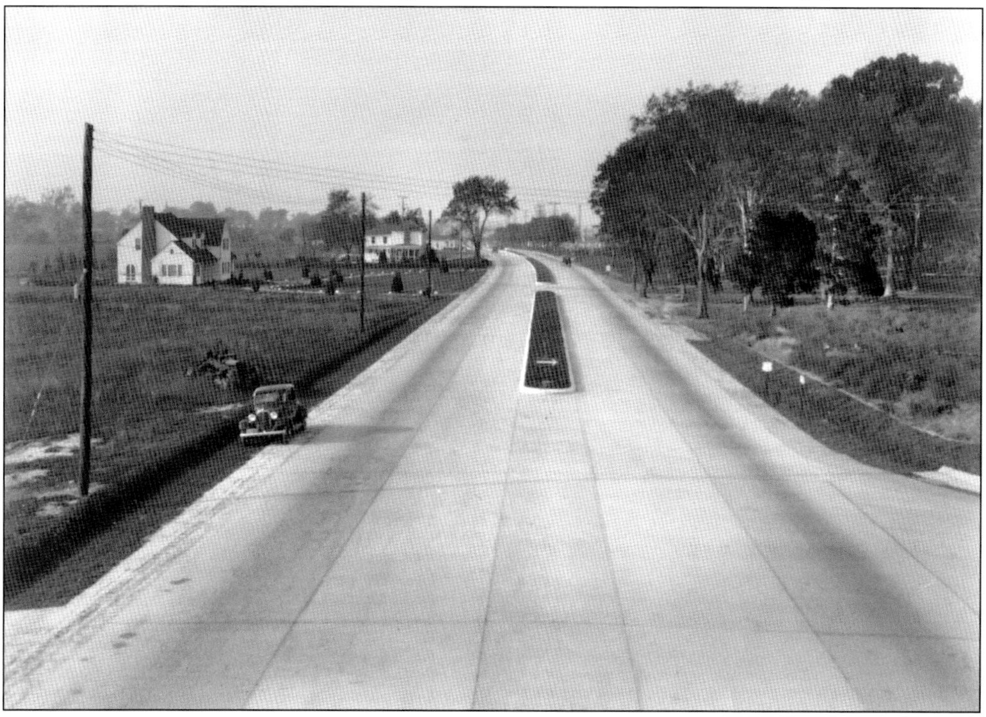

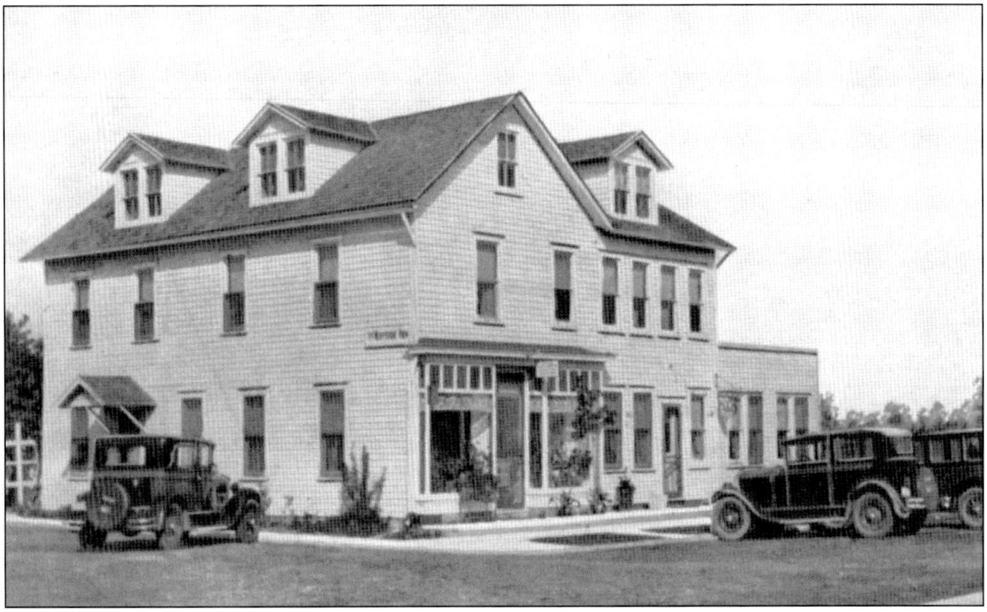

The Wayside Inn opened in 1925 along the freshly laid DuPont Boulevard in Smyrna. They boasted of fresh pies, cakes, and ice cream, all made in their kitchen. They offered special dinners every evening and all-day Sunday, with three different price points: 75¢, $1, and $1.25. The Wayside Inn experienced a lot of change along the Smyrna corridor over the years, including the installation of a beautiful garden for travelers to enjoy. Finally, in 2008, after 80 years of business and several owners, the restaurant closed and ceased doing business as the Wayside Inn. (Below, courtesy of Brooks Keen.)

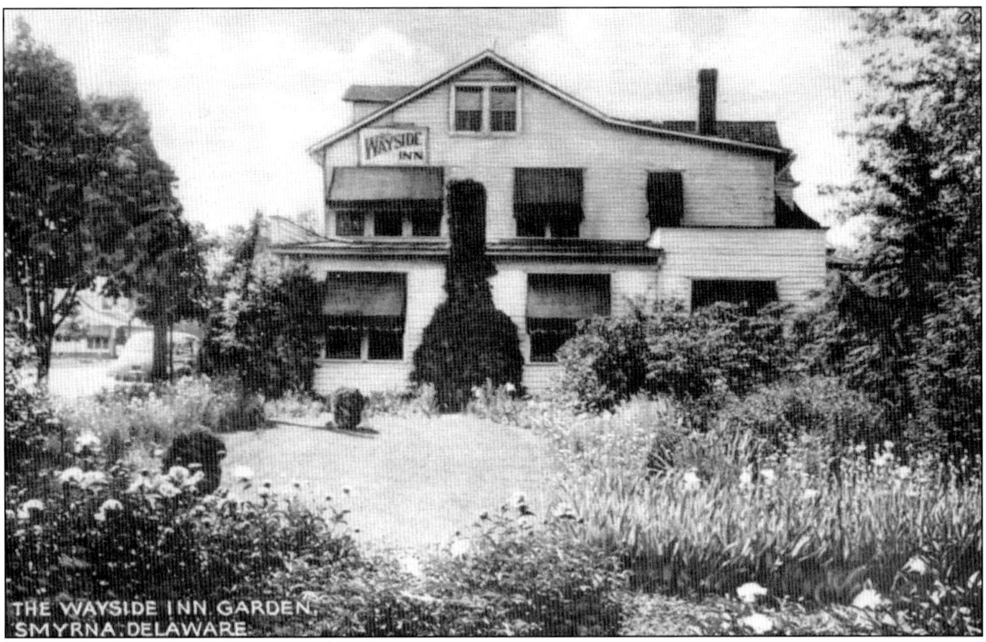

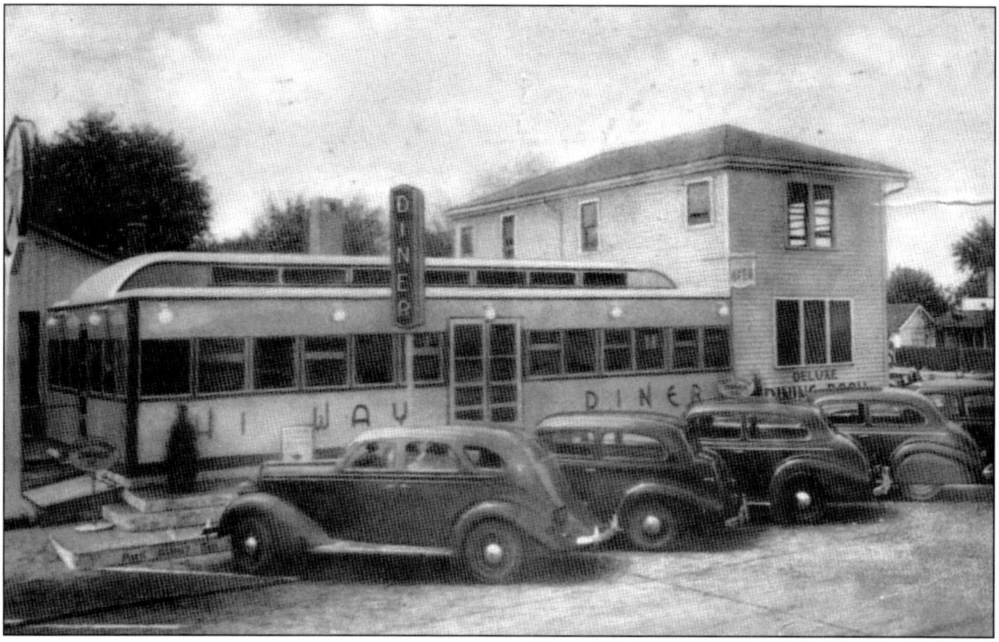

The Hi-way Diner, located on the boulevard, was a Ward and Dickinson dining car built in New York. The Hi-way boasted of a kitchen open for inspection with government inspected meats and Chase and Sanborn coffee. All pies and desserts were prepared in their own kitchen. A special, full-course dinner in the built on "deluxe" dining room would only cost travelers 50¢. (Courtesy of Brooks Keen.)

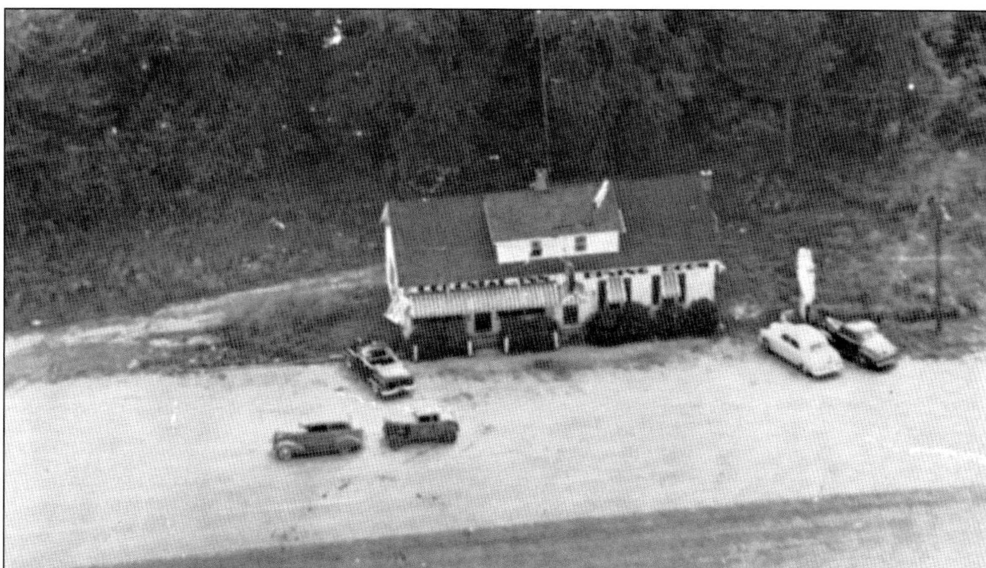

The Colonial Inn was located 3.5 miles north of the town of Smyrna. They offered fine foods and cocktails as well as seafood. The restaurant was open seven days a week from 6:00 a.m. until 11:00 p.m., serving breakfast, lunch, and dinner to boulevard travelers.

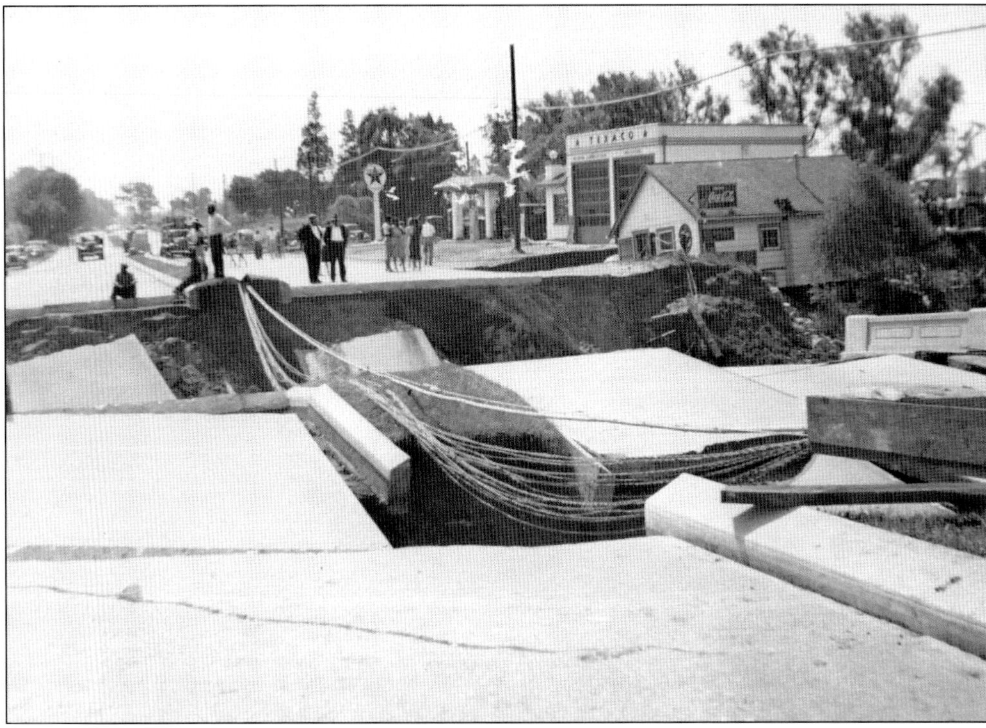

With all new things come new problems. The new DuPont Boulevard in Smyrna was not without its hiccups. In 1940, and again a few other times over the years, the portion of the road that bridges over Lake Como collapsed. Traffic was at a standstill, and a detour was needed.

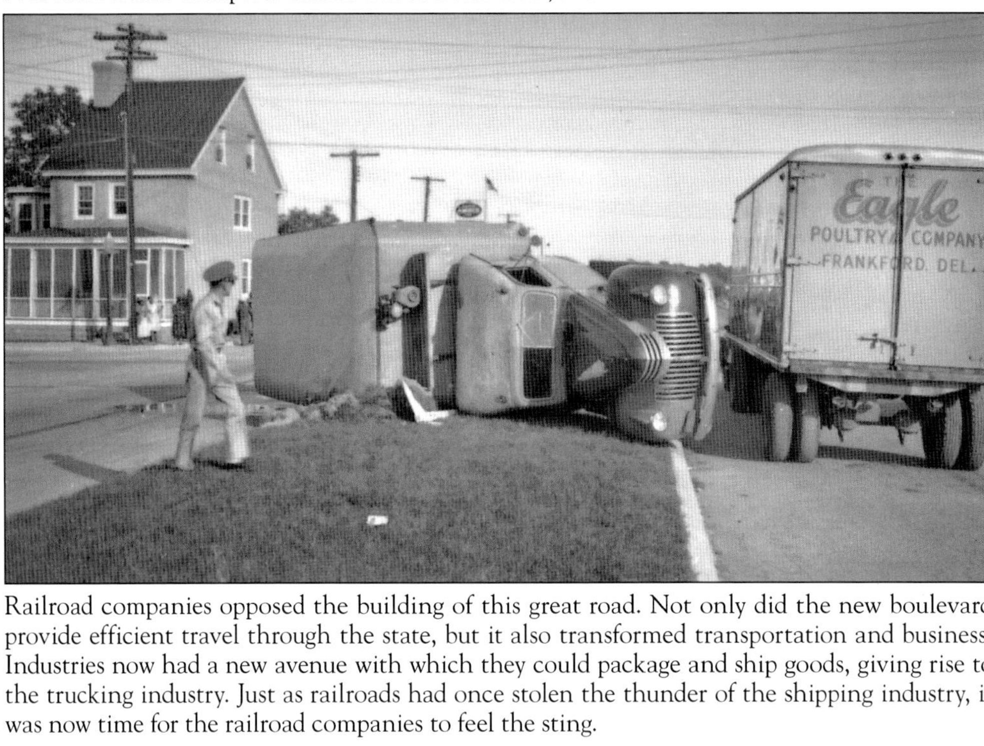

Railroad companies opposed the building of this great road. Not only did the new boulevard provide efficient travel through the state, but it also transformed transportation and business. Industries now had a new avenue with which they could package and ship goods, giving rise to the trucking industry. Just as railroads had once stolen the thunder of the shipping industry, it was now time for the railroad companies to feel the sting.

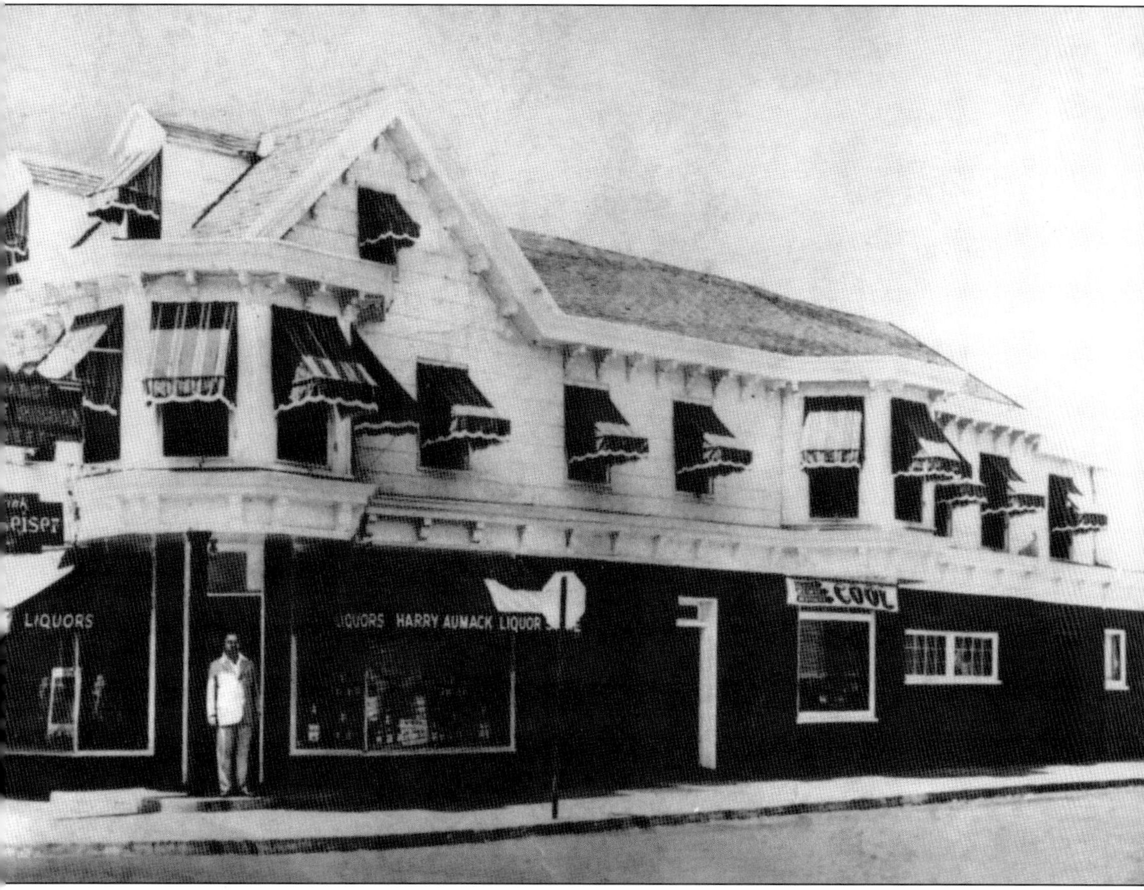

Smyrna Package Goods and Tavern was located on the corner of Commerce and Market Streets. Historically, this property has been many businesses, including a millinery (hatmaking factory) in the late 1800s. Shown here in 1940, the business was owned by Harry Aumack. Like a lot Smyrna business owners, then and now, Aumack was involved in many community interests. He was a member of the Citizens' Hose Company No. 1, just a block away on Commerce Street, and a member of the Smyrna Business Association, where he attended meetings and served on committees with other members of the town. Harry Aumack also sponsored a local softball team. (Courtesy of the Duck Creek Historical Society.)

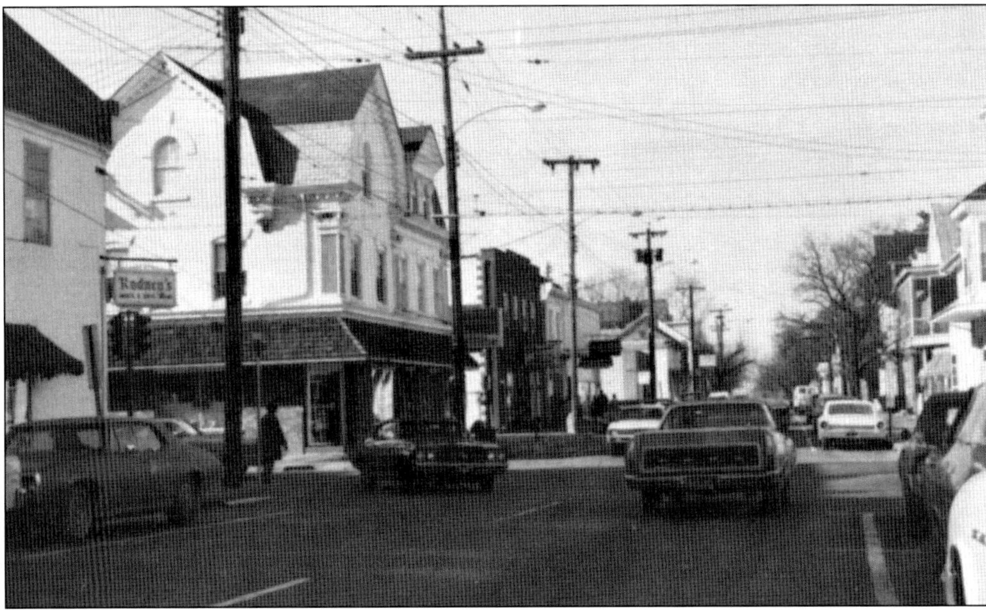

Businesses kept steady in the downtown district of Smyrna, and the town continued to expand. Rodney's, first located in Ward's Hall on Commerce Street next to the Colonial Hotel, moved into the Ball's Corner building. Rodney Schuman previously worked at Wooten's department store before opening his own clothing store for men in town.

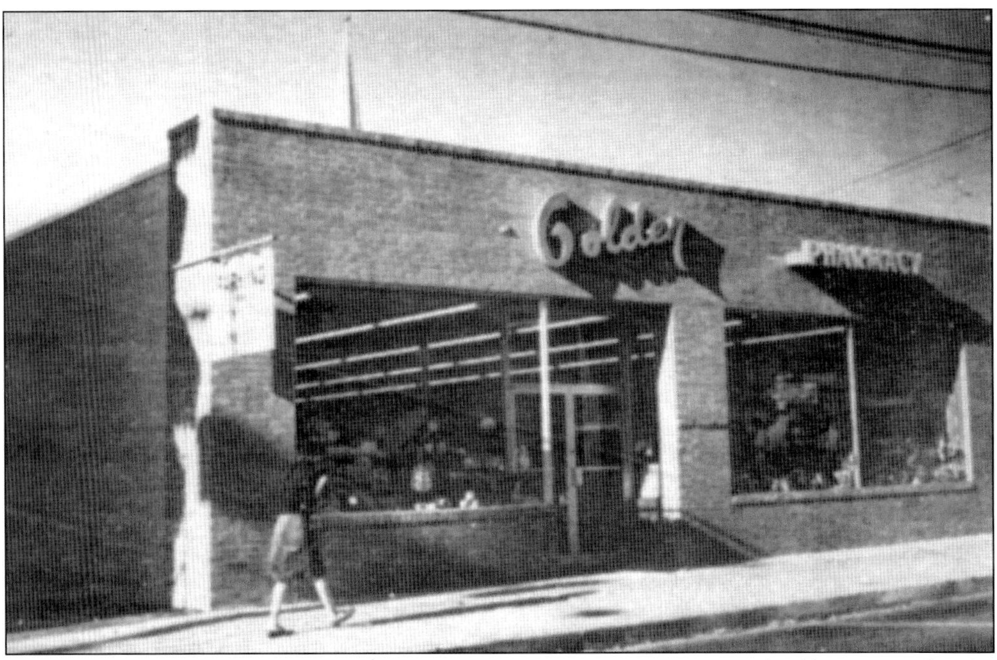

Golden's Pharmacy opened first in the old Clifton and Jones Drugstore building around 1953. Martin Golden renovated and expanded the old drugstore after opening under his name. Golden's stayed there for almost 15 years before moving farther north on Main Street. The new building was much more modern.

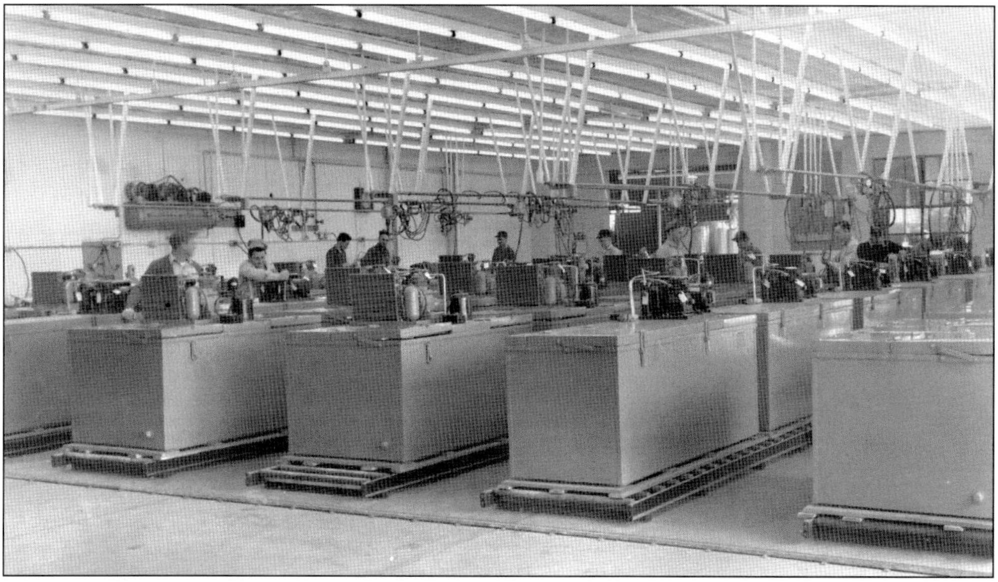

The Wilson Cabinet Company was started in 1934 in the midst of the Great Depression and rose to become a national contender for their revolutionary model for home storage: the Zerosafe quick freezer. In 1948, the factory was devastated by a million-dollar fire. The building was abandoned for a new headquarters. Soon, two other buildings were purchased for new office space, storage, and manufacturing needs. (Courtesy of the Citizens' Hose Company No. 1, Inc.)

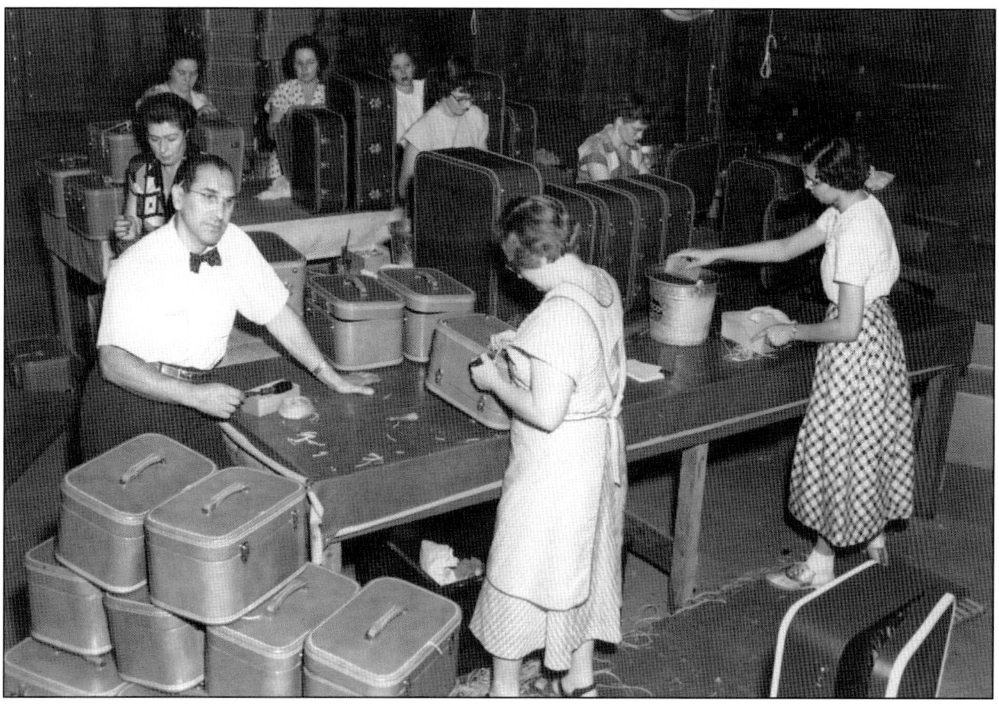

The Belber Trunk and Bag Company of Philadelphia purchased the Wilson Refrigeration Company building on Main Street in Smyrna in 1959. The company set up in Smyrna and manufactured luggage in their new building. The Belber Trunk and Bag Company eventually went on to become a division of the Leeds Travel Wear Company.

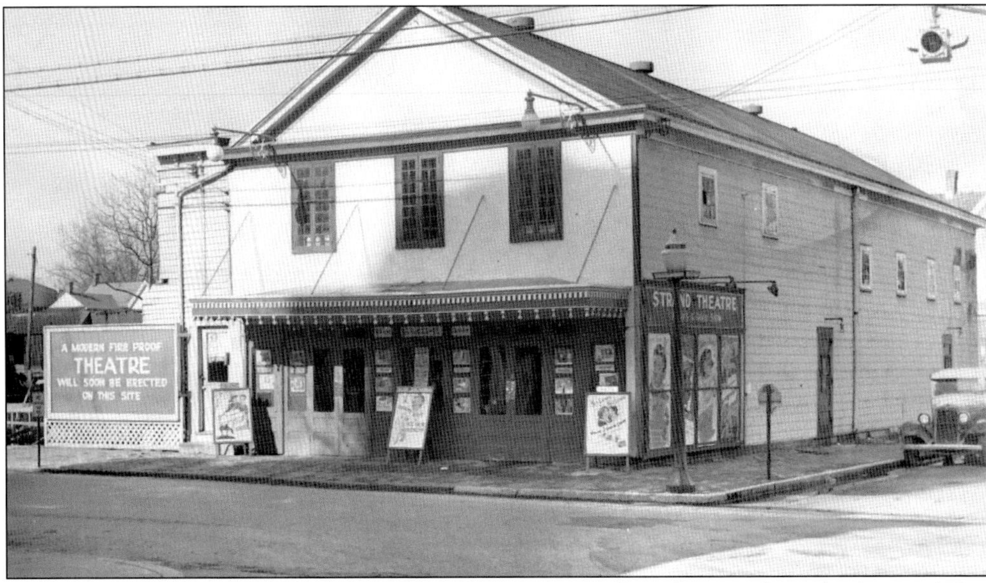

The Strand Theater was located on West Commerce Street, directly across from the Citizens' Hose Company. The theater, just like the Roxy in the old town hall, offered silver screen entertainment for the citizens of Smyrna. After sitting vacant for two years, the theater was torn down in 1950. The location became the parking lot for the new Smyrna Theater next door. (Courtesy of the Citizens' Hose Company No. 1, Inc.)

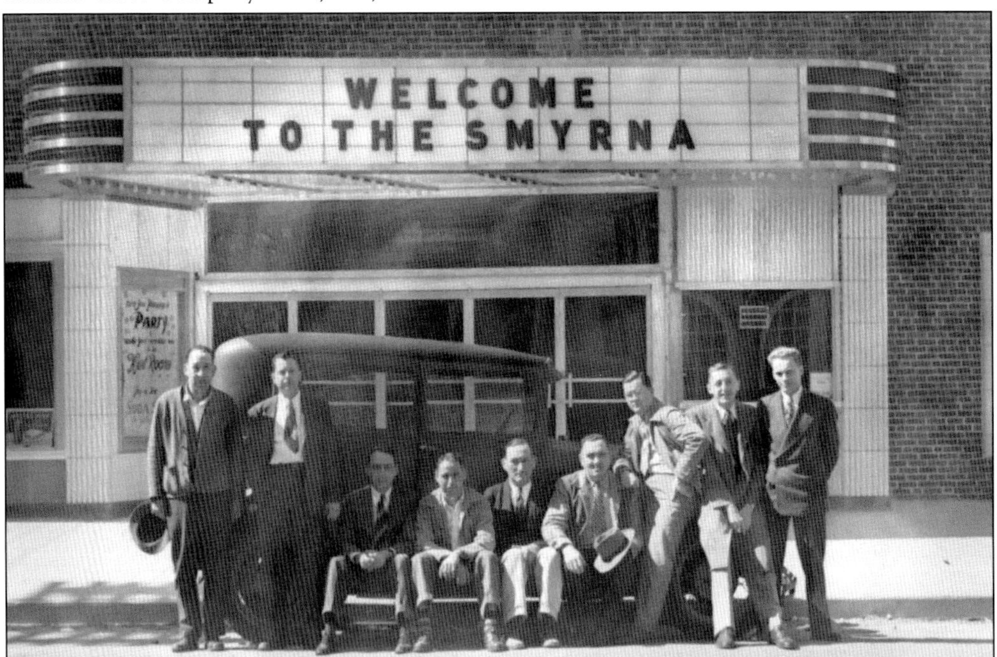

The Smyrna Theater opened directly next to the Strand Theater in 1948. It operated until 1983, when it was sold to a plumbing supply company. This photograph was taken in 1948 of a group of Citizens' Hose firemen, who are, from left to right, Harold Hufschmidt, Wilson Mayberrie, Fletcher Truax, James Truax, William Poore, Horace David, Leland Slaughter, Harry Pusey, and Gi Faries. (Courtesy of the Citizens' Hose Company No. 1, Inc.)

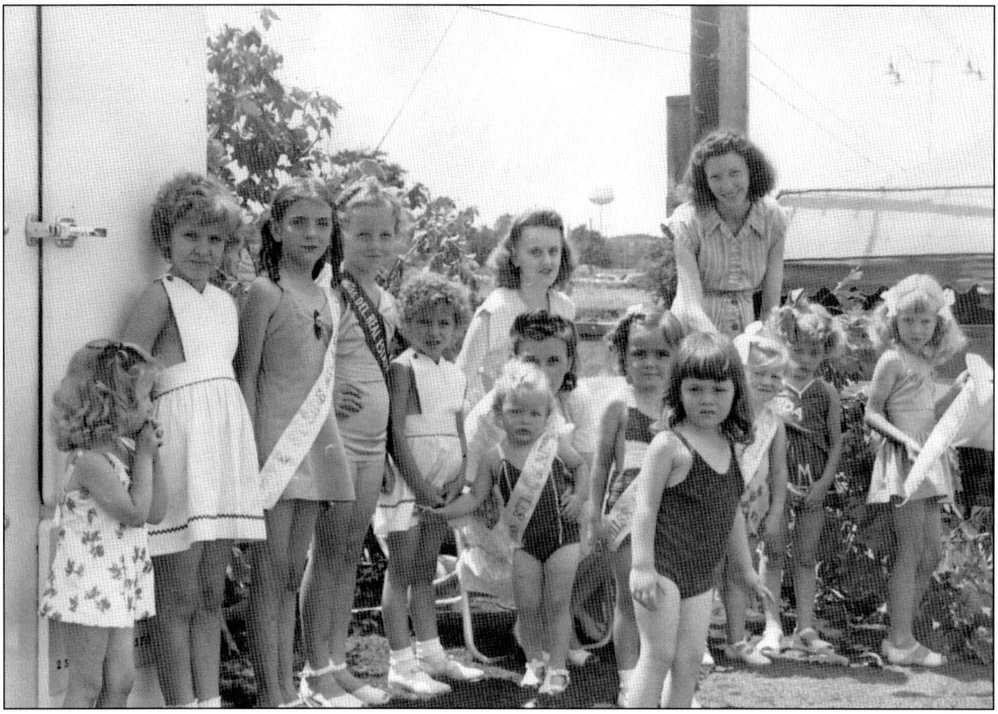

The Citizens' Hose Company in Smyrna was, and continues to be, heavily involved with the Smyrna community. The company used to sponsor a carnival every summer for the town. Rides, raffles, car give-a-ways, contests, and games filled the weeklong fair. This photograph was taken of the children's beauty contest at the fire company carnival at Lake Como in 1946. (Courtesy of the Citizens' Hose Company No. 1, Inc.)

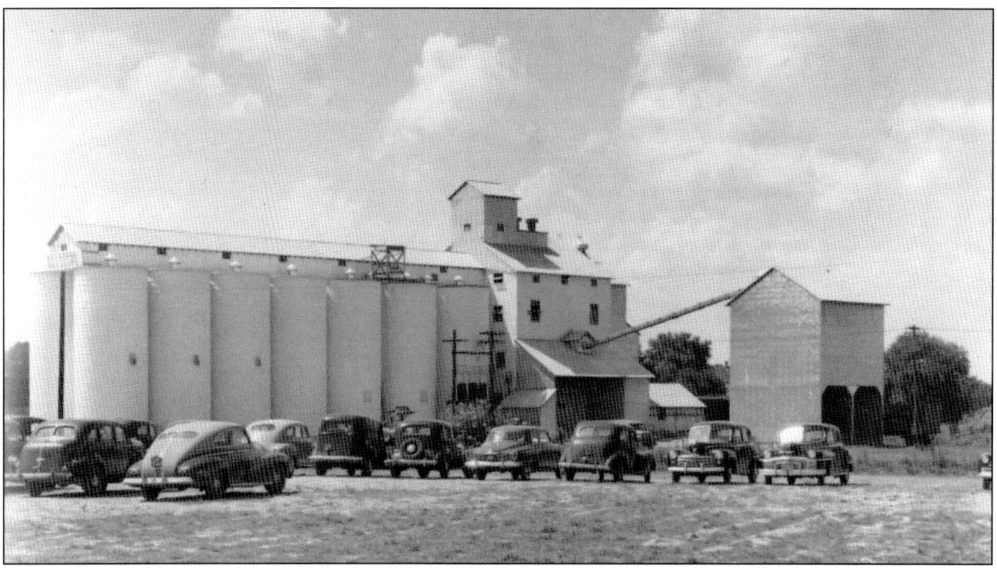

Even with large industries moving into Smyrna, agriculture and grain remained king. The Rothwell Grain Company survived for many years in Smyrna. In May 1957, a large fire broke out at the granary. Both the Clayton and Smyrna fire companies met at the scene. (Courtesy of the Citizens' Hose Company No. 1, Inc.)

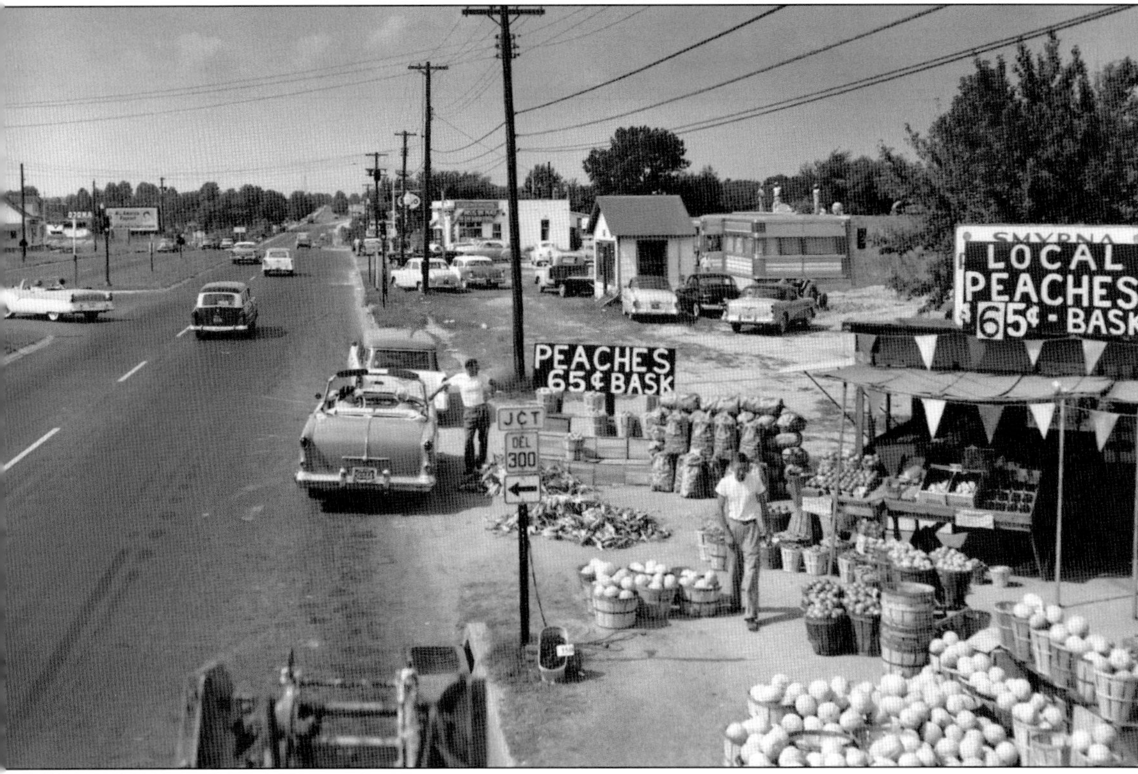

Even with the downfall of the fantastic peach orchards historically in and around Smyrna, peaches, apples, and strawberries still prevailed on a smaller scale. With the introduction of the DuPont Boulevard, stands like this one popped up along the roadside in the summer months. They catered to those traveling from Wilmington to the beaches in Sussex County along the DuPont road, as well as Smyrna locals, as produce of the area was still in high demand. This image shows one such stand around 1950, located on the highway in Smyrna at the intersection of the boulevard and Route 300. They were selling a large variety of peaches, tomatoes, potatoes, and melons. The building slightly north of this fruit stand was the previous diner replaced by the 1965 Smyrna Diner. Just above that is the County Line restaurant and motel.

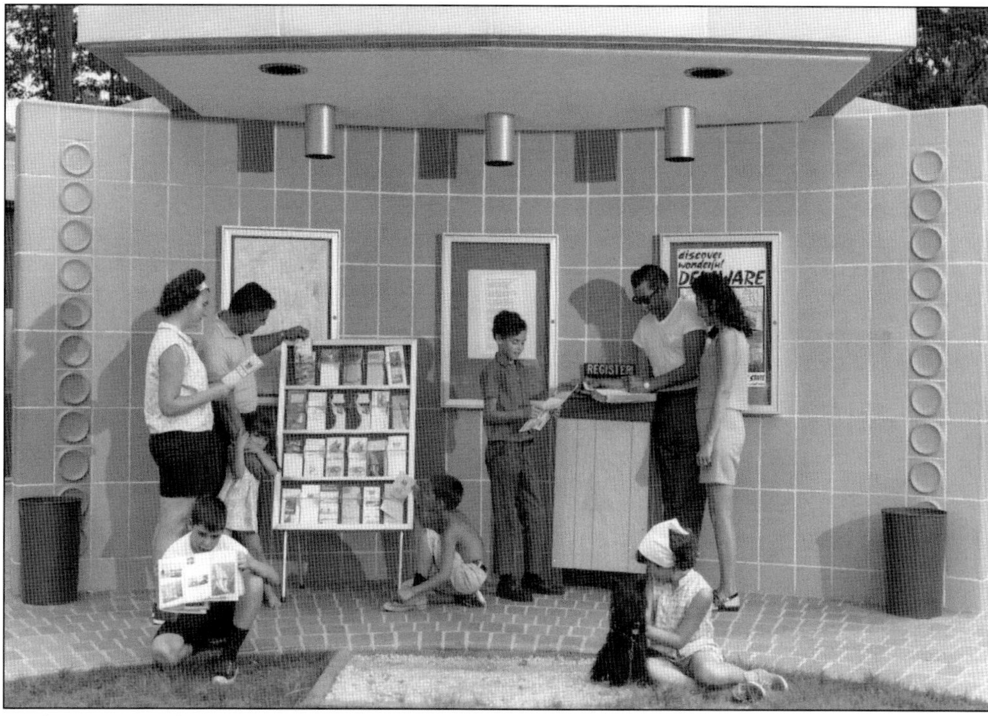

With more travelers traversing through Smyrna, a rest area was started in 1937 by the Delaware Highway Commission. First, it was just a spot of open space for cars to pull off the road, but this eventually grew to include several buildings, picnic areas, and even a short-lived petting zoo. This photograph shows the Smyrna Rest Area in 1960 as visitors stop to gather local information about the state of Delaware.

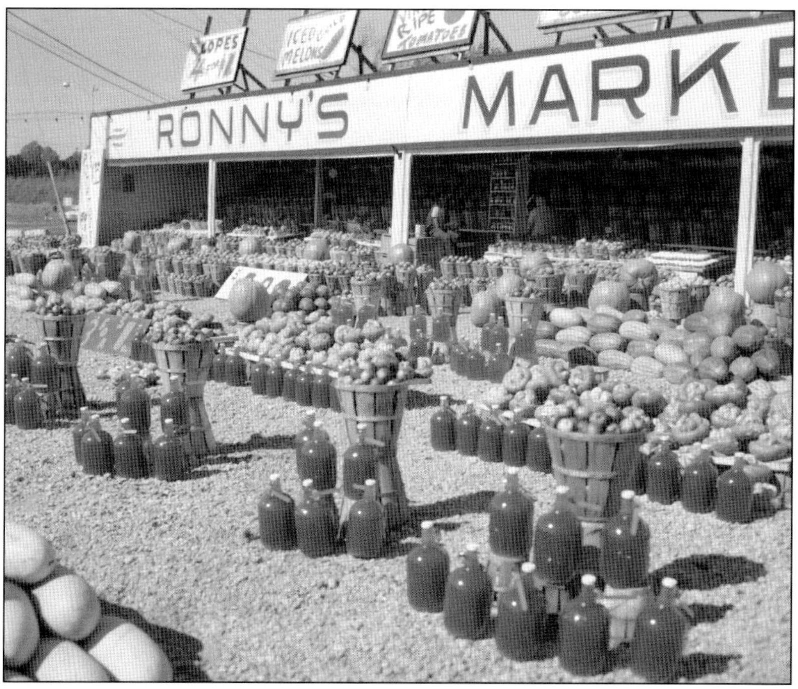

Ronny's Market started as a seasonal roadside market catering to those travelers going south to the beaches, as shown in this photograph from 1960. By 1970, Ronny's Garden World was a thriving business of plants and gardening supplies and is still a fixture along the boulevard today.

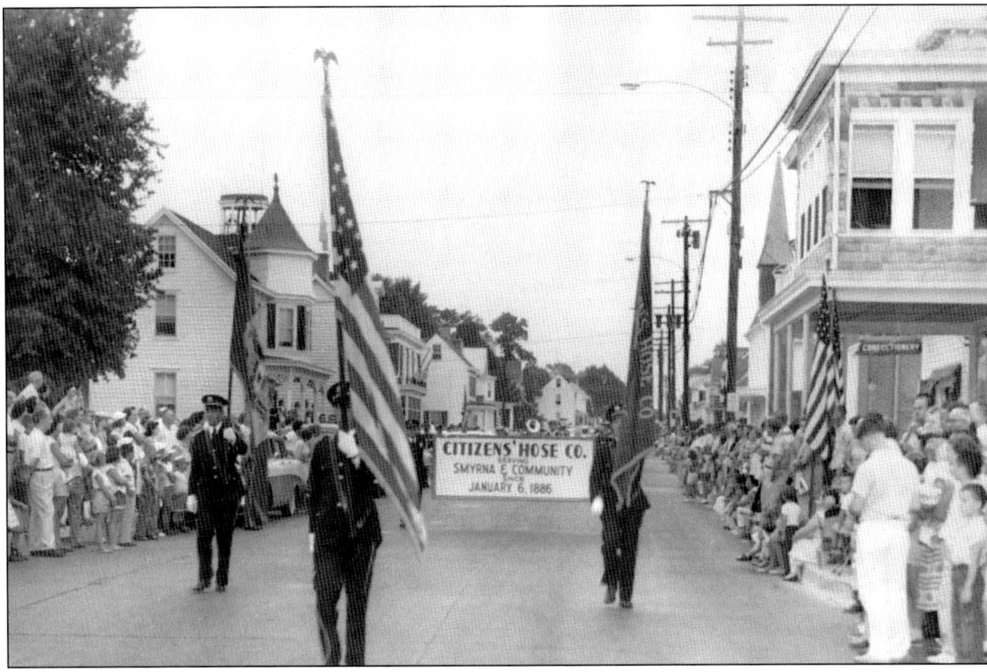

The Citizens' Hose Company No. 1 marching band is shown here in a rededication of Commerce Street in 1957. This photograph taken near the corner of Commerce and Market Streets shows the change of West Commerce Street from the early commercial days. (Courtesy of the Citizens' Hose Company No. 1, Inc.)

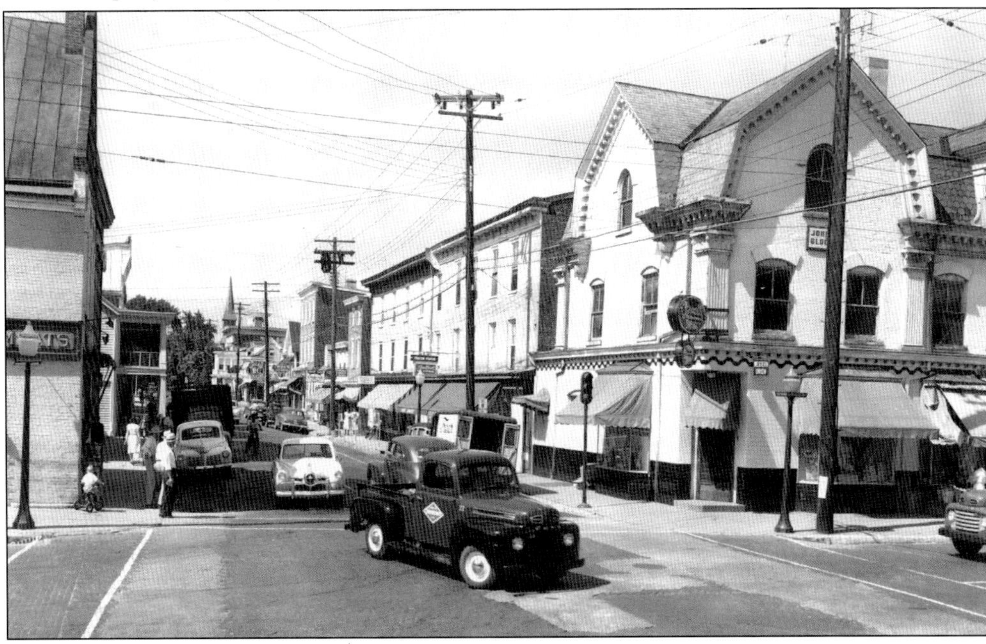

The more things change, the more they stay the same. Still referred to as the Four Corners, downtown Smyrna remains a hub of activity. Although there are considerably less downtown businesses than there were at the turn of the 20th century, industries have continued and many still frequent the intersection of the Maryland Road and the Kings Road.

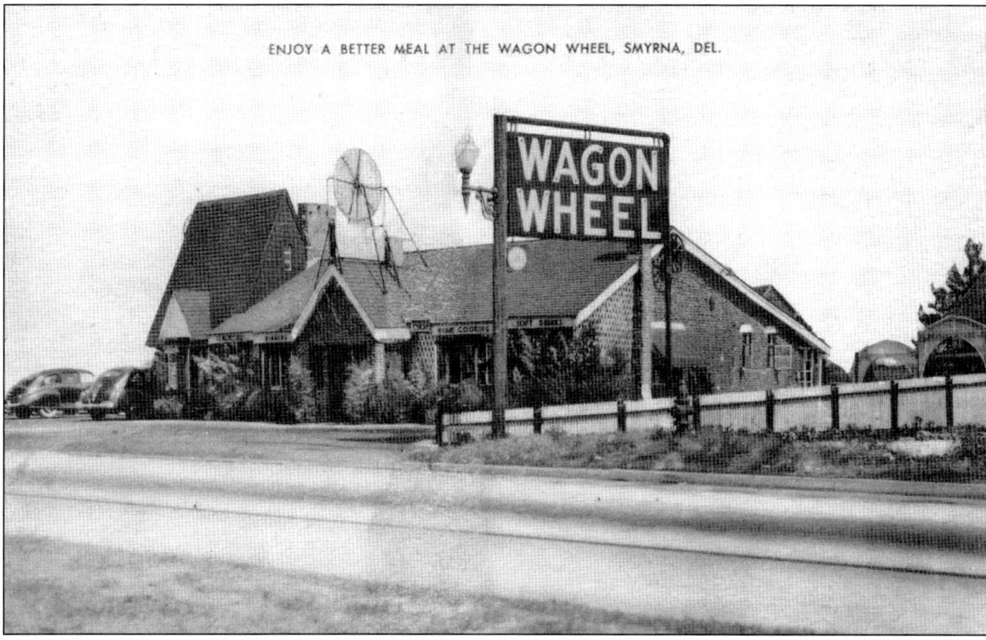

"Enjoy a better meal at the Wagon Wheel" was the slogan for the Wagon Wheel. This restaurant popped up on the DuPont Boulevard corridor more than 40 years ago. Their biggest draw has always been authentic home cooked food, including muskrat. Muskrats are trapped in the marsh toward Bombay Hook and cooked to perfection at the Wagon Wheel. While it sounds strange, to the local hunters and trappers, muskrat is a delicacy.

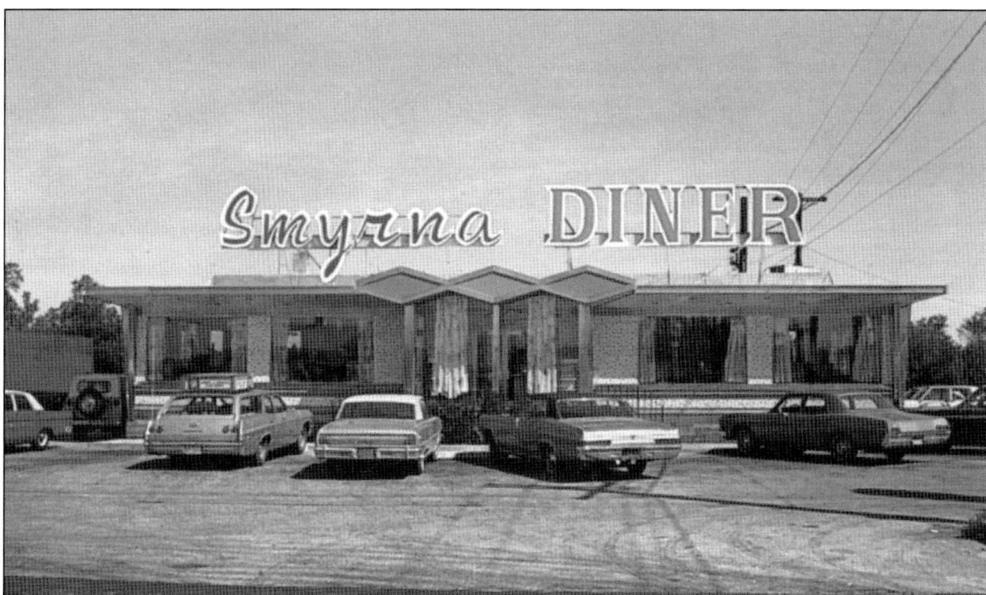

The Smyrna Diner opened in 1965 with a Paramount Diner car, replacing an older, smaller diner that opened in 1954. Over the years, the facade was updated with wood panel overlay. The Smyrna Diner became a local landmark on the DuPont Boulevard, located on the northbound side of the highway.

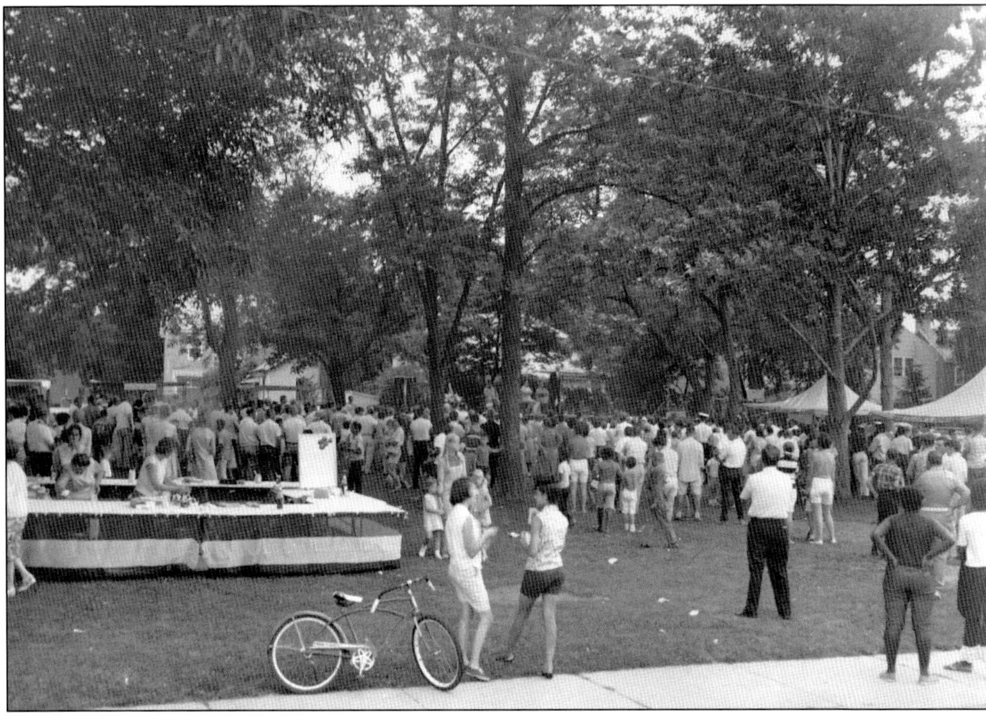

Citizens' Hose Company No. 1's carnival took place in the new park at Market Plaza in 1967. The plaza was cut through in the 1960s, giving a location for a new post office in 1962, a local park, and a new town hall in 1972. The plaza sits between South and Commerce Streets and faces the John Bassett Moore School on South Street. (Courtesy of the Citizens' Hose Company No. 1, Inc.)

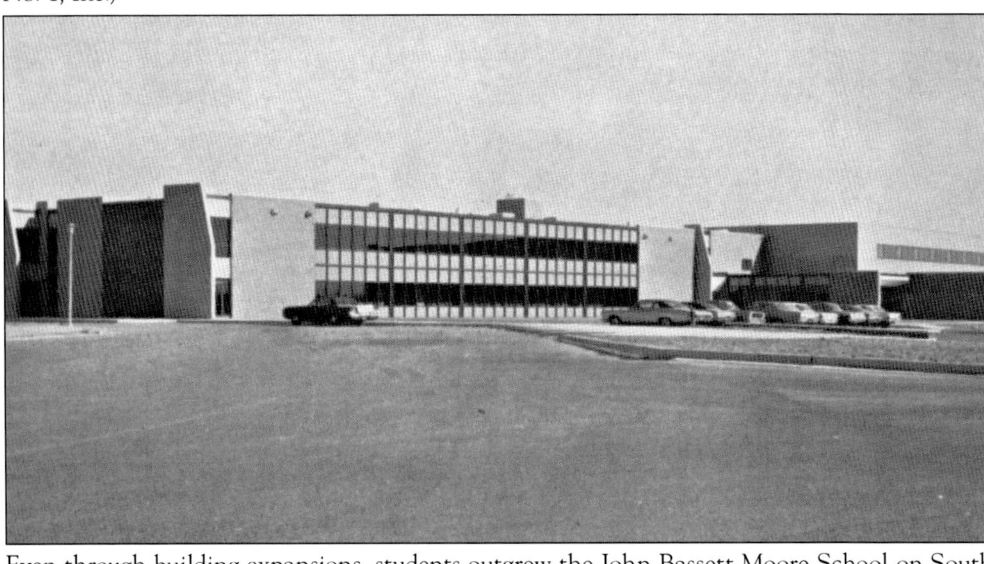

Even through building expansions, students outgrew the John Bassett Moore School on South Street. New schools were needed for all grade levels. The new high school finally opened outside of downtown Smyrna in January 1971. The $4.5-million school was built on the Johnson farm and directly faces Duck Creek. Along the same road, one can find the old Quaker Friends burial ground of Salisbury and Duck Creek Village. (Courtesy of Brooks Keen.)

Four

Clayton

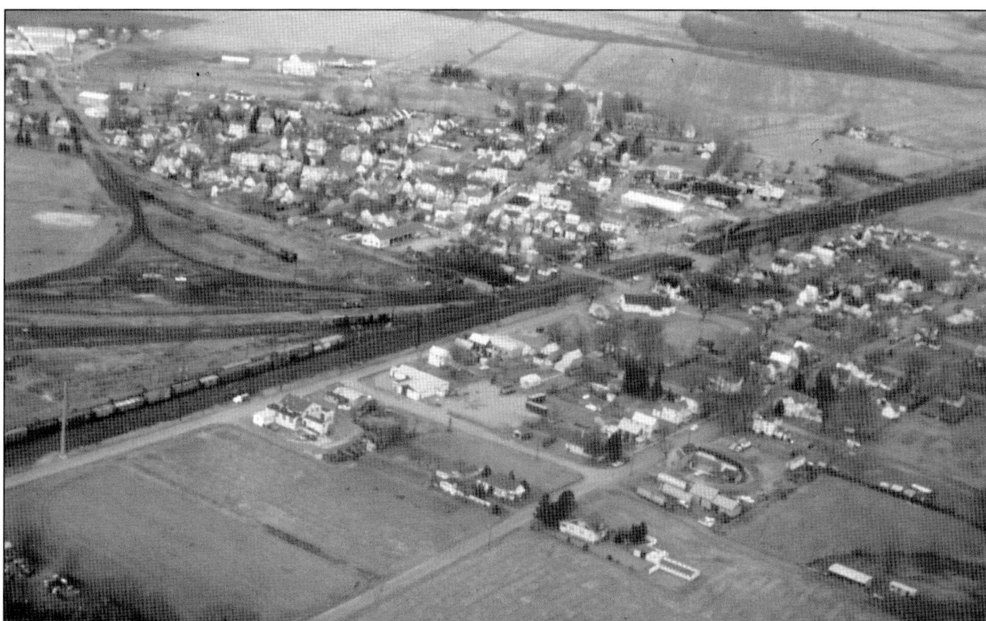

The Smyrna Station community began after the installation of railroad tracks through the Tibbitt farmland west of Smyrna in 1854. By 1860, a small depot, a church, a hotel, and a general store took root. In that same year, the community finally got the name Clayton.

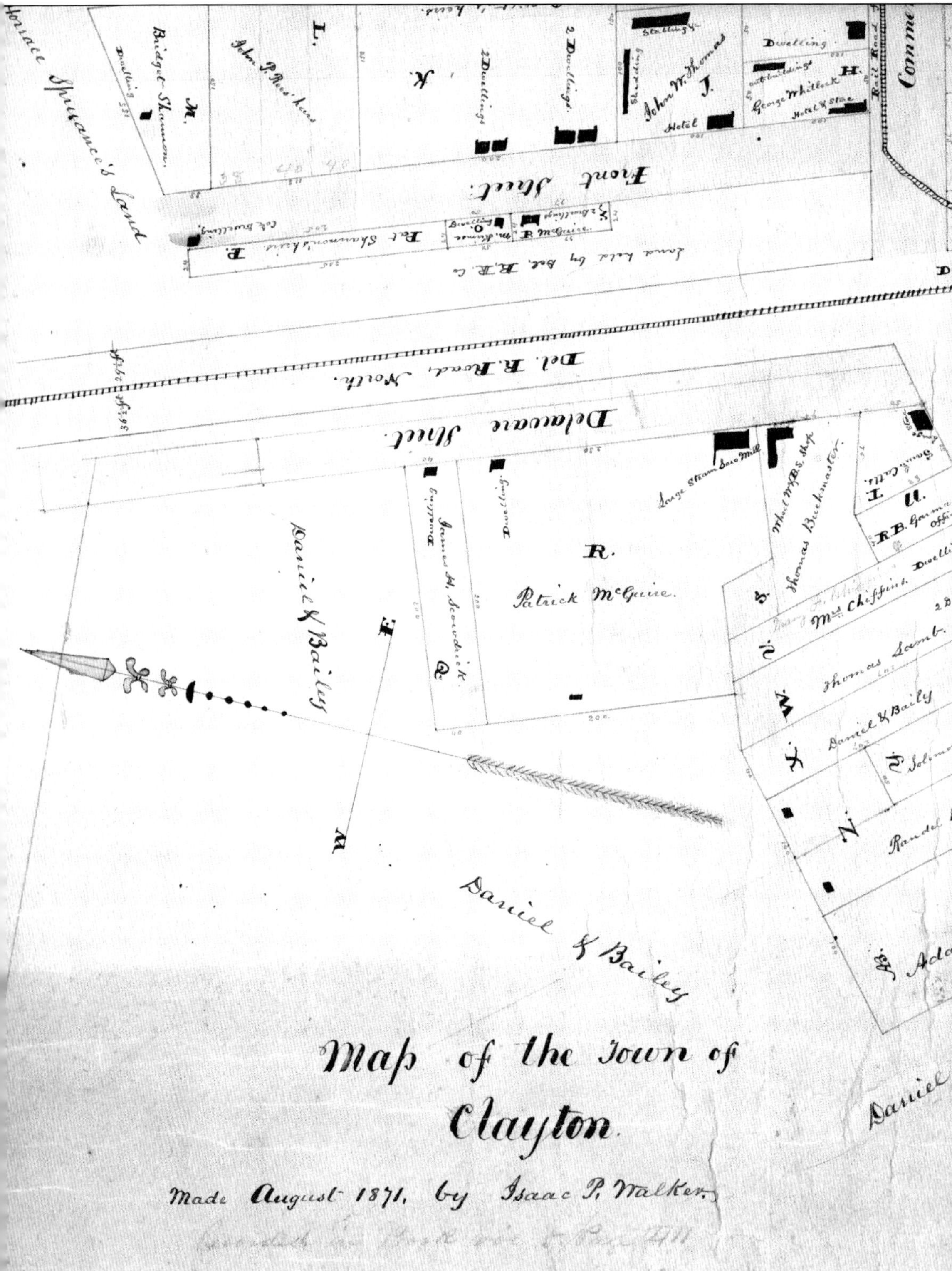

Map of the Town of Clayton
Made August 1871, by Isaac P. Walker
Front Street
Del. R. Road, North.
Delaware Street
Bridget Shannon
John P. Rees' heirs
2 Dwellings
Stabling
John W. Thomas
Hotel
Dwelling
George Whitlock
Hotel & Store
Pat Shannon's heirs
Land held by Del. R.R. Co.
Large Steam Saw Mill
Thomas Buckmaster
Patrick McGuire
James H. Scowdrick
Daniel & Bailey
Mrs. Chiffins
Thomas Lamb
Daniel & Baily

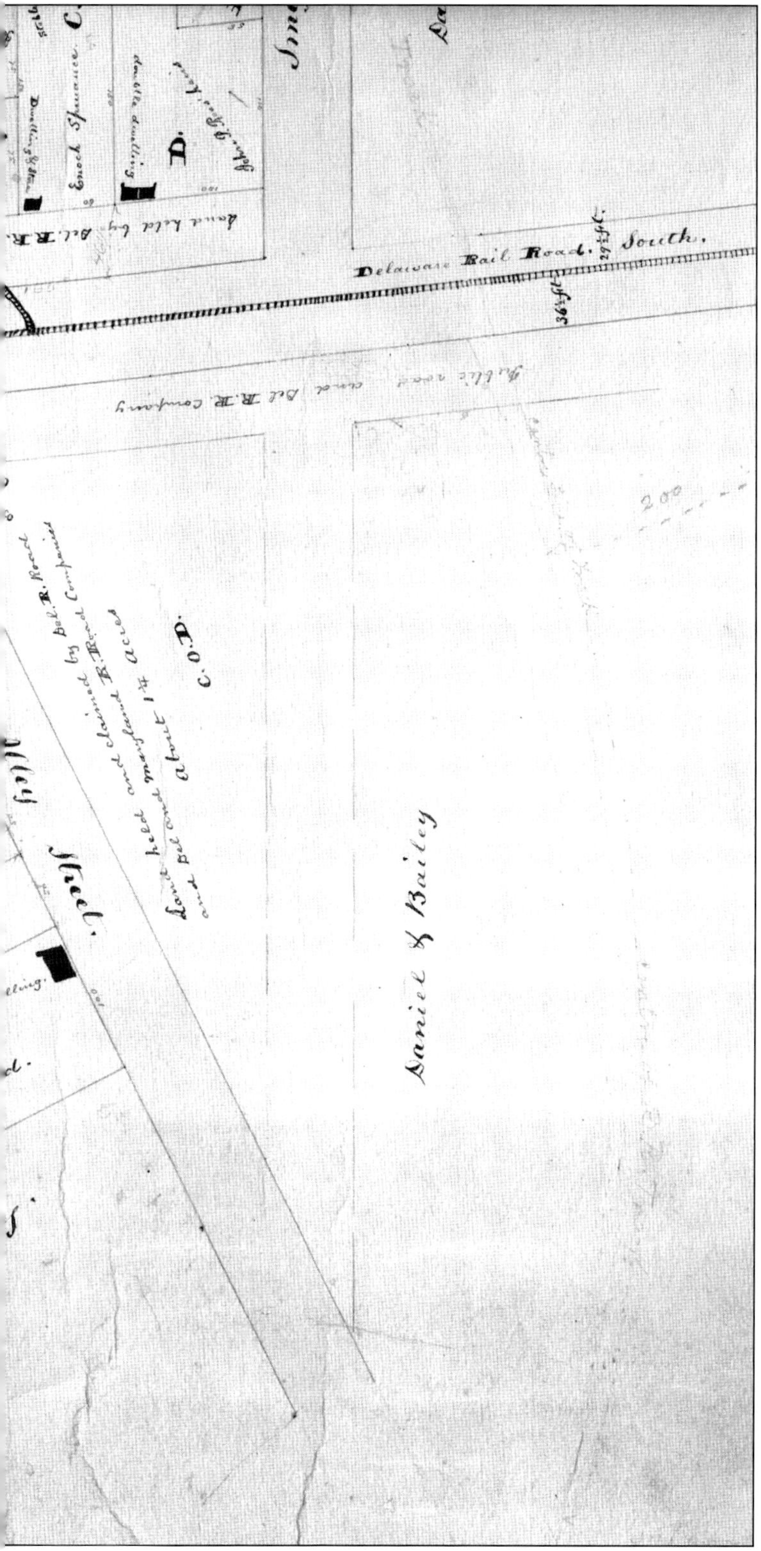

With the introduction of railroad interest west of Smyrna, Richard Tibbitt quickly conveyed property to both the Philadelphia, Wilmington and Baltimore Railroad and the Delaware Railroad Companies. Additionally, parcels were sold to railroad workers and outside businesses. By 1870, still considered a small community with the population of 114, the town was growing considerably with each year. Farmers from outside of town grew peaches and apples that could now be transported by railcar. Taking their harvest into town for export would give them the opportunity to purchase needed lumber, parts for their carriages, visit with the town doctor, etc. Even those who were not farming peaches had a hand in the industry; there was profit to be made in peach basket production as well as picking the fruit at harvest time. The Clayton Fruit and Basket Company was located on Alley Road (Main Street) in 1885.

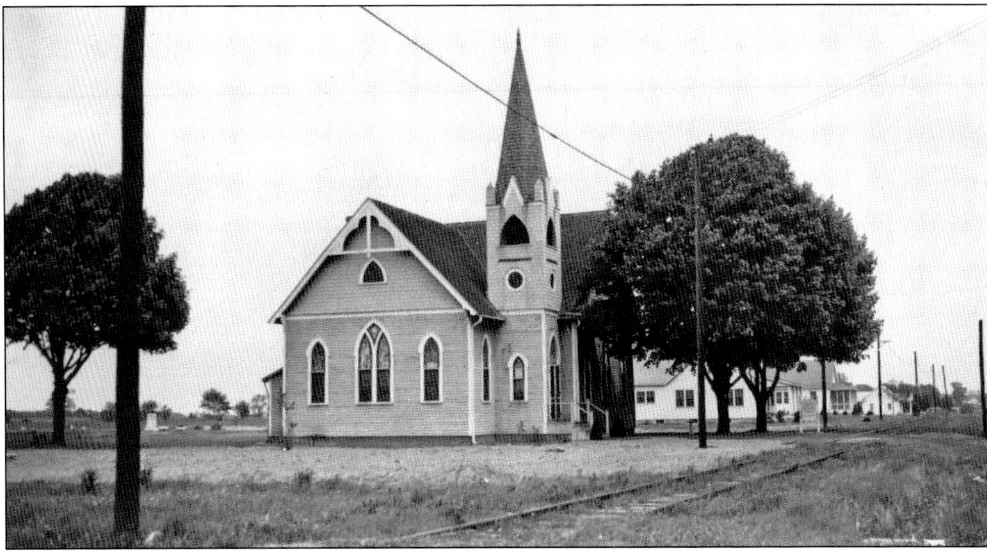

In 1860, Ewell's Methodist Protestant Church was built in Clayton on Delaware Avenue at the urging of Rev. David J. Ewell. By 1869, this church closed due to poor attendance, and in 1870, it rented out the space to a group of Methodist Episcopalians. In 1879, the Protestants reopened their church, and in 1904, they renovated the appearance. It was again revamped in 1942 because of storm damage.

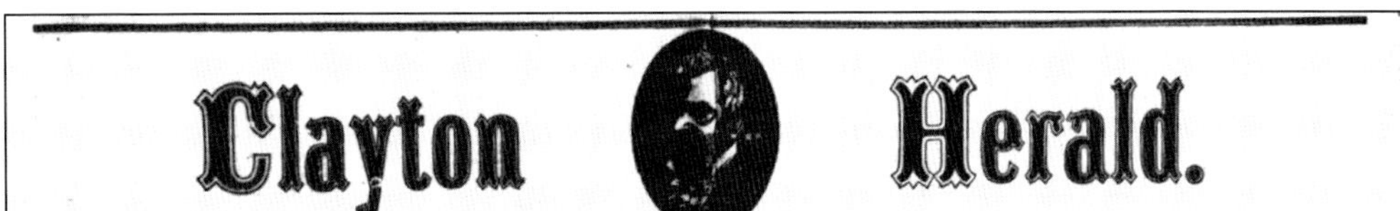

Clayton Herald.

TERMS: Two Dollars a Year, "INDEPENDENT IN EVERYTHING, NEUTRAL IN NOTHING." Invariably in Advance.

VOL. II. CLAYTON, DEL., SATURDAY MORNING, APRIL 25, 1868. NO. 1.

Original Poetry.

SONG OF THE LABORERS.

Selected Story.

THE BROAD WAY.

THE DRUNKARD.

"THE SOUTHWEST."

Extracts from a Traveler's Note Book.

TEXAS.

STRIVE FOR THE BEST.

The Mountain of Lovers.

Wit and Wisdom.

In 1867, the *Clayton Herald* was established by Harriett McConaughy, who was also the editor. The newspaper printed from a building on Alley Street. The paper cost $2 a year and boasted itself to be "Independent in Everything, Neutral in Nothing." Harriett McConaughy was unable to keep the publication profitable, and it collapsed after only a few years.

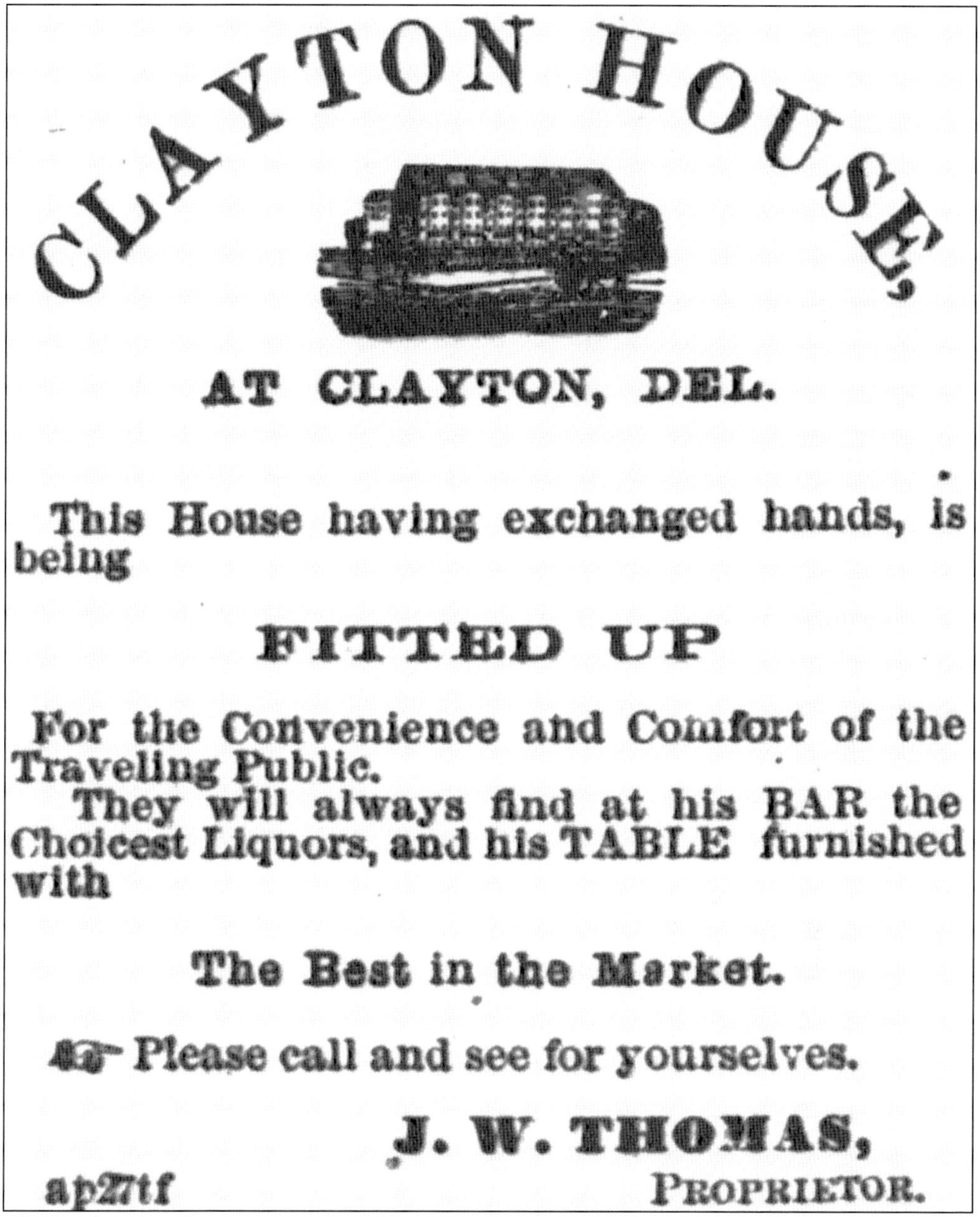

The first hotel in the community was located on Front Street for the convenience of those exiting the railroad cars at the Clayton terminal. In 1870, it was owned and operated by John W. Thomas. Next door, George Whitlock's restaurant and small hotel did well and eventually became the Bingham House. A building down the street housed an eating saloon that transformed into the Hotel Stoeckle, run by Michael Riley. Boardinghouses popped up due to the high demand of railroad workers. The Clayton House could not keep up with the competition as the years wore on and closed their doors. The Clayton House structure remains today as a private dwelling.

Champion Binders and Mowers,

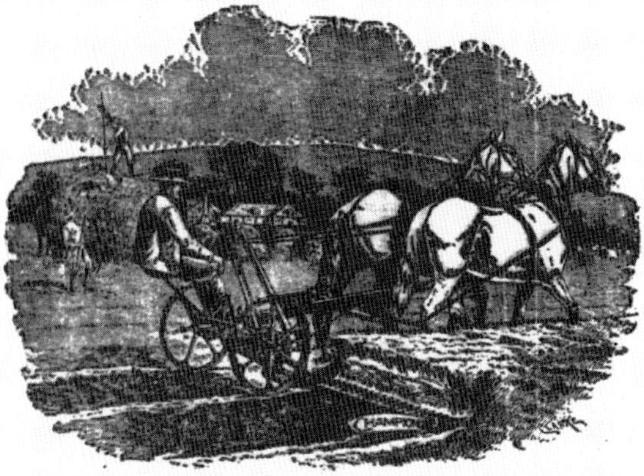

Among the many improvements this year is the new Champion Force Feed Elevator.

Binder Twine, Gasolene, all kinds of Oils, Nails, Forks, Brushes, Spades, Shovels, Rakes, Rope, Lawn Mowers, and everything in the Machinery line.

James T. Saxton,

Smyrna Avenue and Clayton Avenue, Clayton, Del.

James Saxton, an early dealer in agricultural implements in the town of Clayton, was living as a boarder with the Burris family on the 1900 census in Clayton. His shop on the corner of Smyrna and Clayton Avenues carried everything a farmer would need to take care of his fields.

Refreshments & Confectionaries,

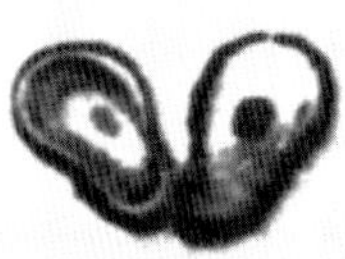

R. PALMATARY,

CLAYTON, DEL.,

Would respectfully state to his friends, and the public generally, that he keeps constantly on hand, a well selected assortment of

Confectionaries & Refreshments,

at his old stand,

OPPOSITE THE DEPOT,

Where he will always be pleased to supply anybody desiring anything in his line.

He also keeps on hand Cigars and Tobacco of the best brands; all of which he will dispose of reasonable for cash.

ap27–1y R. PALMATARY.

R. Palmatary ran one of the confectioneries in the town of Clayton located near the Hotel Stoeckle. A confectionery was a bakery that also sold ice cream, tobacco, and other refreshments. Palmatary's advertisement also shows that he sold oysters. Oysters were plentiful from the Delaware Bay at that time and were sold in many stands.

The Pratt Carriage business was located on Clayton Avenue just after the corner Clements building. Pratt sold carriages made in Springfield, Ohio, by the Mast Buggy Company. Carriages, carriage supplies, and carriage repairmen were as important as car dealerships today. This location later served as storage to the Clements hardware store before a lodging area was built.

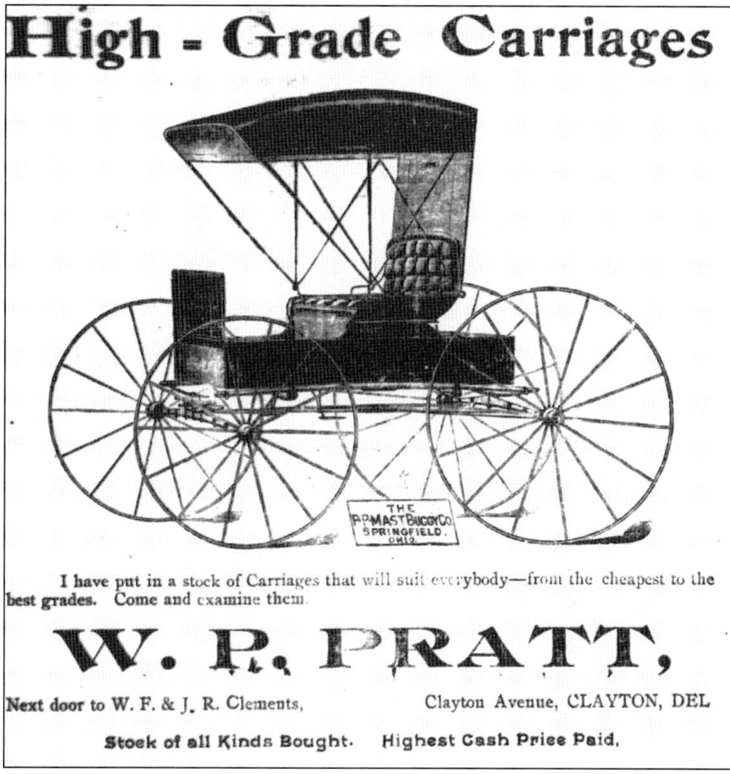

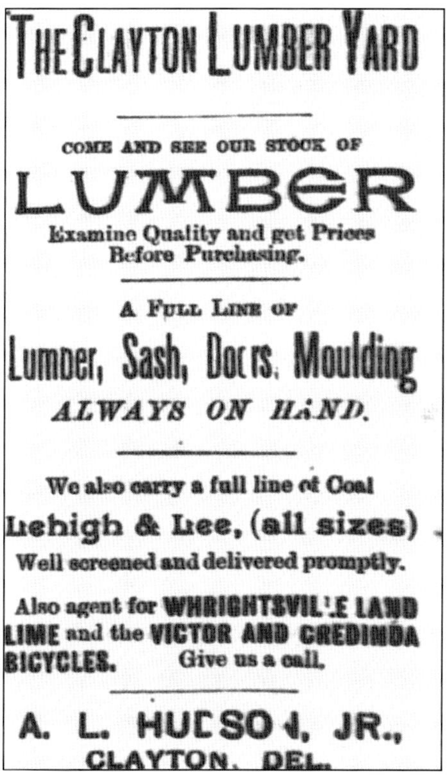

Alfred Hudson, who lived on South Street in Smyrna with his wife, Fannie, held a lumberyard in Clayton. The Clayton lumberyard sold lumber of all sizes to suit any building needs in town. The company also conveniently supplied coal for fuel and lime for farming. A farmer could cover most of his bases with one trip to Hudson's lumberyard.

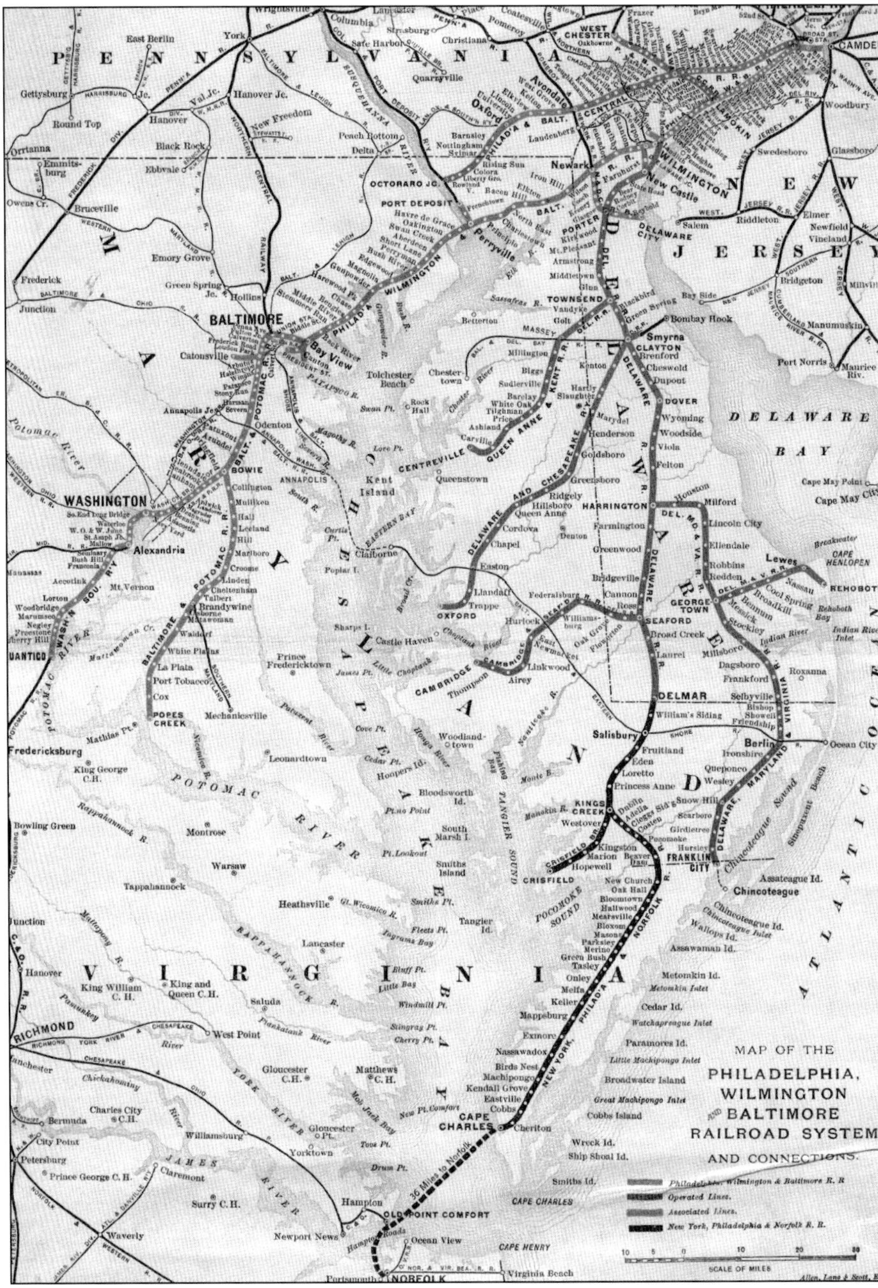

The Philadelphia, Wilmington and Baltimore Railroad Company had an extensive network for connecting tracks. The company was a combination of three others, the Philadelphia and Delaware County Railroad Company, the Wilmington and Susquehanna Railroad Company, and the Baltimore & Port Deposit Railroad Company, which merged together in 1836. By 1857, the Philadelphia, Wilmington and Baltimore Railroad Company took over the Delaware Railroad. Throughout the 1880s, the rail line was at constant battle with the Baltimore and Ohio Railroad Company amid complicated mergers and line usage permissions. Eventually, the lined was owned by the Philadelphia Railroad Company, one of the largest publicly traded corporations in the world at their height.

In 1885, the Philadelphia, Wilmington and Baltimore Railroad Company moved their main office to Clayton. They installed a series of mechanical buildings, offices, loading docks, and storage areas necessary to run their line. They brought with them workers and administrators from Pennsylvania. Many constructed or rented homes in the town of Clayton, while others who lived elsewhere were able to stay in the rail company's dormitory building near the headquarters. As more spur lines were added and connections created, soon the Clayton train station was a vital hub in Delaware. Smaller rail companies like the Smyrna & Delaware Bay Railroad shared the same tracks, allowing passengers to travel from Maryland east through Clayton, Smyrna, Smyrna Landing, and ending at the Bombay Hook (Woodland Beach) terminus.

MARYLAND AND DELAWARE

RAIL ROAD.

CHANGE OF HOURS.

On and after Monday, June 3, '67.

Trains will run as follows:

Going North.

Leave	Greensborough,	6 15 A. M.
"	Goldsborough,	6 32 "
"	Henderson,	6 51 "
"	Halltown,	7 10 "
"	Slaughter's,	7 36 "
"	Kenton,	8 00 "
Arrive	Clayton,	8 20 "
Leave	Clayton,	8 30 "
Arrive	Wilmington,	10 25 "
"	Philadelphia,	11 50 "
"	Baltimore,	3 50 P. M.
"	New York,	6 00 "

Going South.

Leave	New York,	12 00 P. M.
"	Baltimore,	7 25 A. M.
"	Philadelphia,	8 30 "
"	Wilmington,	10 10 "
Arrive	Clayton,	12 15 P. M.
Leave	Clayton,	12 30 "
"	Kenton,	12 40 "
"	Slaughter's	1 04 "
"	Halltown,	1 25 "
"	Henderson,	1 49 "
"	Goldsborough.	2 08 "
Arrive	Greensborough,	2 35 "

Passengers *from* Baltimore purchase tickets for CLAYTON and change cars at New Castle Junction.

Passengers *for* Baltimore will have about two hours to lay over in Wilmington, and take Washington Express.

Round Trip Tickets will be charged half-price, but will only be issued from Greensborough to Clayton and return.

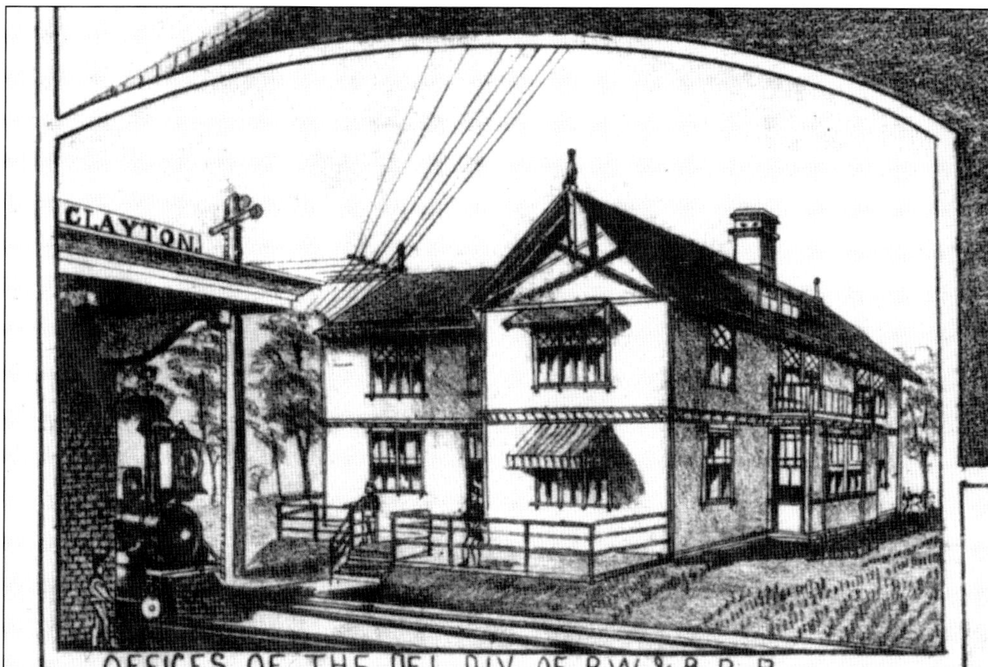

OFFICES OF THE DEL. DIV. OF P.W. & B. R. R.

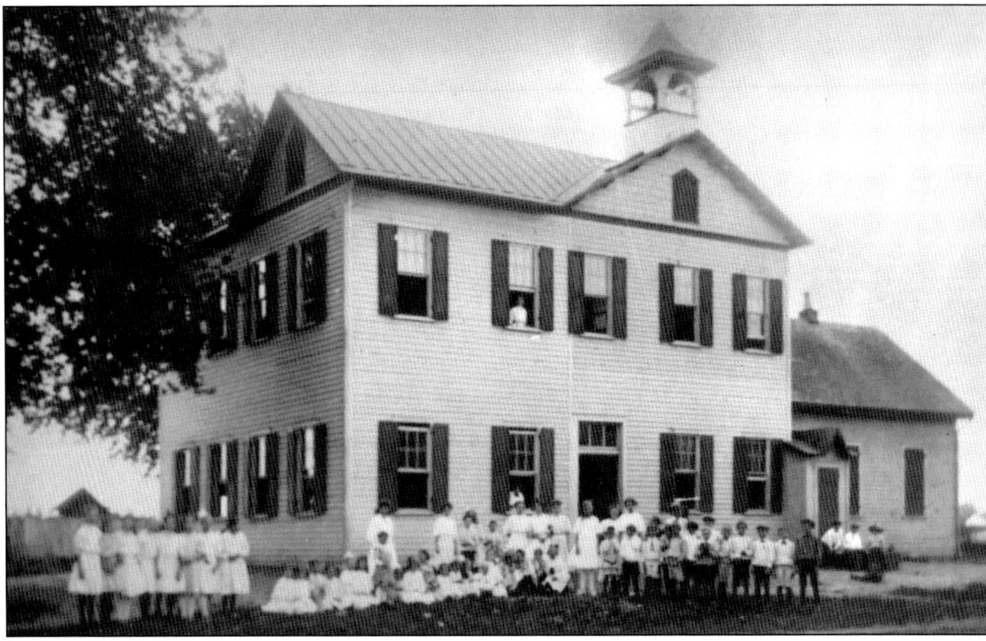

The Clayton Public School was established in 1873 on the same site it occupies today. The construction was made possible by an advancement of funds from A.L. Hudson, the lumber merchant in the town. The cost of the original building was $900. There were 64 students enrolled in the school in 1886, and as the town was expanding, an addition was planned for 1887 to allow room for 80 students. In 1913, the school was reprimanded by the Department of Education for unsatisfactory "water closets" inside the school. As with most small towns, Clayton felt the pressure to keep updated, adequate utilities and town services as the town population quickly rose.

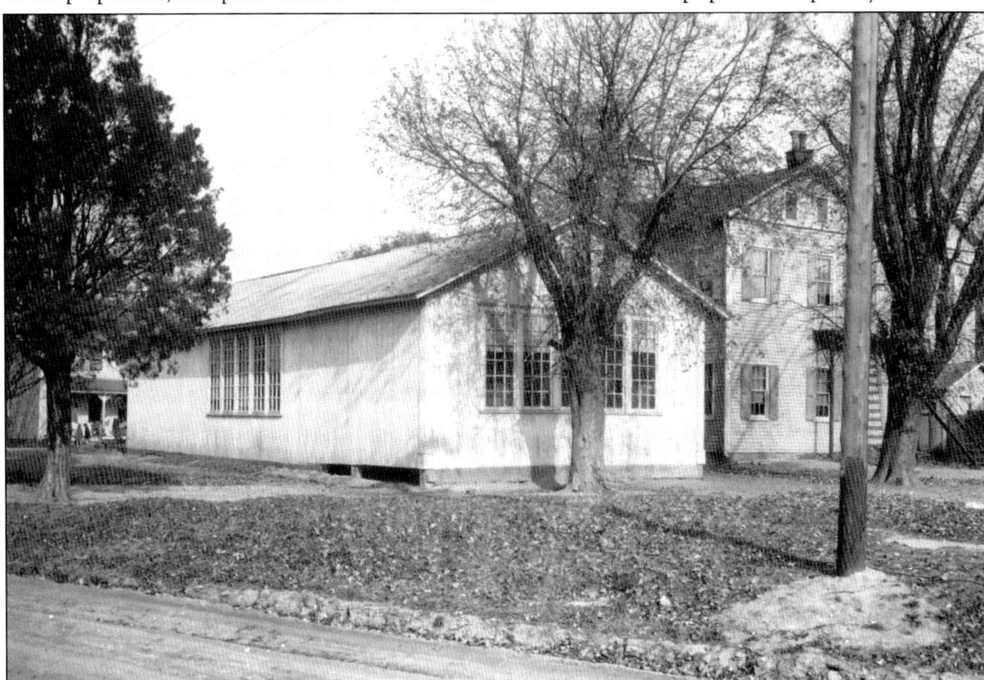

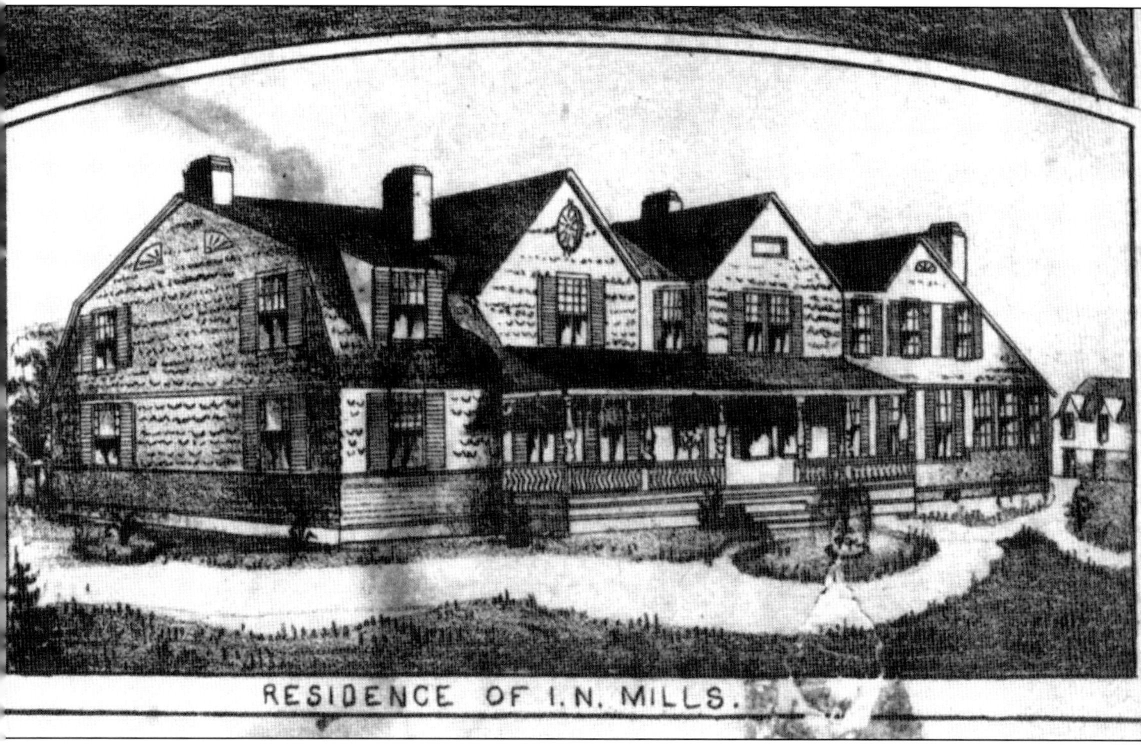

Isaac Newton Mills, a retired railroad superintendent for the Philadelphia, Wilmington and Baltimore Railroad Company, moved his family to Clayton when the railroad company shifted their offices to the little town. Mills was born in 1836 in Pennsylvania and began work at the railroad company as a brakeman before a series of promotions landed him the job of superintendent. He retired in Clayton, where he remained with his family until his death by a stroke in 1913. He and his wife, Annie, had two daughters and built a large mansion on the corner of West Street and Clayton Avenue; they owned a significant portion of property adjacent to their home on what is now Clayton and Washington Avenues. Years after Isaac and Annie Mills passed away, the mansion was converted into two apartments before the building was removed from the property.

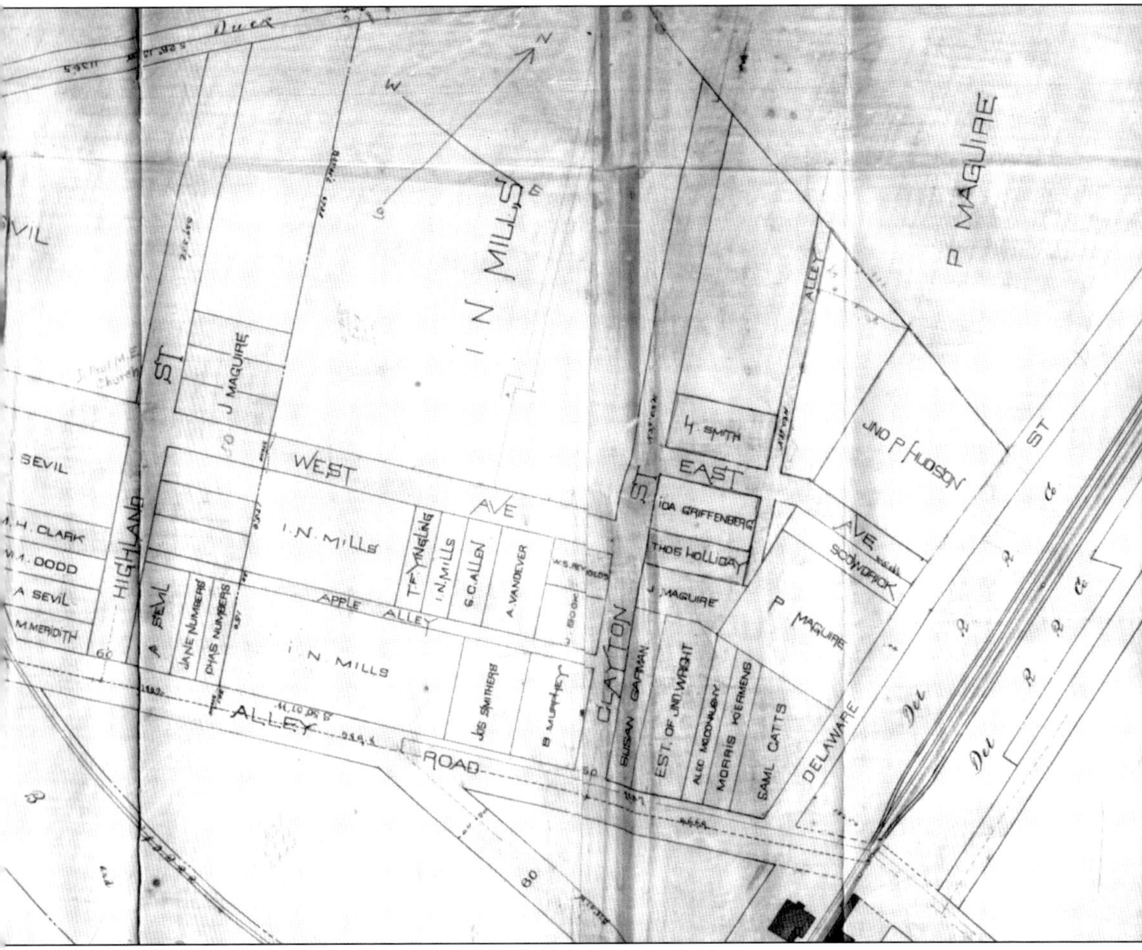

In 1887, the State of Delaware officially incorporated the Town of Clayton and laid out the town survey. At this time, life was booming in small-town Clayton. The main street, called Alley Road, was a tree-lined lane with many houses and businesses. In 1887, the town had two hotels, the Bingham House, run by William Whitlock, and the Hotel Stoeckle, run by Michael Riley; 60 houses; three general stores run by Abel Sevil, George Brockson, and W.S. Reynolds; two millineries; three confectioneries; a wheelwright; a blacksmith; a lumberyard; butcher; and a drugstore run by Dr. Charles G. Harmonson. The town population had grown to 400.

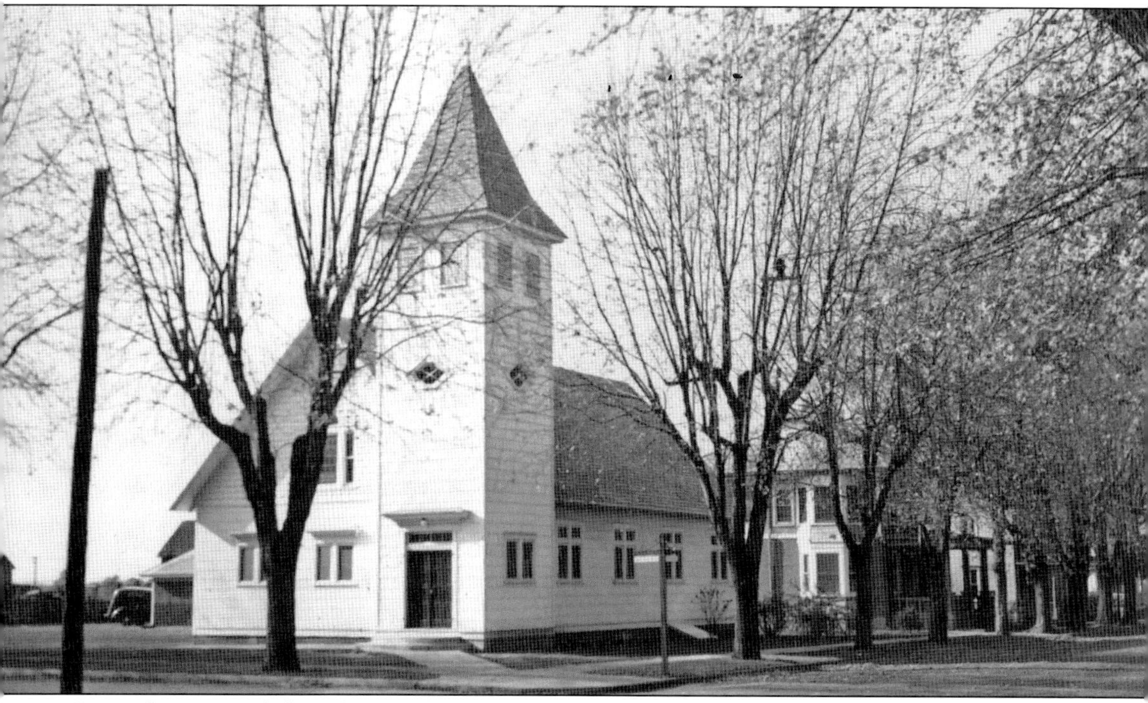

In December 1887, Abel Sevil, a merchant and landowner in the town, donated land on the corner of Highland Avenue and West Street to build the St. Paul's Methodist Episcopal Church. The church was a meeting place for a popular Sunday school service that previously met in a rented space owned by John Hudson on Alley Road. The church was built mostly by donations from the citizens of Clayton, and the bell was offered by a member of the Philadelphia, Wilmington and Baltimore Railroad Company. Members of the Wilmington St. Paul's church choir assisted with setting up services. In 1940, the church was rededicated.

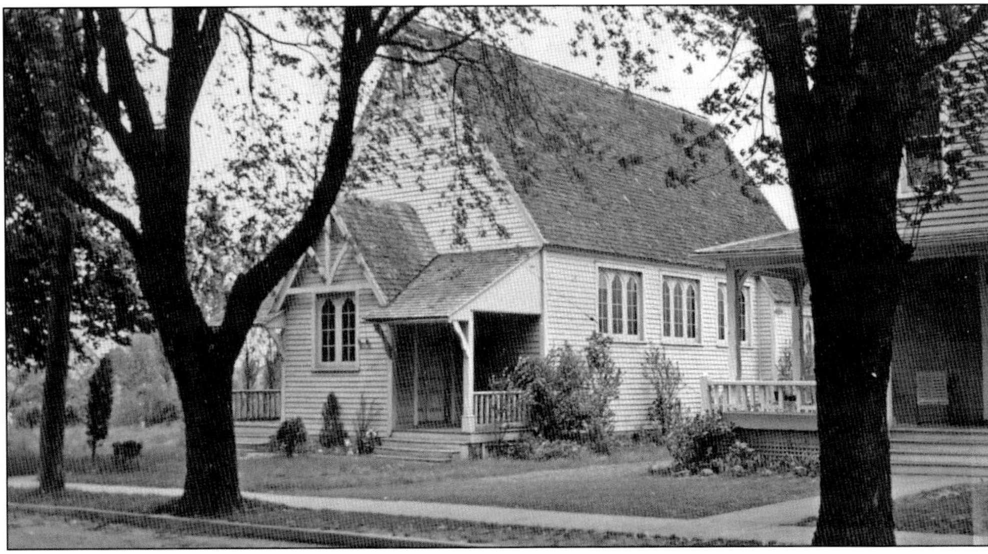

In 1889, I.N. Mills gave land and lumber to the Trinity Protestant Episcopal Church on Clayton Avenue. By 1891, the church was officially open. It was well attended by workers of the railroad and quickly became known as the "railroad church." In 1917, the church was made a mission under St Peter's Church in Smyrna, but by 1930, the services were abandoned, and the building fell into disrepair. It was soon purchased by Dr. Richard Comegys, the town doctor, who lived with his family on Clayton Avenue. He was a member of the church prior to the stopping of services and decided to renovate the building for his medical practice. This building has continued to serve as a long-standing medical office.

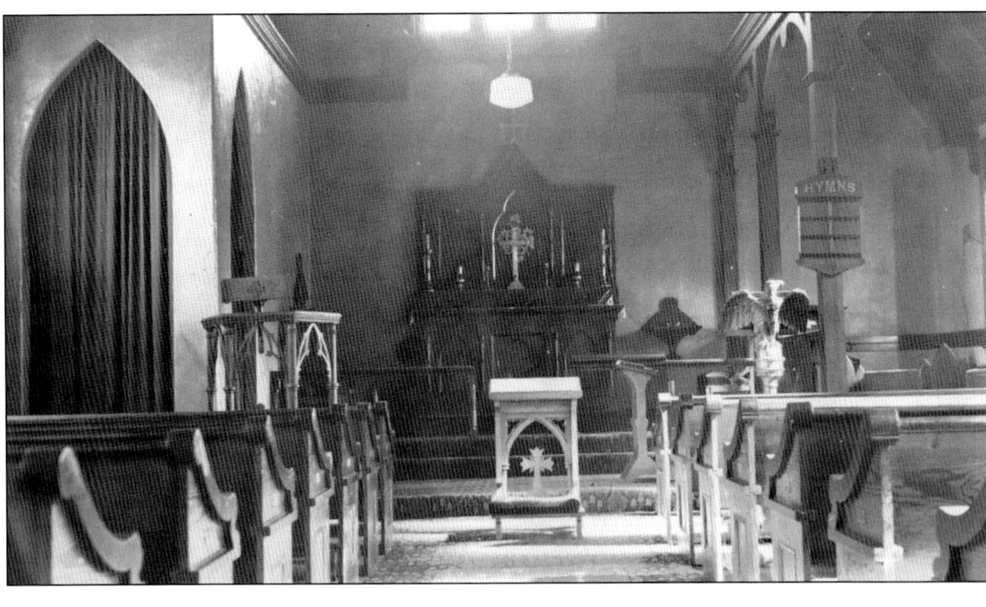

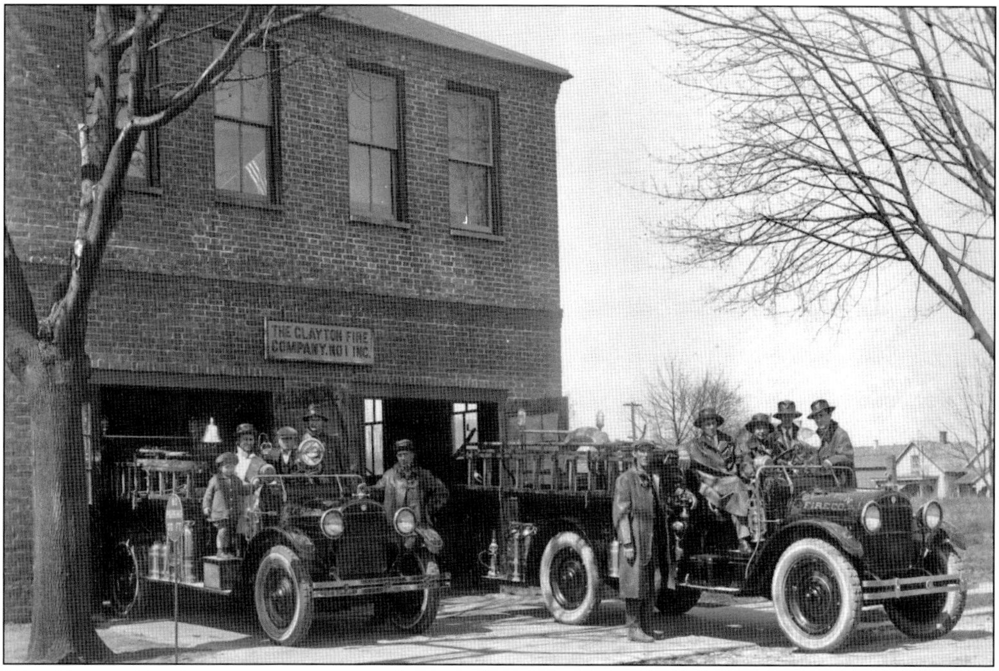

The Clayton Fire Company was originally started in 1891, in part by donations from the Philadelphia, Wilmington and Baltimore Railroad Company and town contributors. Originally, the firemen kept their water truck on the north side of the first floor of the Hotel Stoeckle. The company was incorporated in 1923 and took use of the first floor of the Town of Clayton building on Railroad Avenue. The town council used the upper floor of this building for meetings. The fire company, shown here in 1925 in front of the old hall, moved to its current location in March 1968.

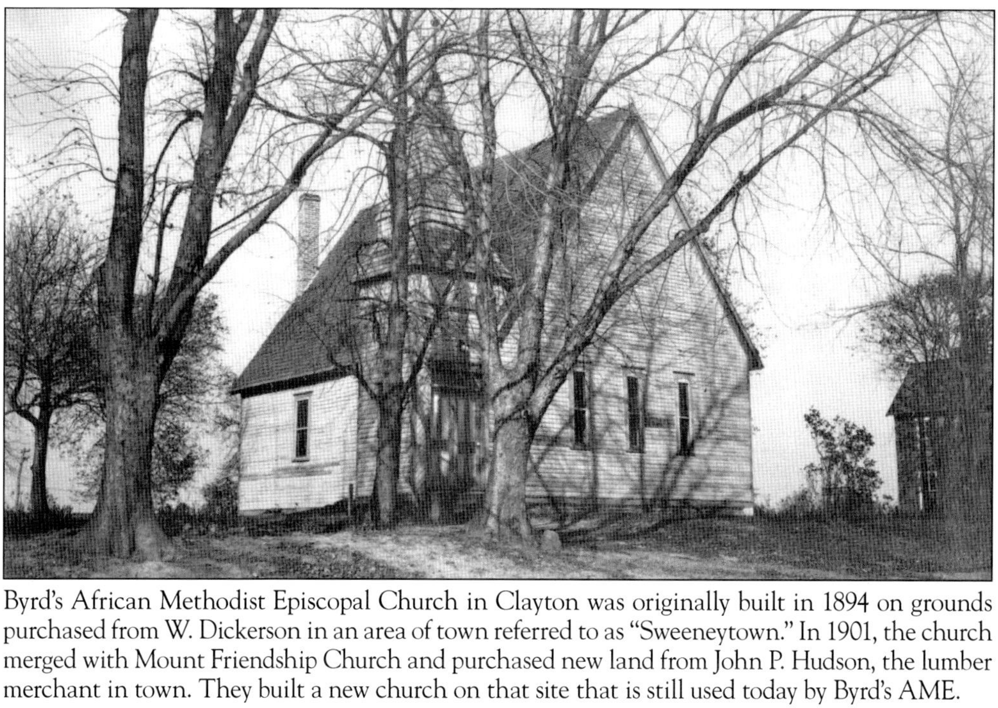

Byrd's African Methodist Episcopal Church in Clayton was originally built in 1894 on grounds purchased from W. Dickerson in an area of town referred to as "Sweeneytown." In 1901, the church merged with Mount Friendship Church and purchased new land from John P. Hudson, the lumber merchant in town. They built a new church on that site that is still used today by Byrd's AME.

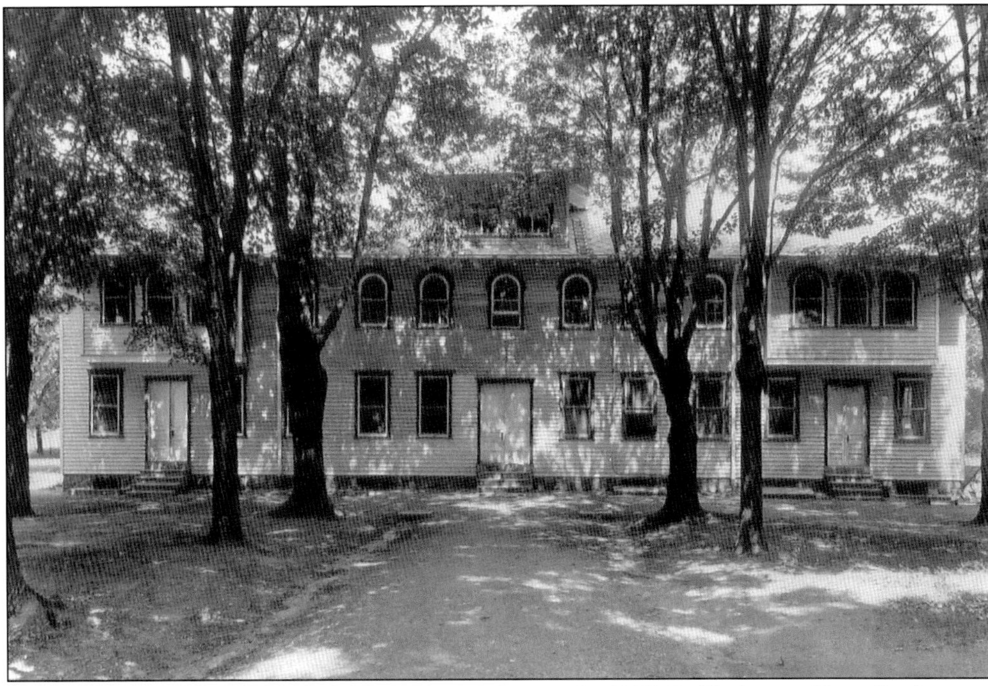

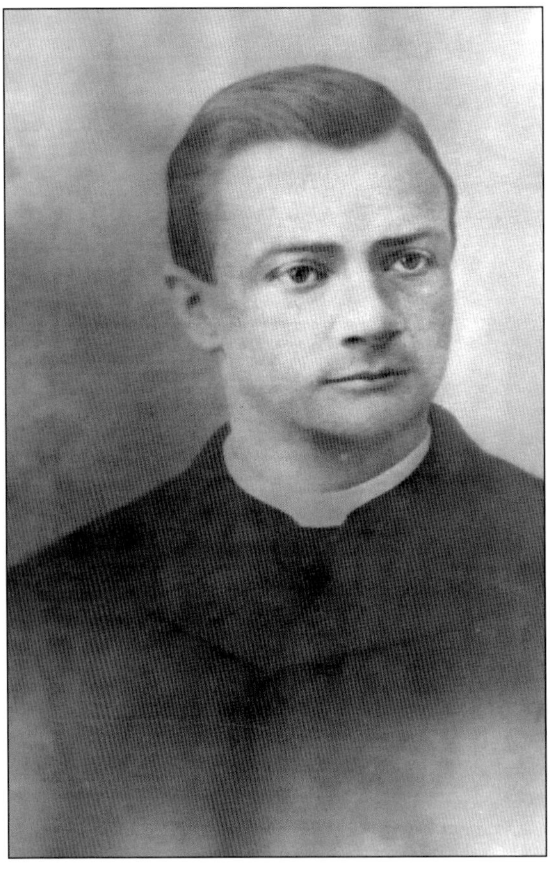

In 1895, Sr. Katharine Drexell of Philadelphia purchased 400 acres of land on the northern edge of Clayton for St. Joseph's Diocese in Wilmington. The acres were accumulated from parts of different farms owned by William Tunis, Ella Bowers, Tilghman Foxwell, and Nathaniel Severson, among others. Sister Drexell graciously gifted this land to the new school. (Courtesy of Phil Voshell.)

Father De Ruyter, a Belgian priest, established the St. Joseph's Industrial School in Clayton in 1896. The only original portions of the campus remaining are the chapel and the stone arch that welcomes the weary souls into the school grounds. The industrial school was first opened to help African American youth to better their lives and to grow the Catholic faith. (Courtesy of Phil Voshell.)

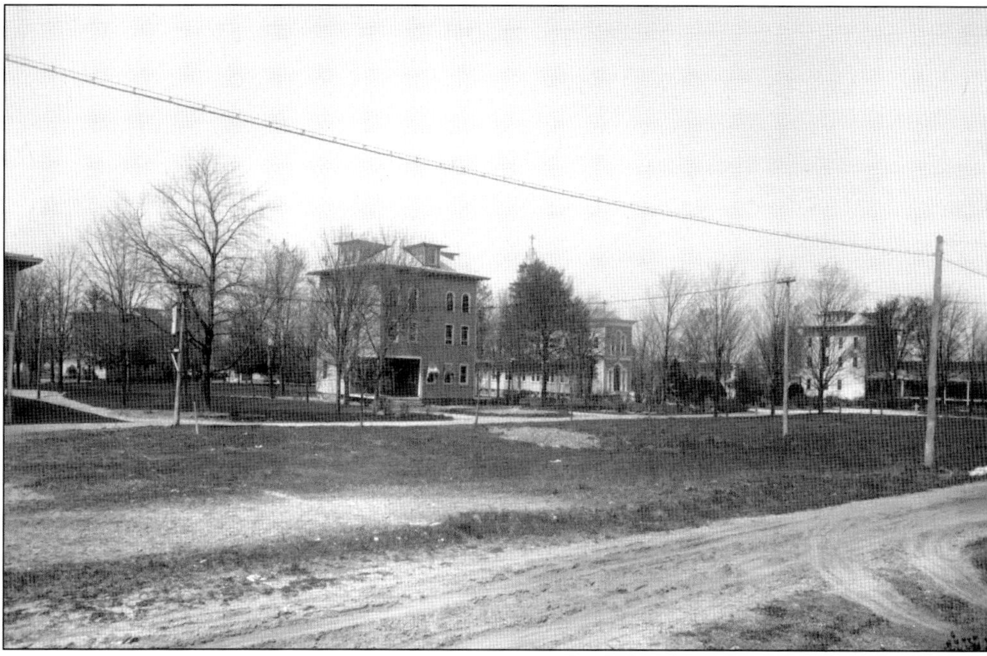

The industrial school, a completely self-sufficient commune, boarded and taught boys from 14 to 17 years of age. There, they experienced spiritual knowledge through tasks at the school. Tending to the animals, gardening, tailoring, carpentry, and other vocational training, in addition to their scholarly learning, helped them to become full stewards of the Lord.

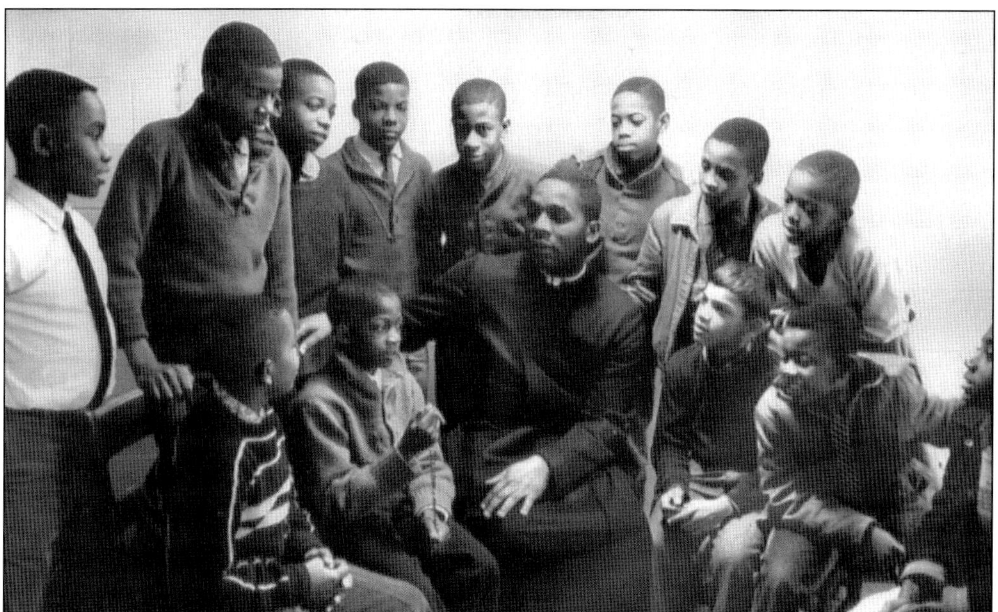

The teachers at the St. Joseph's Industrial School were comprised of both laymen and Catholic priests. The school became very popular, and young men from as far as Texas came to live at the institution. Some of the men went on to become teachers in the Catholic faith, returning to their home; St. Joseph's School in Clayton produced a new generation of followers. (Courtesy of Phil Voshell.)

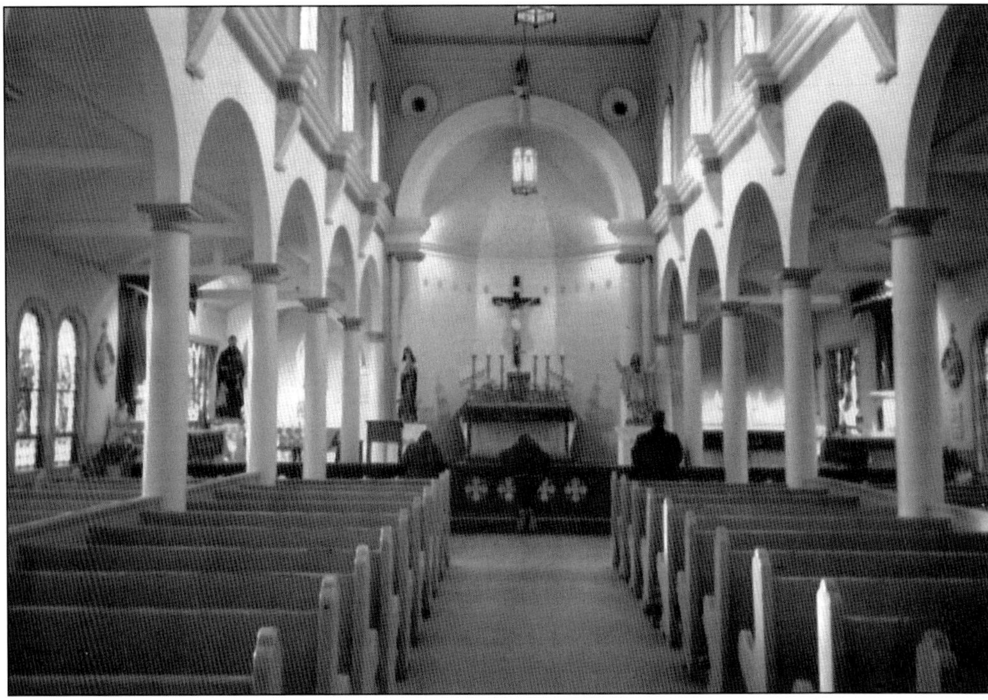

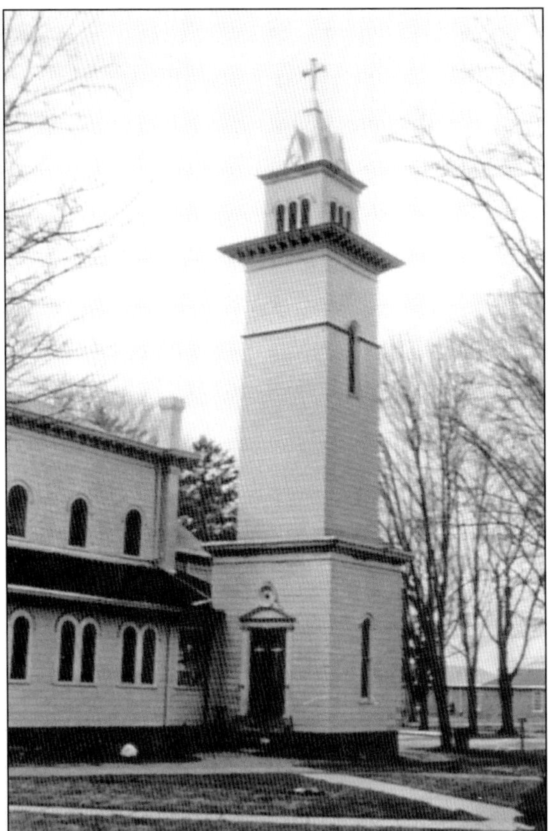

The parish chapel, built in 1896, is the only surviving structure of the original campus. The chapel was made available for residents of both Smyrna and Clayton to attend services, along with the members of the school, in 1914. Local Catholics congregated there and were married at the parish until St. Polycarp's in Smyrna was reopened in 1968. The local congregation switched locations at that time. The chapel holds 53 stained-glass windows and engravings of the Fathers and boys that used the chapel for so many years. The historic chapel is now sitting idle among the shadows of the tall campus trees. (Courtesy of Phil Voshell.)

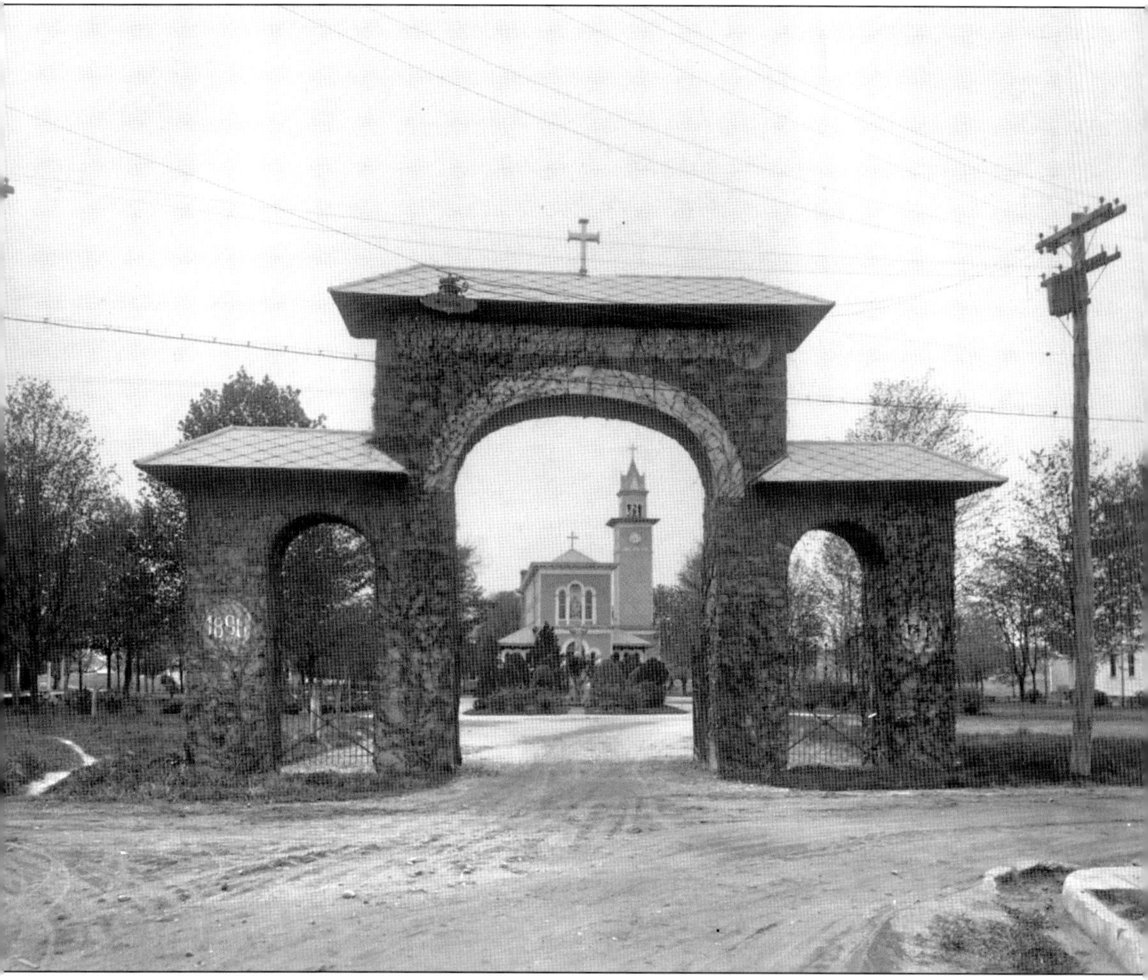

The years took their toll on the industrial school. Weakened enrollment and loss of charitable funding eventually meant the demise of the Catholic institution. A series of fires devastated the school. One in particular occurred on May 10, 1956, with a blaze so large that eight different fire companies came to assist the Clayton company. The large building was completely destroyed with only one loss of life. In recent years, a group was founded with the hope of reviving the old campus and giving it new purpose for the community of Clayton. The group, however, had trouble generating necessary funds to retain any such project, and the campus is currently lingering statuesquely at the north end of Clayton Avenue, a reminder of the once bustling school, inviting the passerby in to sit under its many shade trees.

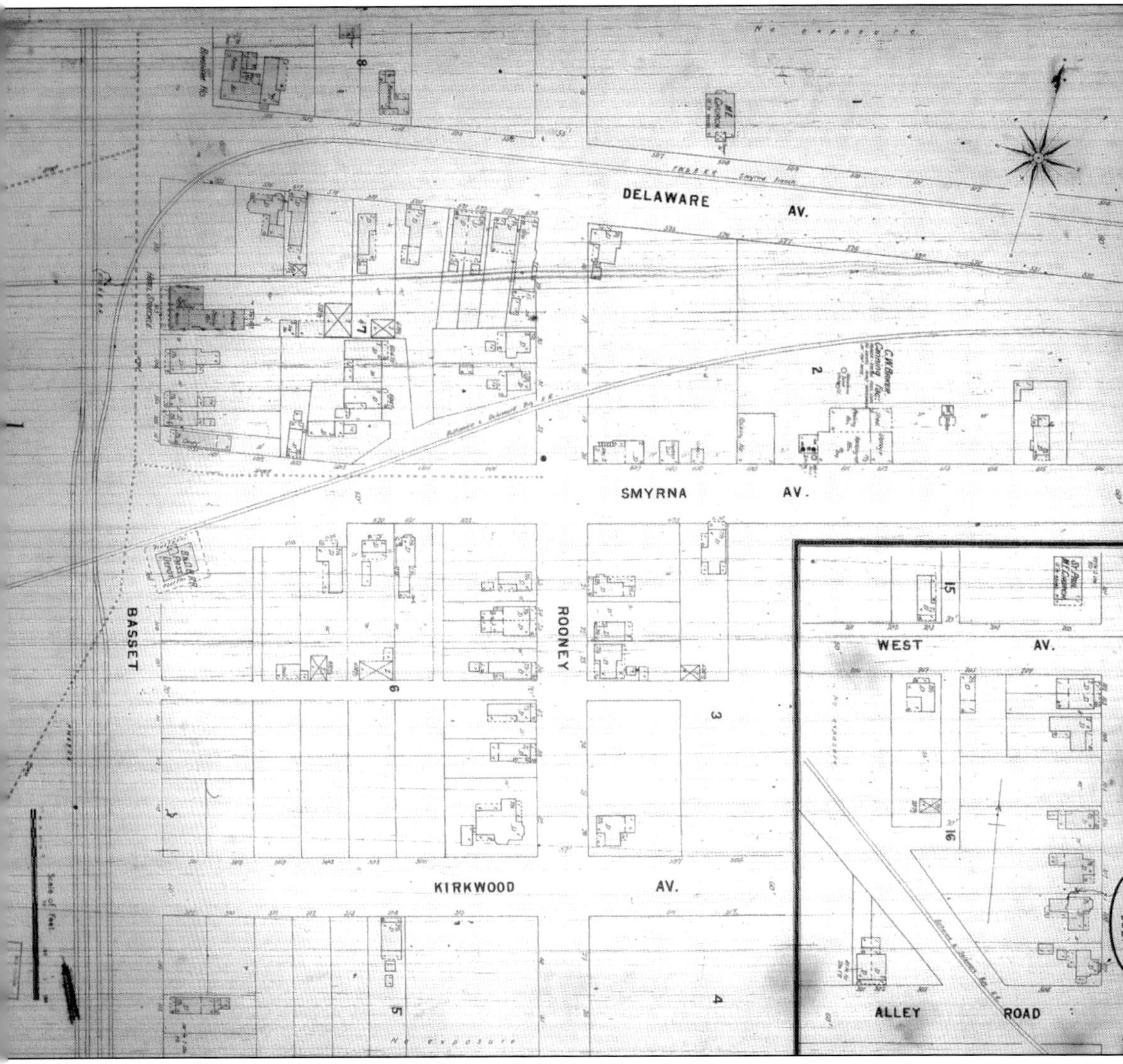

Still a mostly agricultural community, canning companies were a necessity to preserve the harvest and were extremely popular in small towns. In 1881, Hardcastle and Jones began in the town of Clayton, generating 300 baskets per day. The Smith and Carson cannery began in 1888 and produced 1,300 cans a day. In 1898, the Clayton Canning Company was opened by Charles Winfield Baker on Smyrna Avenue. The Clayton Canning Company canned tomatoes, peaches, and corn. Like most canneries, business hours were kept seasonally to allow for the canning of the freshest produce. From Aberdeen, Maryland, Baker opened his first cannery in his hometown before branching out. He manufactured two types of product grades, each with their own brand name and label. In 1909, he went into business with George A. Walls of Sudlersville, Maryland.

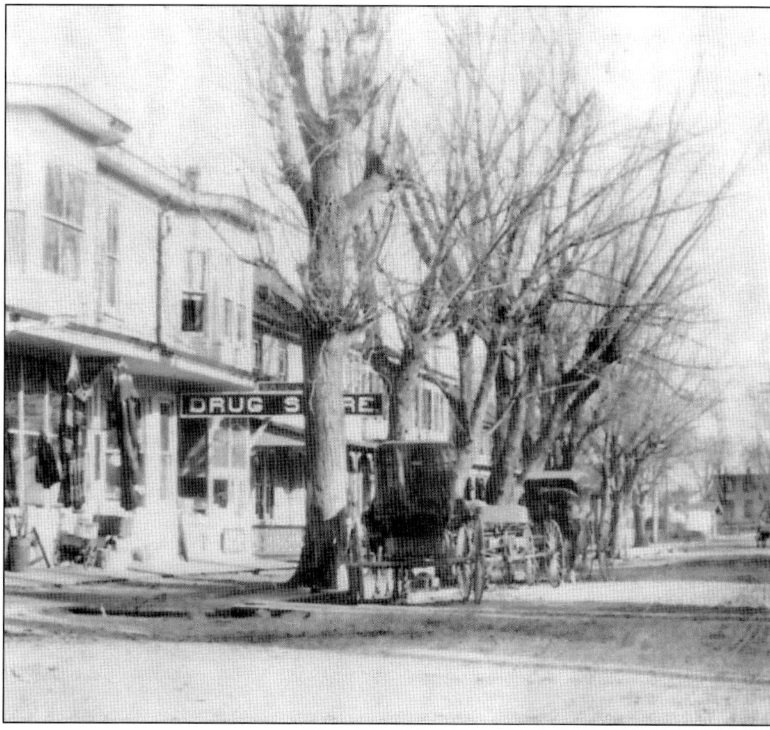

The Keys' drugstore is shown here on the left, just before a row of dwellings that no longer exist on Main Street. The butcher worked directly across the unpaved street. A large building for the railroad workers can be seen at the end of the street. This was one of the postcards created by Keys to sell in his drugstore. (Courtesy of Virginia D. Cubbage.)

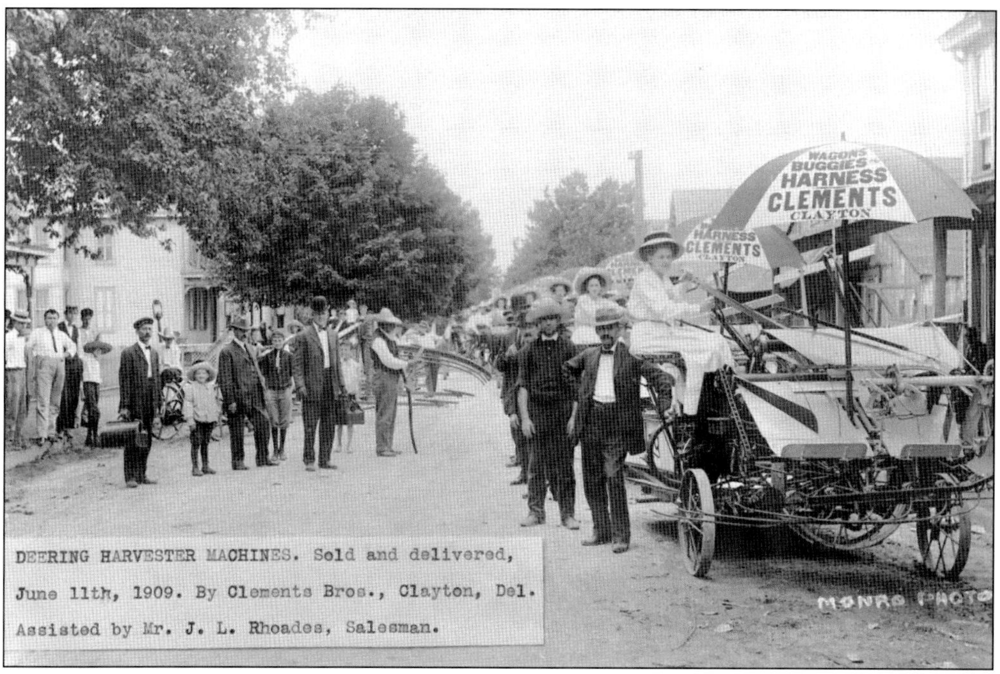

William and James Clements held a long-standing business in the town of Clayton. They supplied citizens with carriages, farm equipment, cultivators, hardware, and paints. The brothers grew up on a farm in Kenton. In 1900, James was living with his brother William and his wife, Florence, above the hardware store on Alley Road. Seen here with a new shipment of harvesting machines, Clayton residents lined the streets to see them paraded through town.

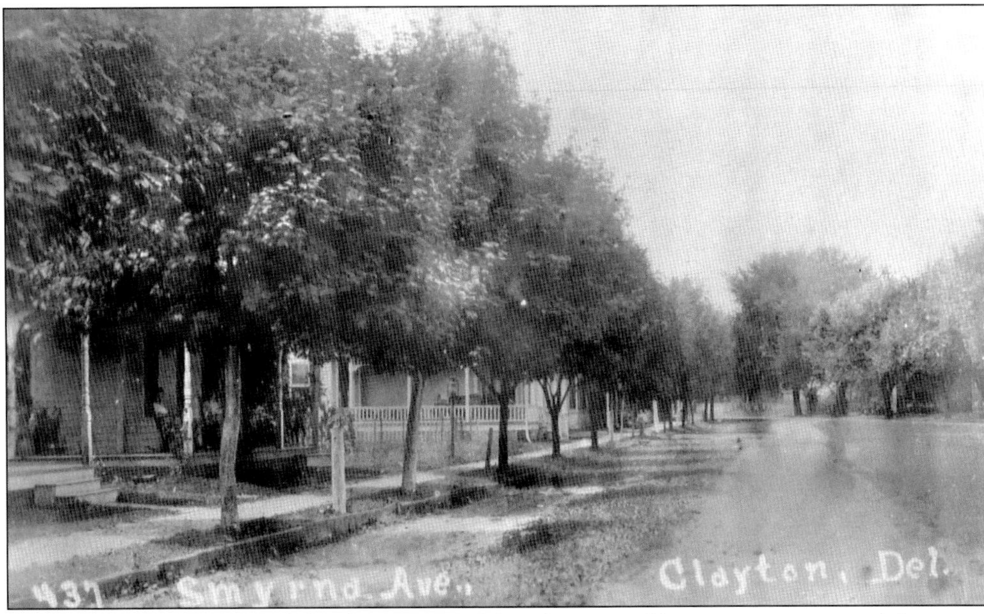

Walter R. Keys, who owned the drugstore on Main Street in Clayton, commissioned four views of the town of Clayton in 1911 to be photographed and printed as postcards for sale in his store. Originally, the cards were printed without any wording to indicate their location, so Keys fashioned rubber stamps to imprint each card. Above is one of his cards, showing Smyrna Avenue in the early 1900s.

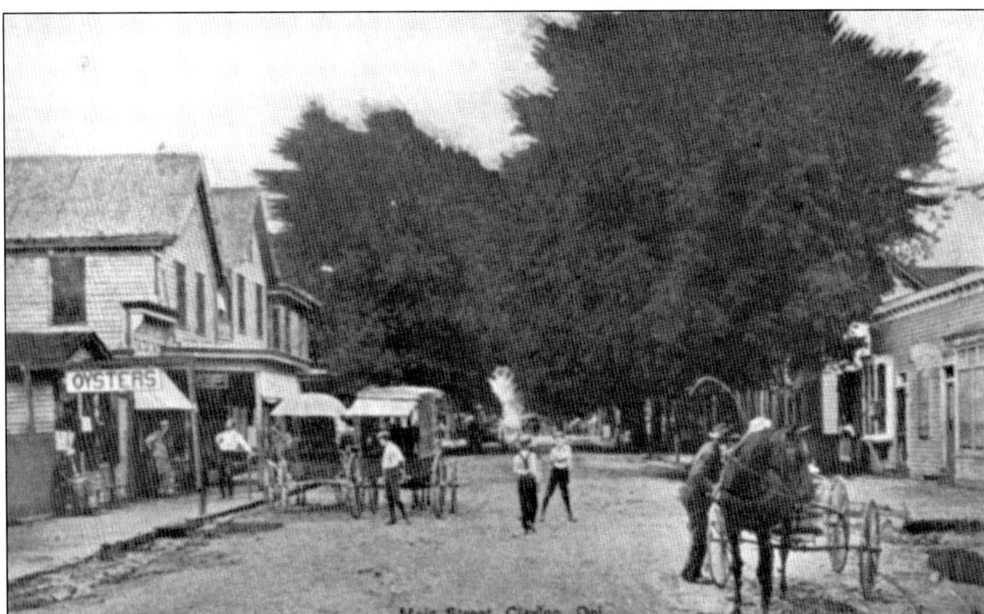

Main Street Clayton in 1910 was a bustling place. Trees lined the sidewalks, trains rushed in and out of town along their busy connecting tracks and schedules, and merchants sold their wares to out of town railroad passengers and farmers coming into town for errands. Still with unpaved roads, wagons navigated Main Street to reach the many established businesses there.

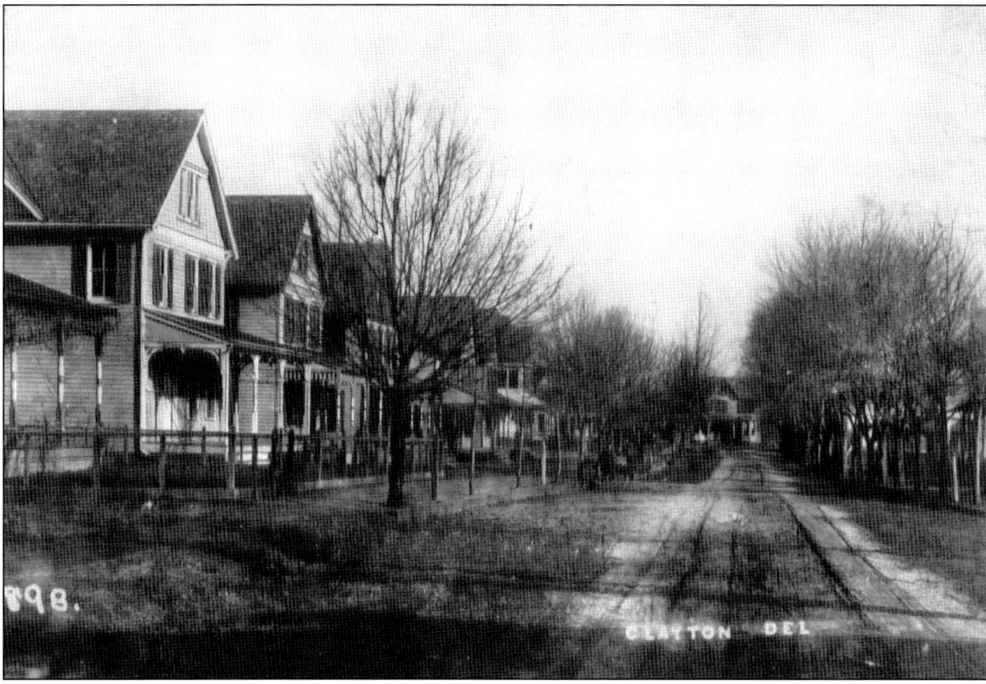

Postcards were heavily used in the first half of the 20th century. Nearly every traveler would pick up cards to send a quick note to family and friends outlining their travel plans, sending well wishes, or asking friends to visit. The images above and below are two more of the Walter Keys's cards. The photograph above shows a view of West Street from the west looking east to Clayton Avenue. Large trees that lined the street obstruct the view of the Isaac Mills's mansion that sat on the left corner of that street. Below is the opposite vantage point on the same street, looking west.

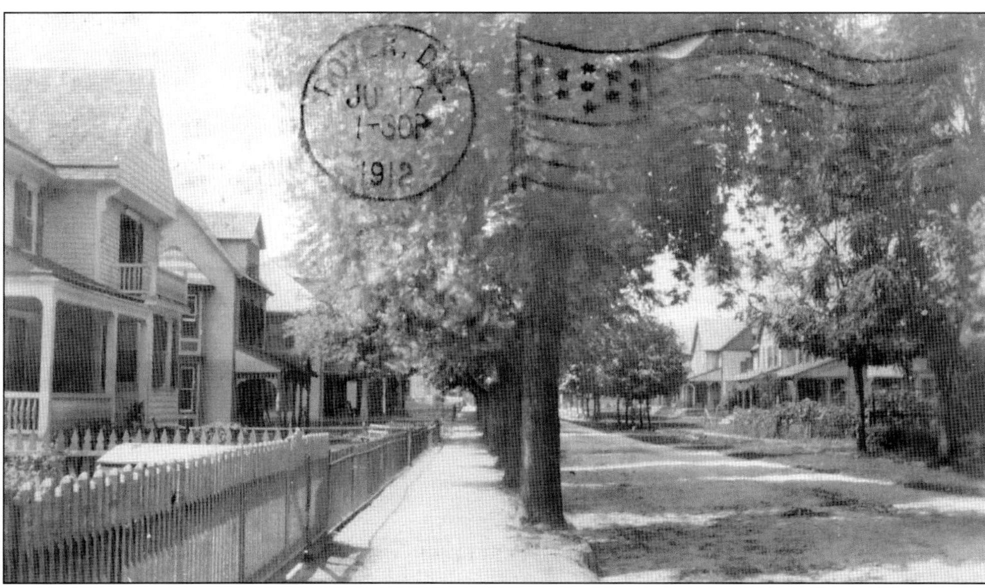

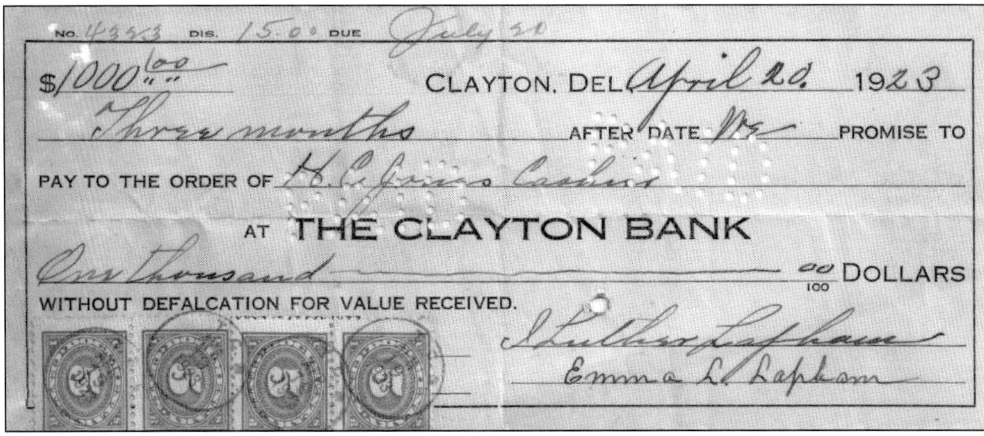

NO. DIS. 15.00 DUE

$1000 00/100 CLAYTON, DEL April 20. 1923

Three months AFTER DATE PROMISE TO

PAY TO THE ORDER OF

AT THE CLAYTON BANK

One thousand 00/100 DOLLARS

WITHOUT DEFALCATION FOR VALUE RECEIVED.

I Luther Lapham

Emma L. Lapham

As the town grew, new institutions were needed to keep money in the town of Clayton. In 1913, the Clayton Bank and Trust Company was founded by merchant Abel Sevil. The board of directors included other business owners in the town, such as James R. Clements, Walter R. Keys, and Dr. Charles G. Harmonson. The Clayton Bank and Trust Company advertised in the *Smyrna Times* about the pride of home ownership, boasting that it could help residents become substantial citizens, adding: "Your own home is your castle. That's where you'll want to take your bride and make your little nest." Above is a 1923 bank note, and a below is a photograph of the bank from 1963. The Clayton Bank and Trust Company became PNC Bank of Delaware in 1992. The building currently holds the Town of Clayton administration offices and police department. (Both, courtesy of the Duck Creek Historical Society.)

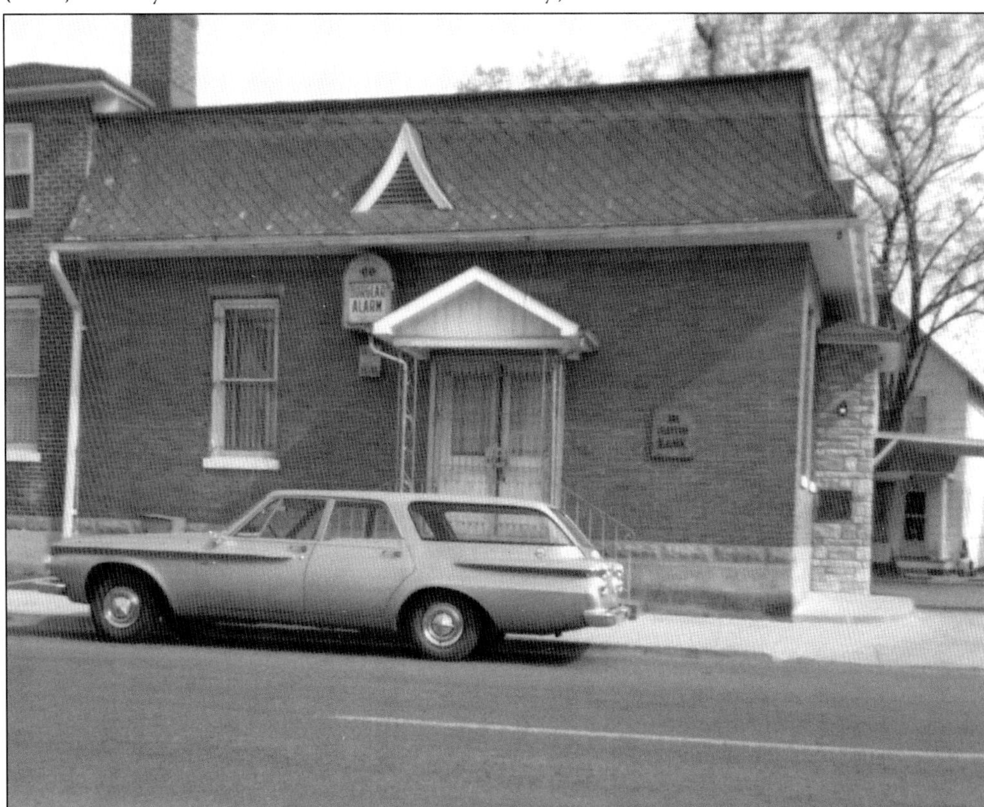

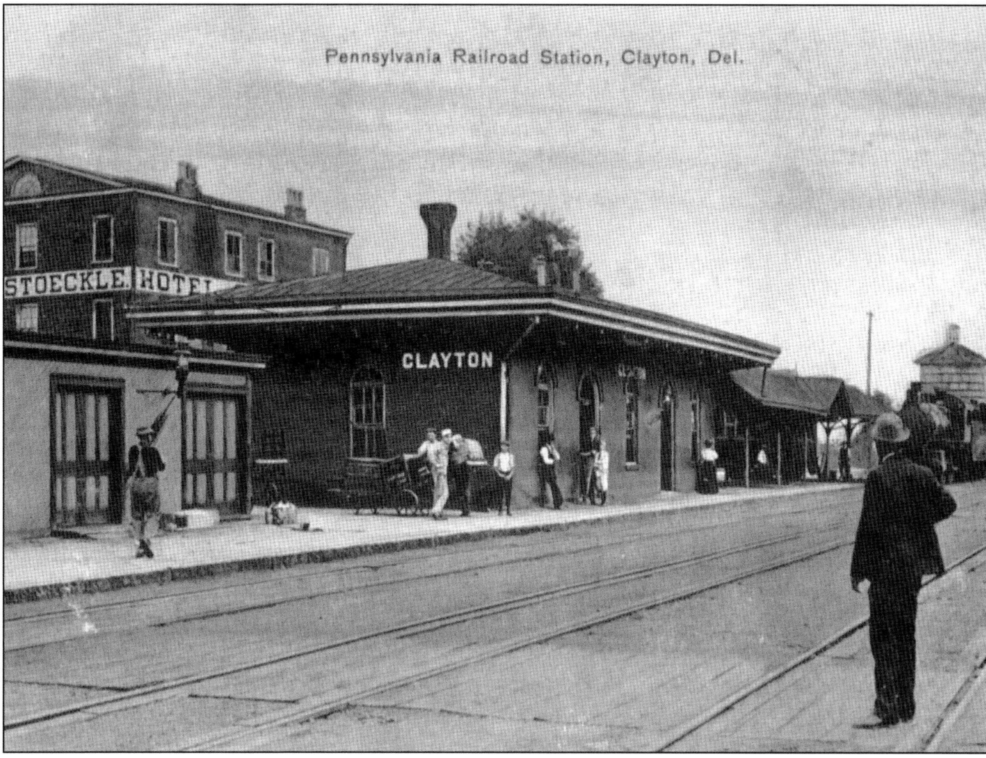

The current Clayton railroad station was built in 1885 to replace a smaller depot previously used at the same location. The station contained a ticket office, baggage rooms, a waiting room, and the stationmaster's personal office. The Hotel Stoeckle can be seen in the background. After a fire on the second floor, the hotel was converted to a one-story structure, making the building almost unrecognizable today. (Courtesy of Brian Hill.)

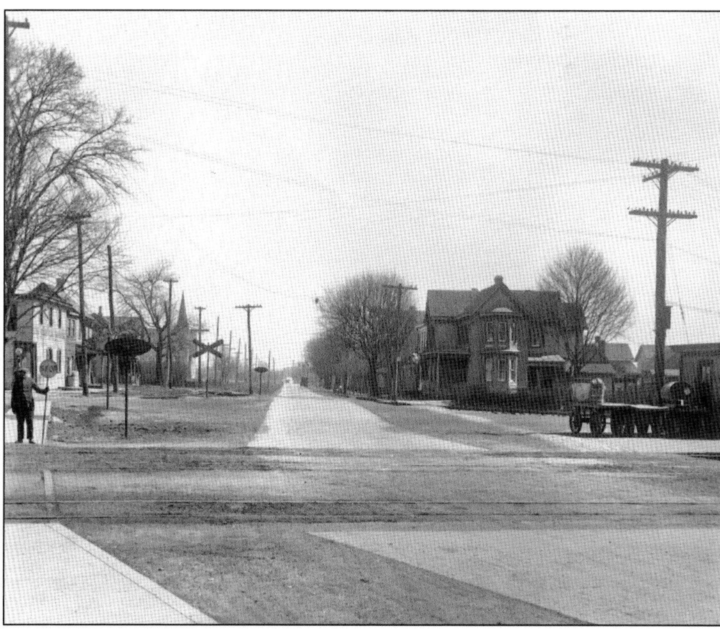

In 1922, the Philadelphia, Wilmington and Baltimore Railroad closed their Clayton office. Their business heeded to the Pennsylvania Railroad Company, who occupied the busy tracks until filing for bankruptcy in 1970. Conrail now uses the tracks through town. The closing of the offices was a loss for the town; however, many of the rail workers remained transplanted as Clayton residents.

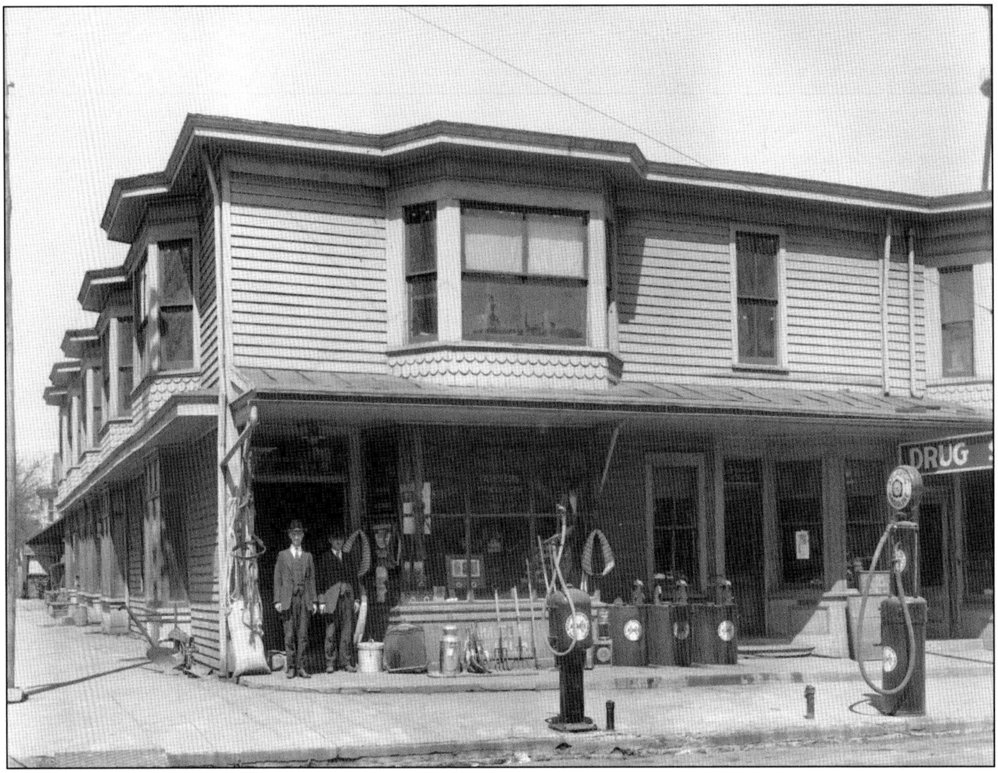

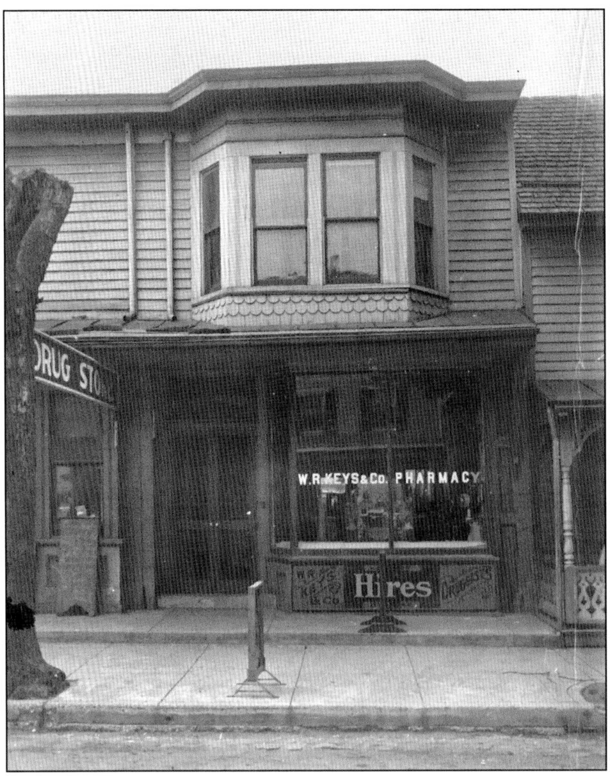

From Clements Brothers Hardware, where the brothers sold harvesting machines, to the Clements Supply Company, James and William Clements were long-standing citizens of the town. James Clements went on work as a trustee of the Clayton School and served on the board of the Clayton Bank and Trust Company while continuing to run his company.

Walter R. Keys held a pharmacy next to the Clements brothers' store on Main Street. Keys lived in the upstairs of the drugstore prior to the 1900 census. By 1940, he moved his residence to West Street. Keys served in all offices of the Delaware Board of Pharmacy and was an active member of the Clayton community, sitting on the Clayton Bank and Trust Company Board of Directors.

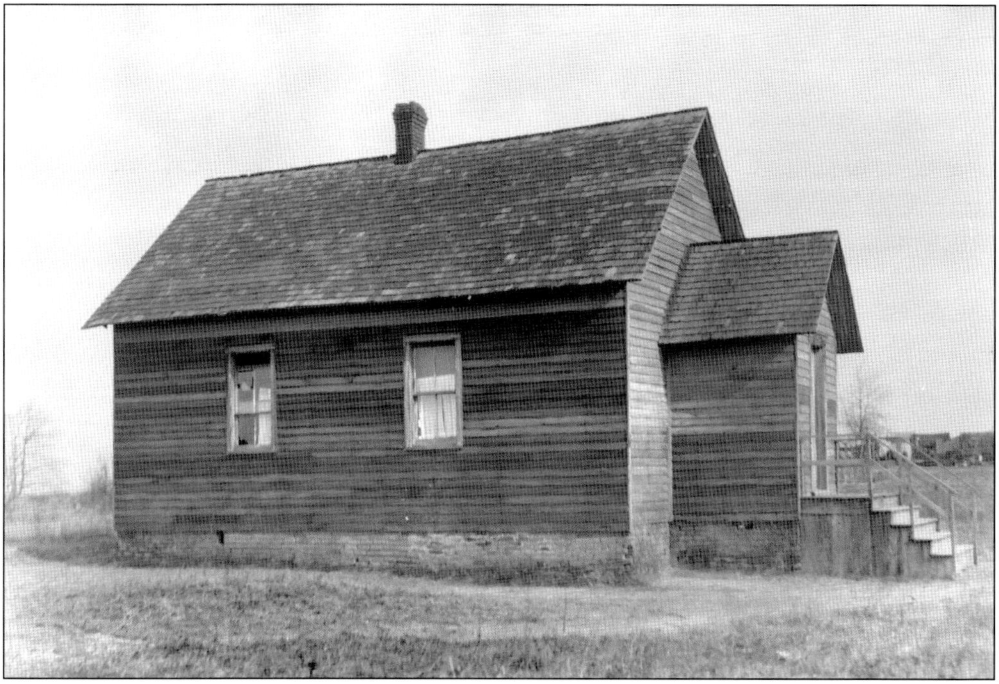

A school for minority children was built in the town of Clayton. Conditions of the small school were not ideal. In 1913, the Department of Education held an inspection of the institution. It was said to be at adequate standard, with the water closets needing attention.

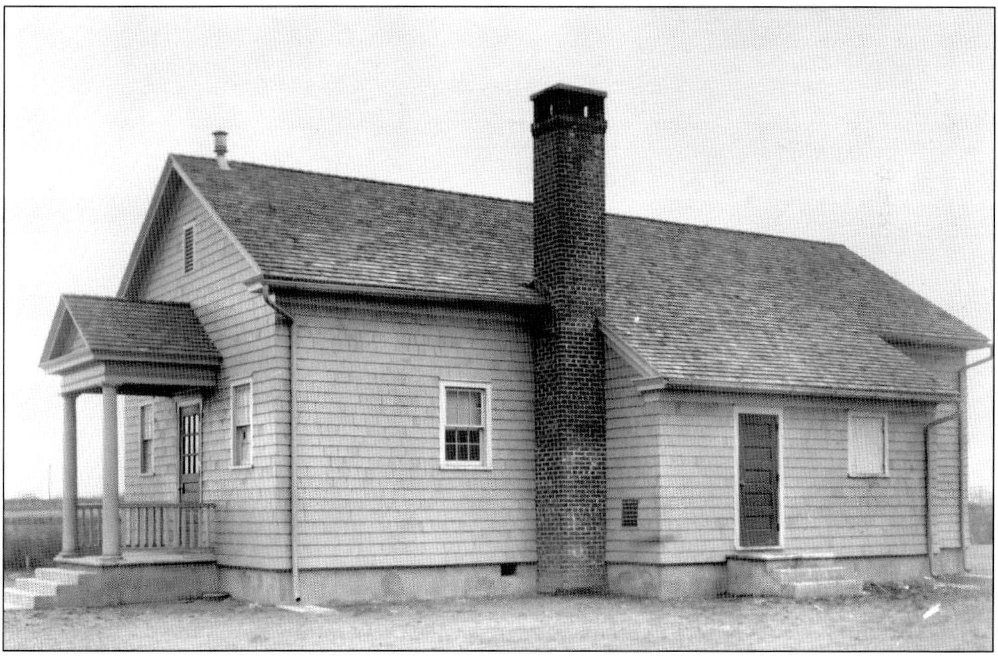

A new Clayton Colored School was built in May 1922 through the Pierre S. DuPont initiative. The total cost for construction was $6,516. The school was only one room and taught all grades. While this new building replaced an older one in town, they continued to only employ one teacher for all children.

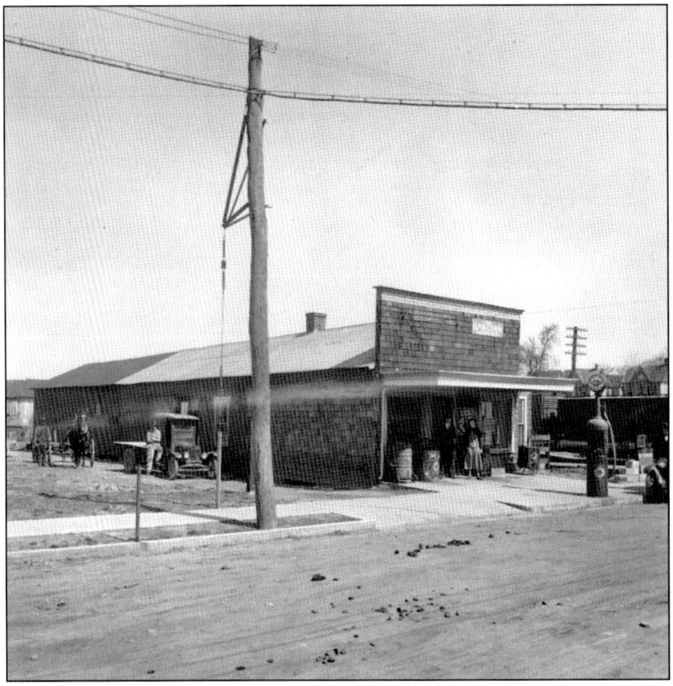

Rynear Williams Slaughter, born in May 1886, was the sixth child of Ezekiel and Mary Lydia Ford Slaughter, who lived as farmers in Smyrna. Rynear went to Smyrna High School and in 1913 set up a butcher shop in the town of Clayton. In 1916, he married Mary R. Garrison, daughter of Gamaliel Garrison in Kenton. Once married, they lived on Clayton Avenue. Rynear experimented with many business ventures and opened a very profitable lumberyard in Clayton. Slaughter held many prominent positions in community groups in Clayton, Smyrna, and Dover.

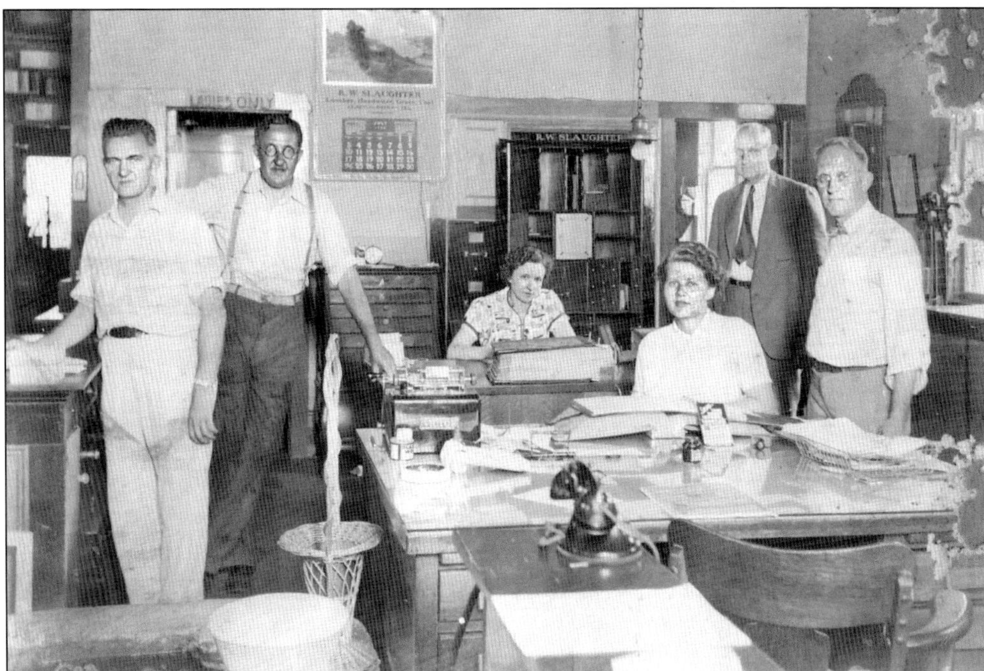

Rynear W. Slaughter, who was known to enjoy wearing a bow tie, is seen here inside his lumber office with employees. Standing on the left side of the room are Earl Carter and Raymond Mabrey, Slaughter's salesman and manager. The woman sitting at the back desk was Helen Goldsborough, a longtime employee of Slaughter. Along with his office, he held a small gift shop for patrons as well as a small cement fishpond that interested every child who entered the building. (Courtesy of Thelma and Preston Knight.)

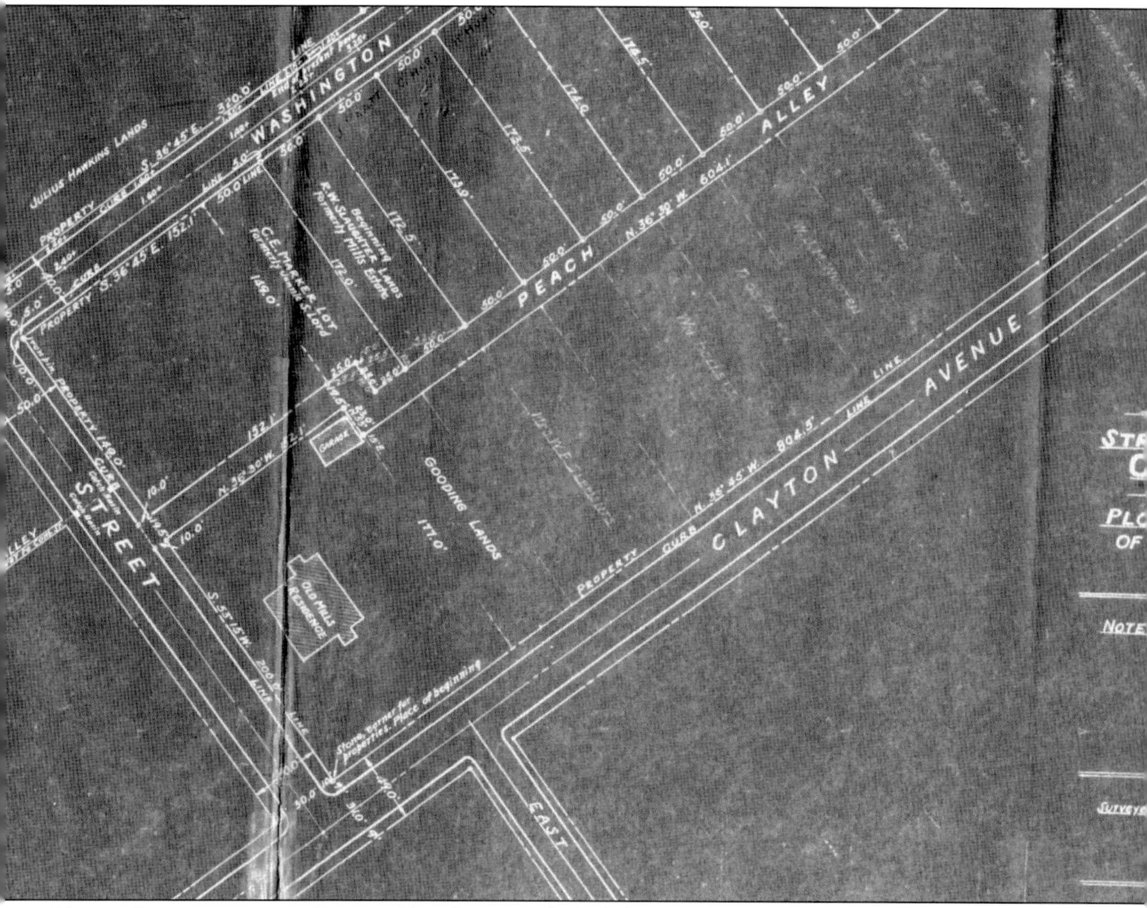

Always the entrepreneur, Rynear Slaughter purchased the Isaac N. Mills estate a few years after the death of Isaac's wife, Annie. In 1938, he planned a grand subdivision called Evergreen Acres on Washington Avenue that boasted of water and sewage service. Located parallel to Clayton and Highland Avenues, the street took up what was once the farm and woodlands of Isaac and Annie Mills. The lots sold quickly and with ample lumber from the Slaughter Lumberyard, eight houses were built along the avenue.

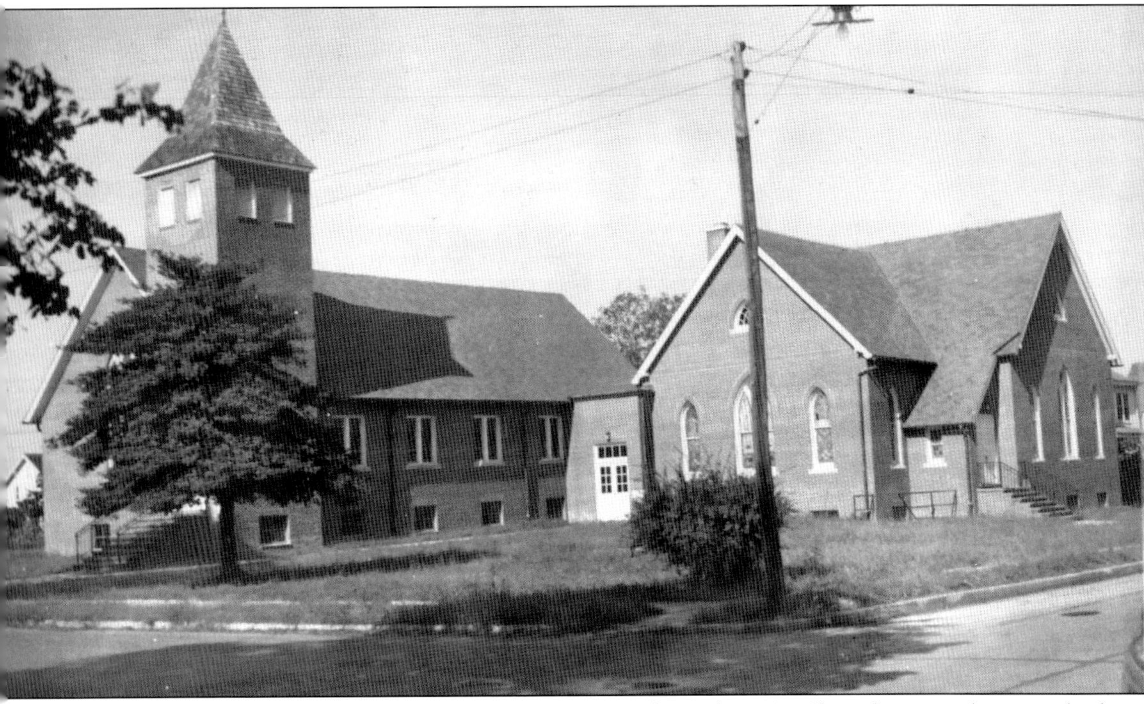

With Trinity Methodist Episcopal Church converted to a doctor's office, the town that once had three Methodists churches in close proximity to one another now had them all united under one roof. In 1951, under the direction of the United Methodist Church, Ewell's Methodist Protestant Church (located on Main Street) and St. Paul's Methodist Episcopal Church (located on the corner of Highland and West Streets) moved to join together. The new location would be on the corner of West Street and Clayton Avenue. This was the same spot where the Isaac Newton Mills mansion once stood. In 1918, the land was purchased with the intention of building a Catholic parish. At the onset of World War I, that idea was abandoned and Catholic parishioners instead started attending the chapel on St. Joseph's Industrial School campus. The uniting of these two churches was no small feat. Each building was put on rollers and taken down their respective streets. It is said that St. Paul's structure was moved through the "fields" of Highland and Washington Avenues, where houses were not yet built. Ewell's Episcopal Church made the journey over the railroad tracks and eventually onto Clayton Avenue. Once both on-site, the churches were married together to form the building that seen now. Ewell's-St. Paul's United Methodist Church was born.

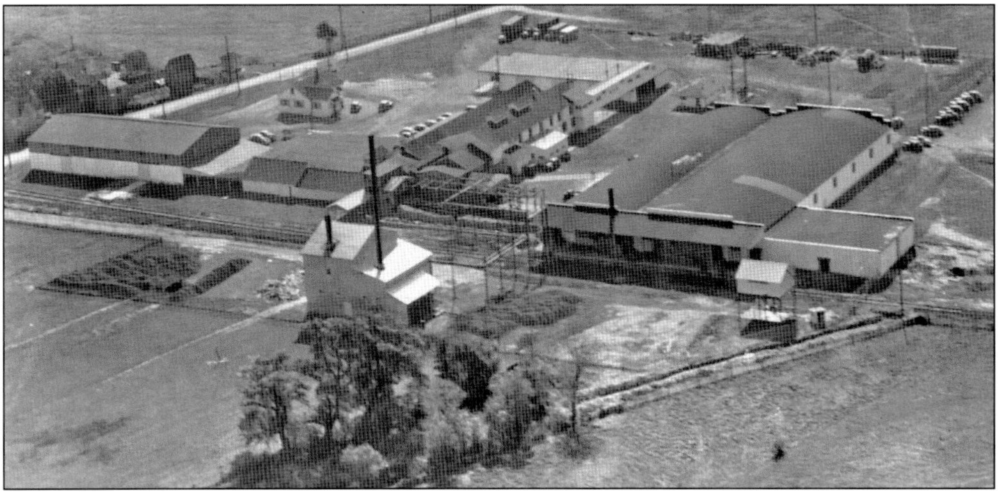

Wheatley's Canning Company operated in Clayton from 1930 until 1969. Walter Lee Wheatley ran a successful canning business in Federalsburg, Maryland, before opening a business in Clayton. In 1940, he went into business with his son, Walter Leslie Wheatley. Walter Leslie ran the company after his father's death in 1945 until 1969. In that year, canning gave way to vegetable flash freezing. The canning factory was changed to a freezing facility for the Campbell's Soup Company. This is now the Hanover Foods Corporation at the western edge of the town. (Courtesy of the Citizens' Hose Company No. 1, Inc.)

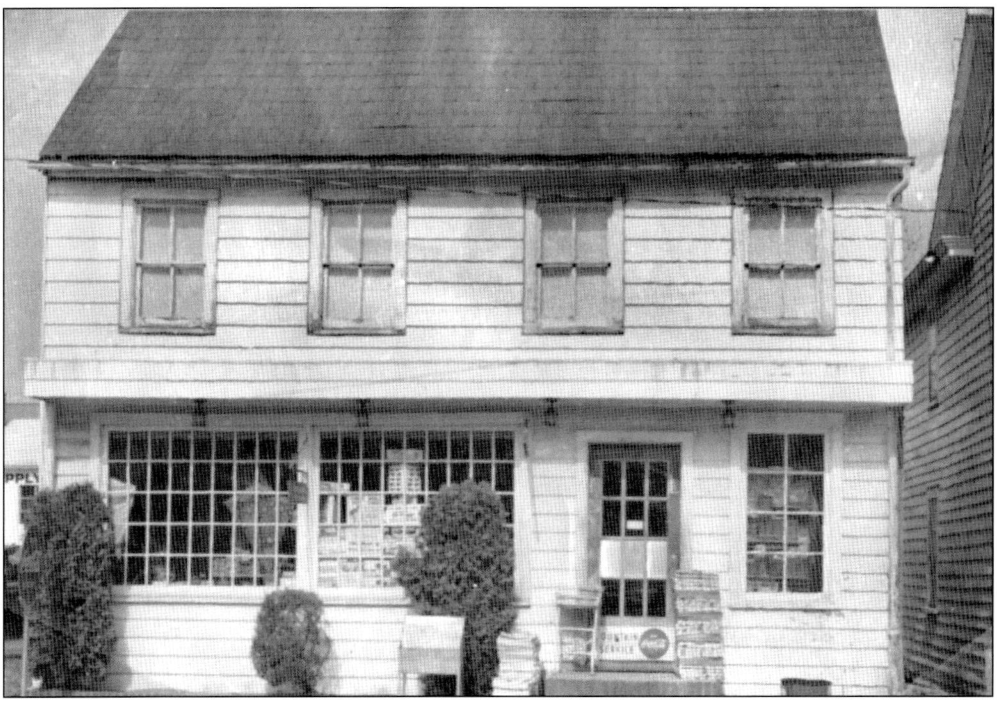

Many Clayton residents fondly remember some of the last small businesses to cater to the town, such as a corner store, barbershop, and hardware store. Above is Clarkie's Candy Shop, owned by Jon Clark. This shop was located just past Walter R. Keys's pharmacy on Main Street. Many adults in town today recall riding their bikes to Clark's store on many a nice afternoon. (Courtesy of Heather Jones.)

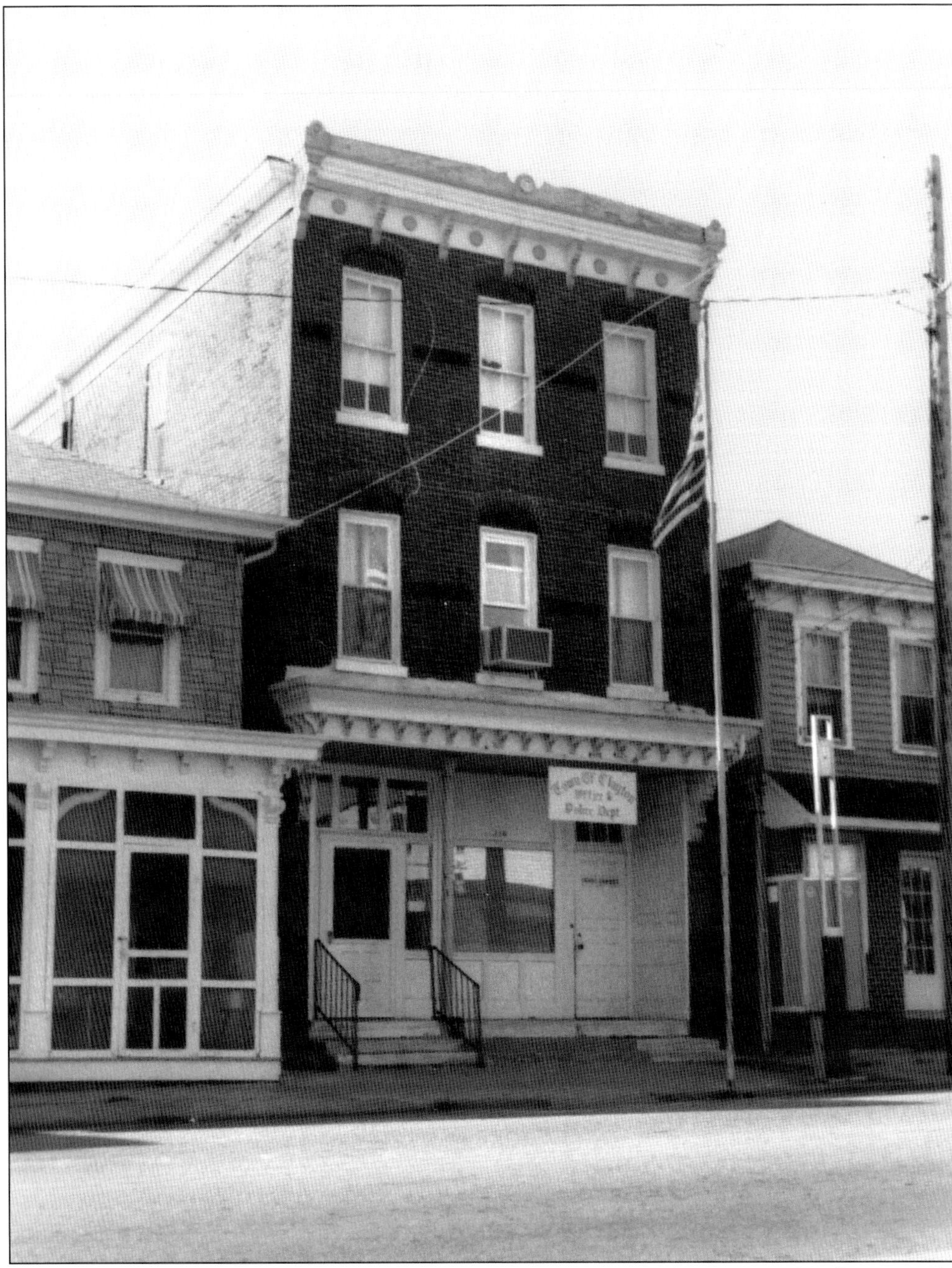

The old Clayton Town Hall now sits quietly on Main Street, currently home to a locally run coffee shop. This building served as a jail and post office in conjunction with housing the town offices. A large steel safe still remains on the first floor and partial prison bars can be found on a back window, reminders of the building's rich history and of the history of the town of Clayton. The town has grown and changed since 1860, but the small-town charm has remained ever present. With fewer businesses, Main Street now serves as a perfect backdrop for a summer evening stroll while admiring the 19th- and early-20th-century architecture and listening for the train whistle to ring through the streets. (Courtesy of the Town of Clayton.)

Five

Woodland Beach

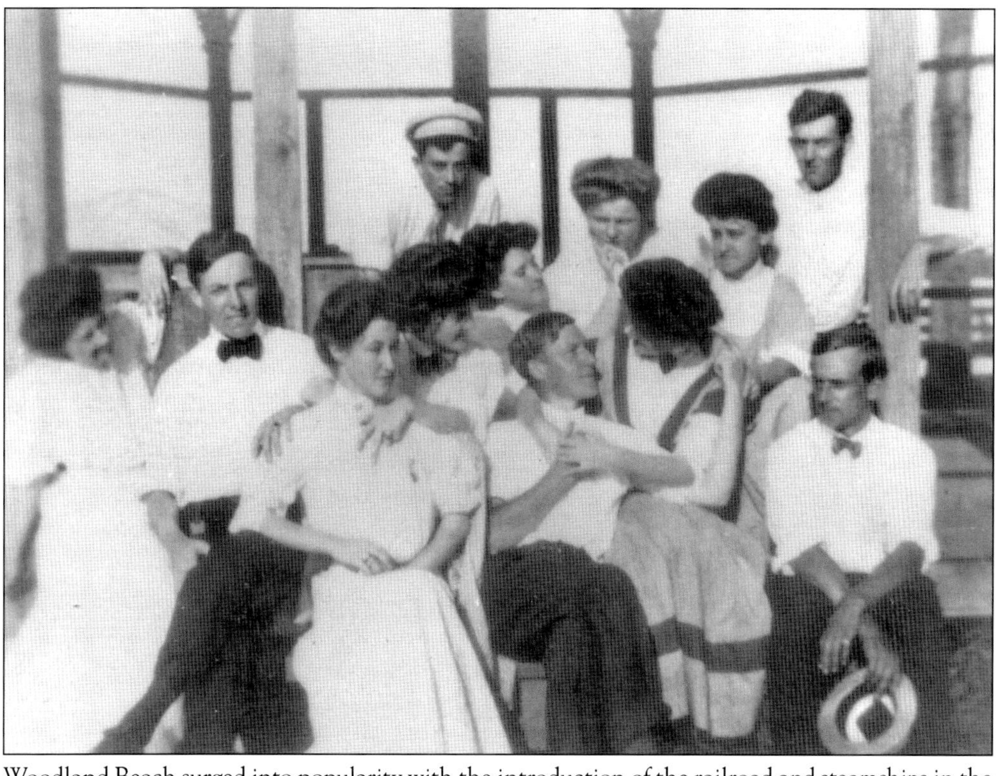

Woodland Beach surged into popularity with the introduction of the railroad and steamships in the later half of the 1800s and into the early 1900s. Each season was opened with a highly anticipated dance at the large dance hall. Families and young people regularly flocked to the resort each year for new opportunities to make wonderful memories. (Courtesy of Roy James Jr.)

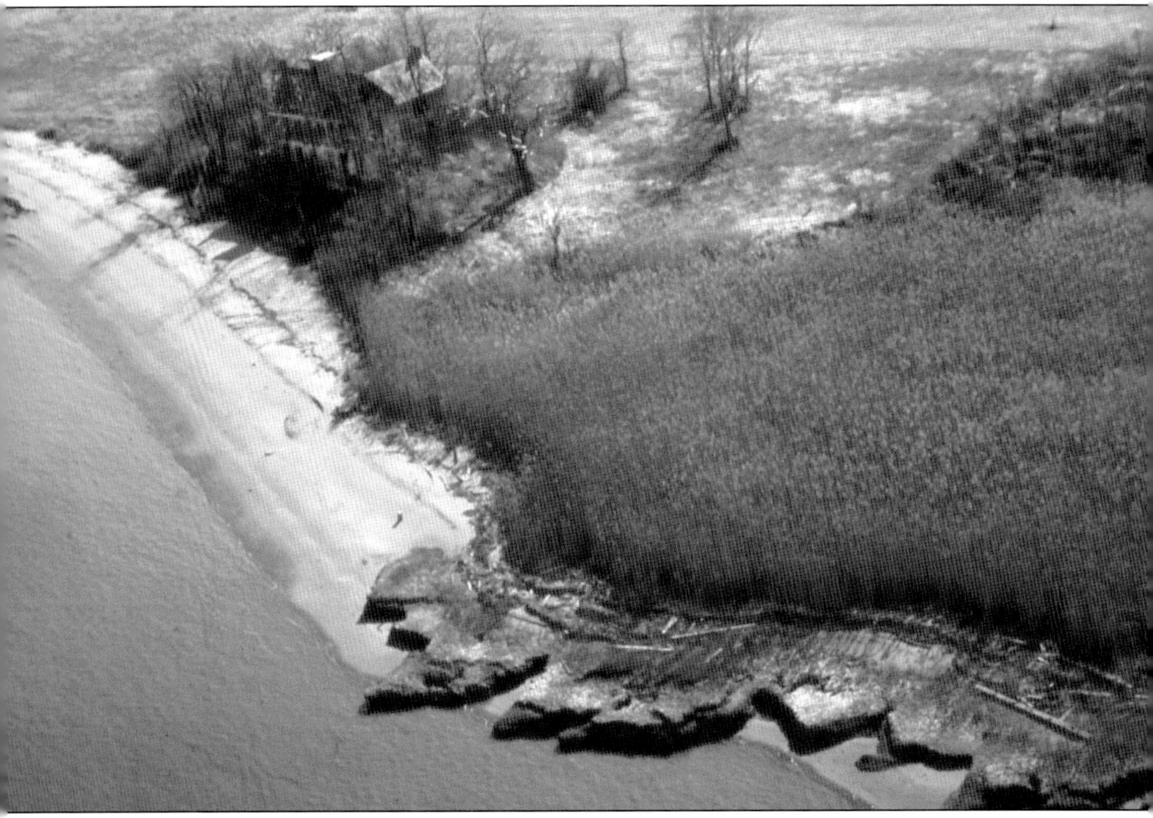

The Bombay Hook Lighthouse was a small wooden house, originally constructed at the time of the Revolutionary War, at the mouth of the Duck Creek River and the Delaware Bay. In 1682, Ephraim Herman dug the first canal in the American colonies through the marsh here, creating the "thoroughfare." This allowed large boats to enter the river from the coast. The lighthouse was initially installed to provide a first defense for the towns of Duck Creek Village, Duck Creek Crossroads, and Green's Landing from the British. In 1813, a militia from Smyrna was sent to help defend the light keeper from British soldiers who were entering into Duck Creek to raid farmland. A hotel was installed just south of the lighthouse by John Brick in 1848. The hotel was later taken over by Eli Logan when he purchased lands on Bombay Hook.

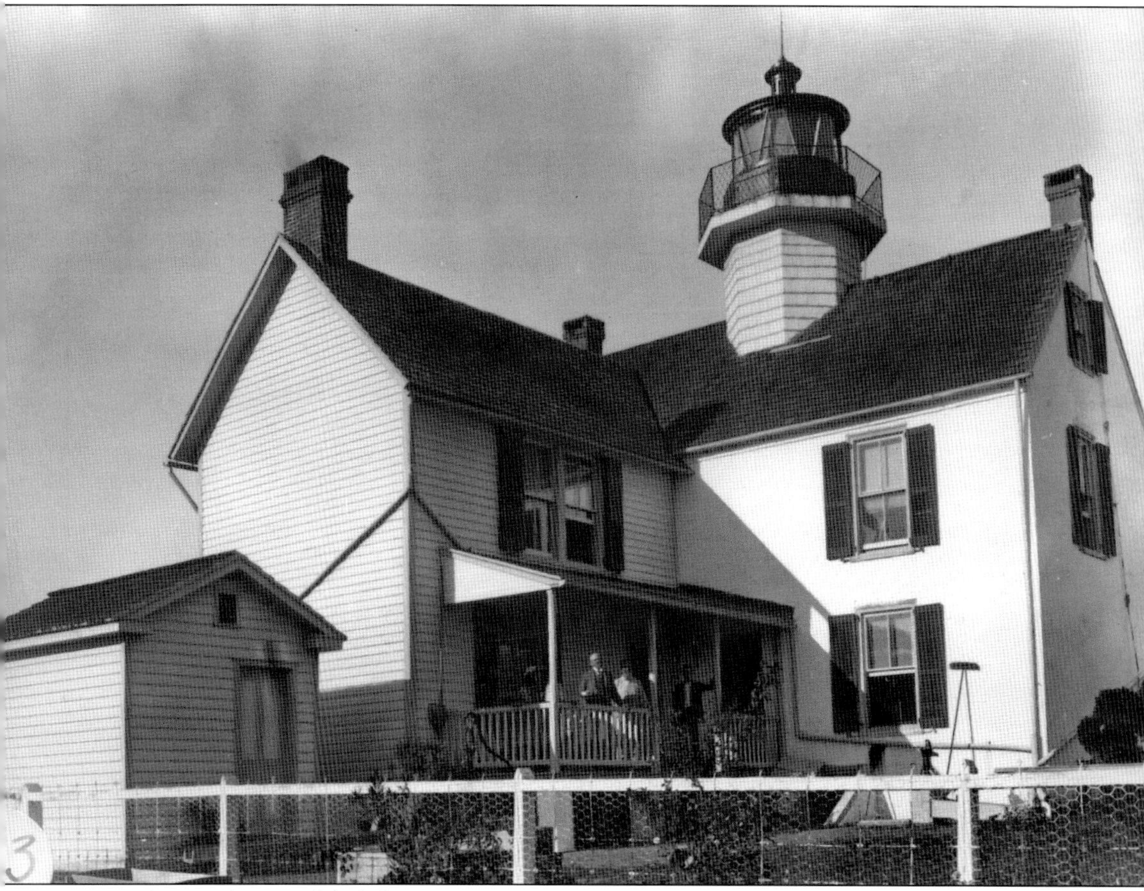

By 1831, the Bombay Hook lighthouse structure had been completely replaced, and in 1841, it was improved upon to create the two-story building shown in the above photograph. The first official lighthouse keeper was Duncan Stewart, followed unofficially by his daughter Margaret before her appointment in 1854. Capt. Joseph Benson of Smyrna was appointed keeper by President Lincoln in 1862 and held that position until his death in 1908. Above is Captain Benson with his family in September 1902. Benson and his wife, Elizabeth, raised 11 children in the lighthouse home. By 1974, the lighthouse had been abandoned and fallen into disrepair. The State of Delaware, present owner of the lands, decided to demolish the remains of the building along with the hotel ruins. (Courtesy of the Duck Creek Historical Society.)

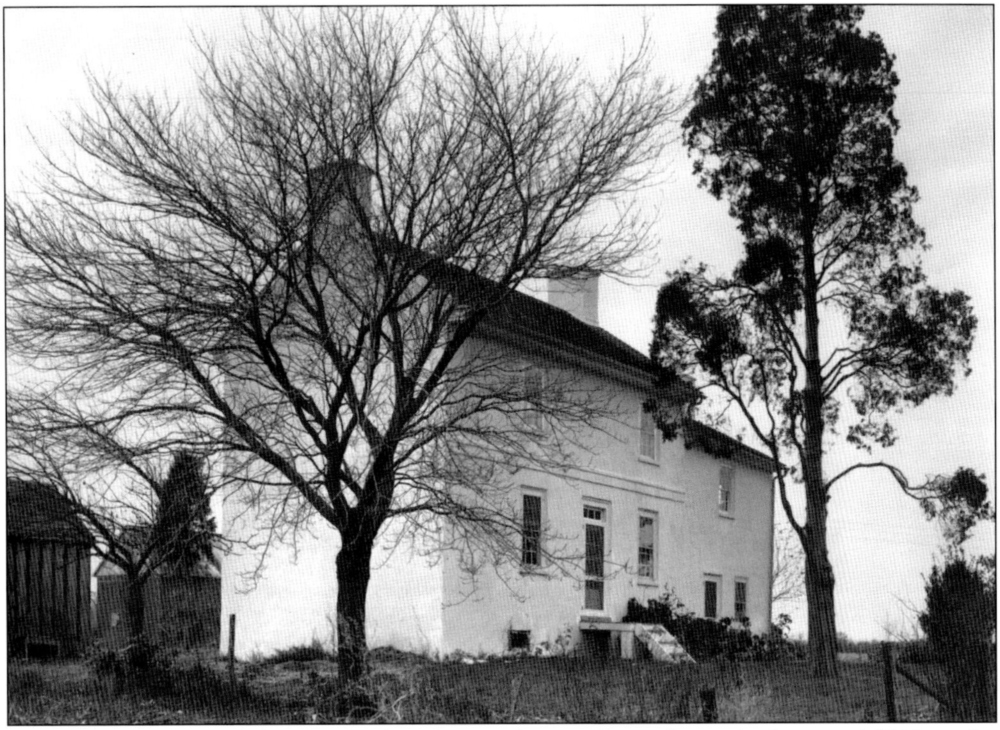

Just down from the lighthouse was the Thomas Sutton House. It was built around 1740 on the tract of land called Newberry near Taylor's Gut. Robert Palmatary was the first landowner of this parcel in 1684. After a string of owners, Samuel Sutton purchased the land and house in 1853 before Thomas Sutton took the property over in 1856. The front of this home sat near the roadway leading from the lighthouse to the Pearsons Cove farm. After the great storm of 1878, the road leading to Woodland Beach was not replaceable. Farmland was lost to the marsh, and the road was rebuilt as it lies today, going around a large portion of new marsh. This put the Sutton home into isolation. The home is now owned by the State of Delaware and is associated with the Woodland Beach Wildlife Area.

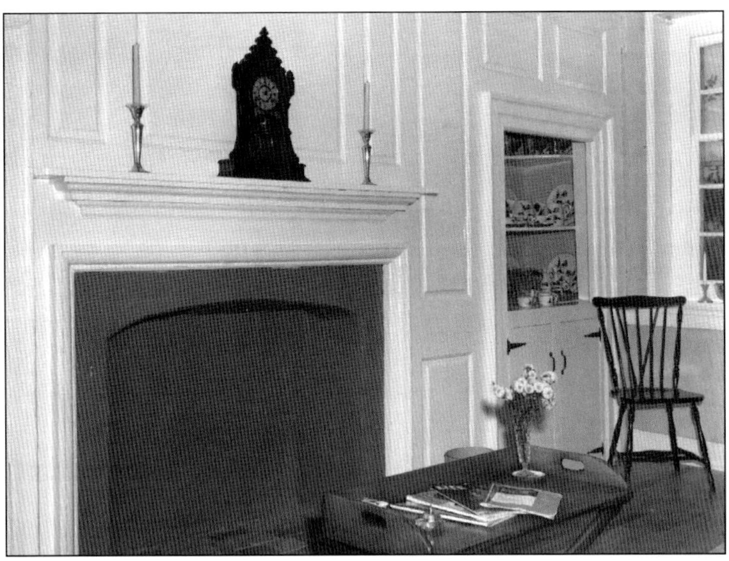

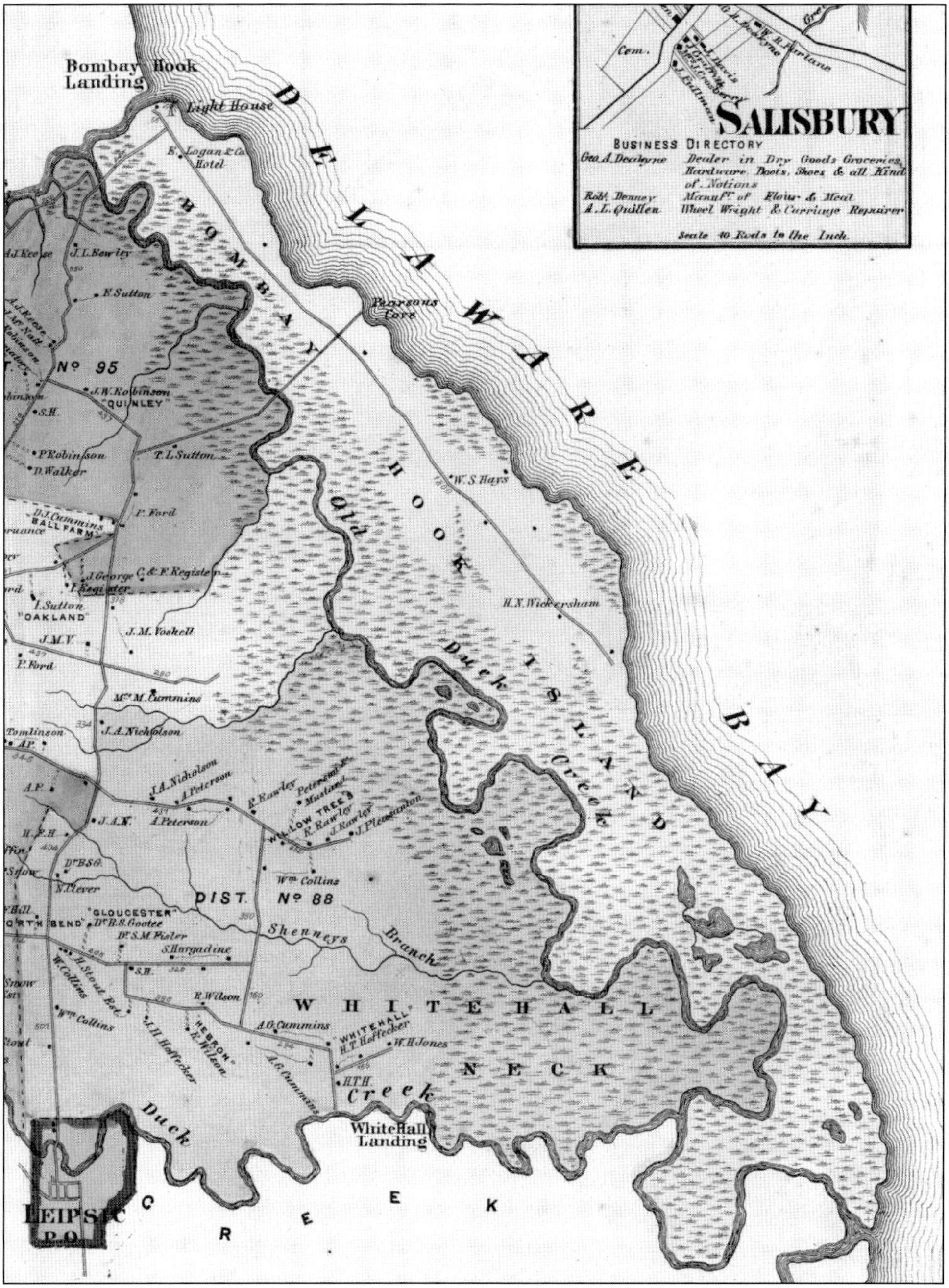

This portion of the Beers Atlas of Duck Creek Hundred in 1868 shows the Bombay Hook lighthouse, hotel, and Pearsons Cove property. Eli Logan, a yeoman from Chester County, Pennsylvania, purchased land on the northern end of Bombay Hook in 1860 and took over the hotel previously owned by John R. Brick in 1862. William S. Hayes, a leather manufacturer from Wilmington, Delaware, owned the Pearson Cove farm and acreage in the center lands of Bombay Hook. Hayes jointly purchased his property in 1860 as part of the Eli Logan, Henry Wickersham, and William Hayes deed. William Hayes sold the Pearsons Cover property in 1876 for $7,068 to James L. Bewley of Philadelphia.

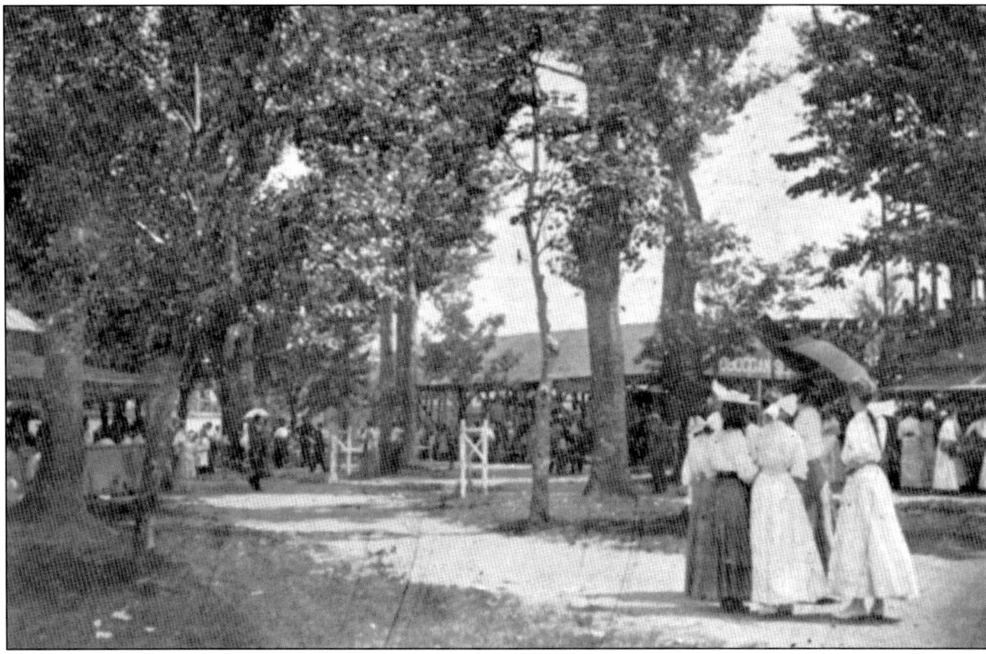

The Woodland Beach Hotel was originally built under the ownership of James W. Spruance, a developer, from Smyrna, Delaware, who purchased the acreage from James L. Bewley. This large building had a porch on both stories that wrapped around the hotel to allow all visitors an amazing view of the gentle water and quiet park. Situated in a grove of tall trees, the hotel was always shaded. In 1878, after a great storm took out most of nearby Collins Beach to the north, James R. Mott (owner of Woodland Beach in that year) purchased the remains of the Collins Beach hotel and floated it down the bay to Woodland Beach, where he used the structure to add to his impressive accommodations.

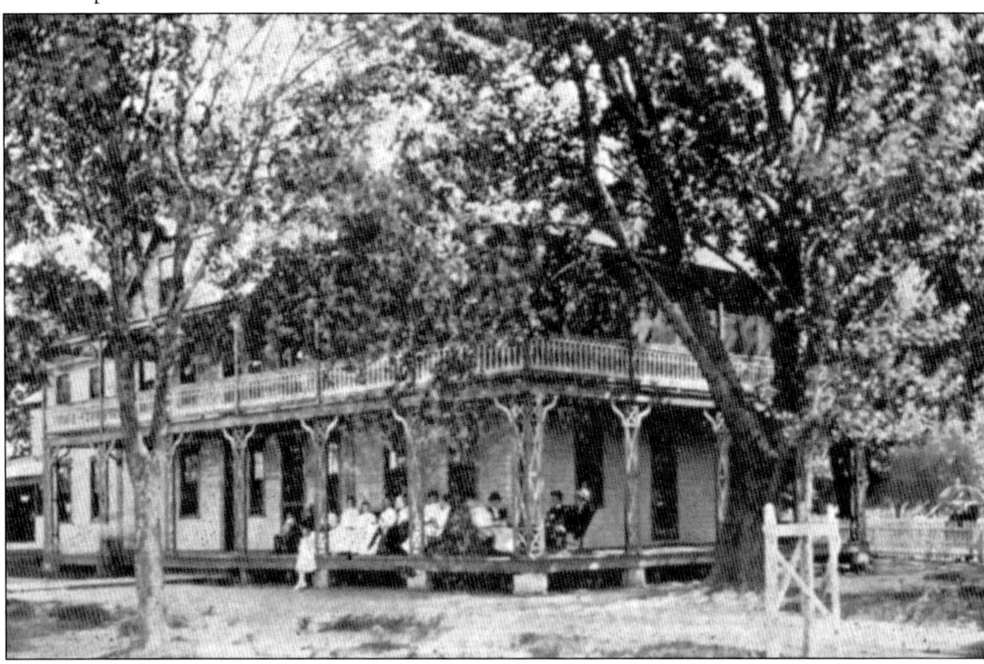

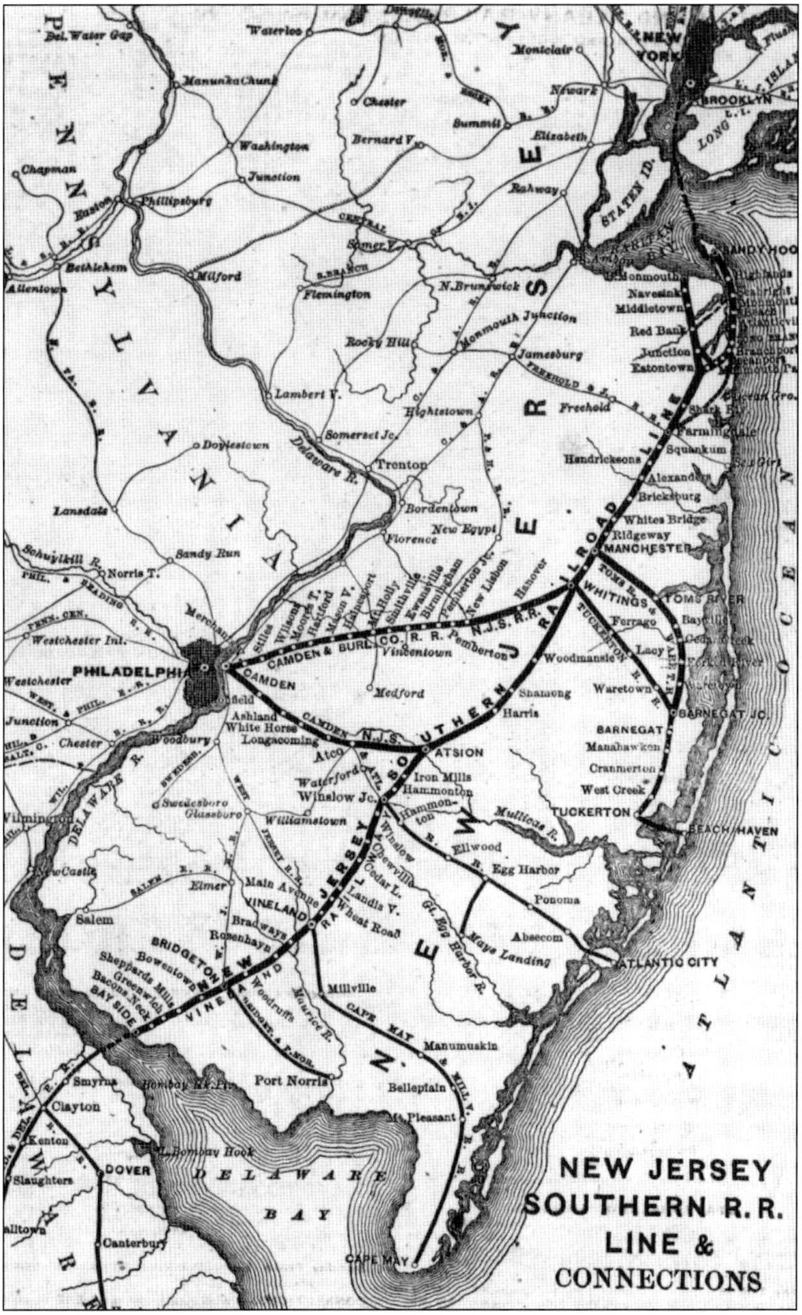

James Spruance also installed a pier for the Smyrna and Delaware Bay Railroad. The rail line began operation in 1873 and ran from the Maryland line through western Delaware, through the Clayton Depot to the Bombay Hook Landing at Pearson's Cove. From that point, passengers could take a ferry across the Delaware Bay and continue onto the Vineland Railroad in Bayside, New Jersey, or enjoy a lovely afternoon at Woodland Beach. The railroad company was incorporated with several prominent landowners on the appointed commission. The line ran seasonally from 1873 until 1883 when it was merged with the Baltimore and Delaware Bay Railroad Company. Then, in 1888, the line was abandoned.

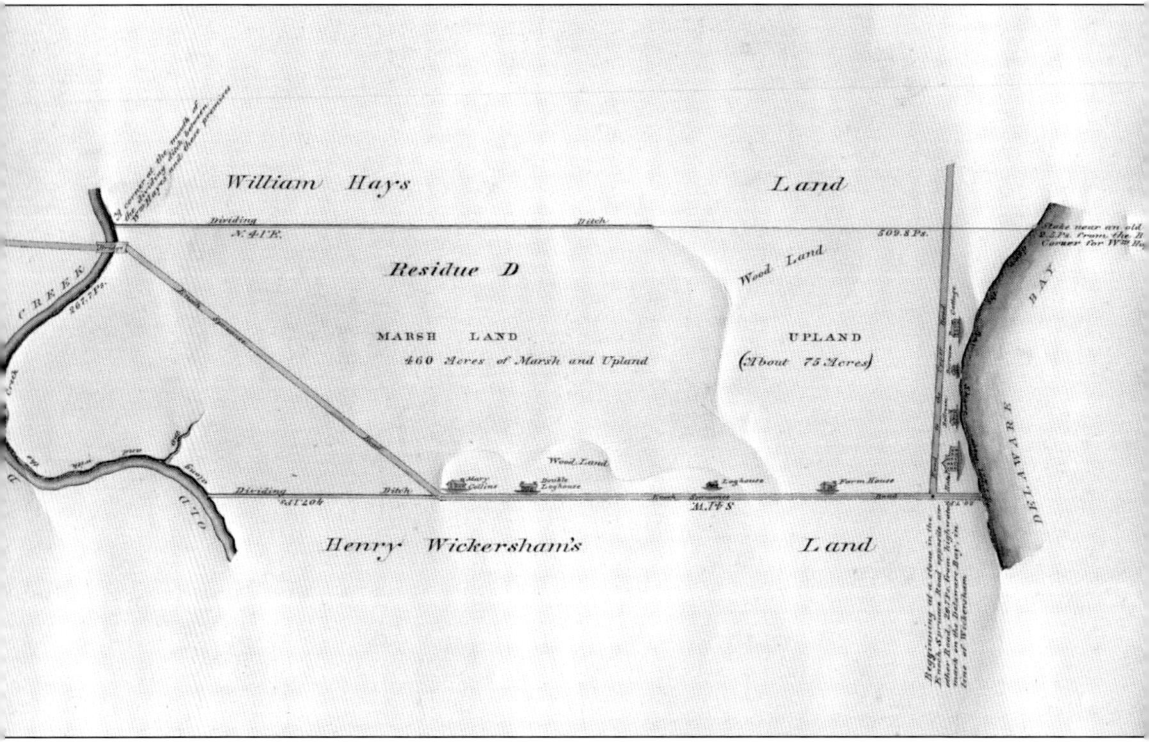

Enoch Spruance, James's brother who was also from Smyrna, was a merchant involved in many business ventures. Enoch set up Fraland Grove just two miles down the beach from Pearsons Cove. Perhaps this was sibling rivalry, or maybe both saw the opportunity for a sandy playground. Fraland in its own right enjoyed great success while it existed. The Fraland Hotel was listed in the Delaware State Directory for the year 1879–1880. Levi Grieves and his brother leased Fraland from Spruance after a successful venture at managing Collins Beach resort and a season at Fraland. According to an article run in the *Smyrna Times* in June 1879, Fraland Grove "is superior perhaps to any on the coast of the Bay, and all it has needed to make it a popular resort has been tact and energy." Unfortunately, after rough storms and a fire at Fraland, the popularity waned and the spotlight shifted back to Pearsons Cove.

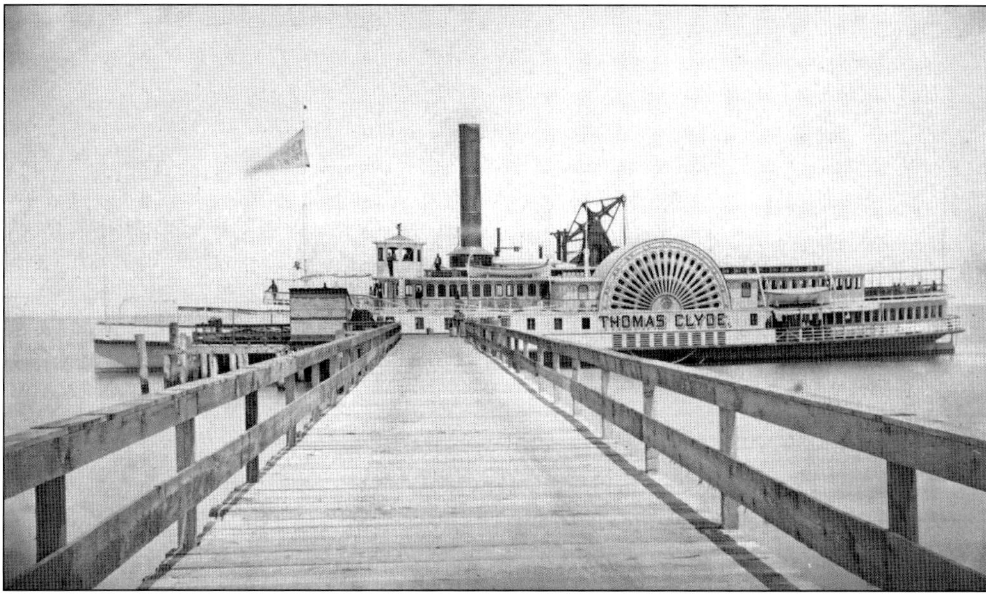

The Reybold family, from Delaware City, had many successes in the business world and were very well known. They owned shipping companies and parts of railroad companies; in addition, they owned farm land, had tenants and raised sheep, pressed castor oil, and most famously grew peaches. Maj. Phillip Reybold lived on a grand estate called Lexington and was known as the "peach king." The Reybold family built the *Major Reybold* and well-known *Thomas Clyde* steamships to primarily transport their peach crops. Some claimed that William Reybold's interest in the Bombay Hook property was solely to further their peach orchard business. Groves were planted around the beach community, and they referred to the resort area merely as the picnic grounds. The Thomas Clyde steamer became a regular in the Delaware Bay, and the ship's popularity became the talk of the Delaware Valley. (Below, courtesy of the Duck Creek Historical Society.)

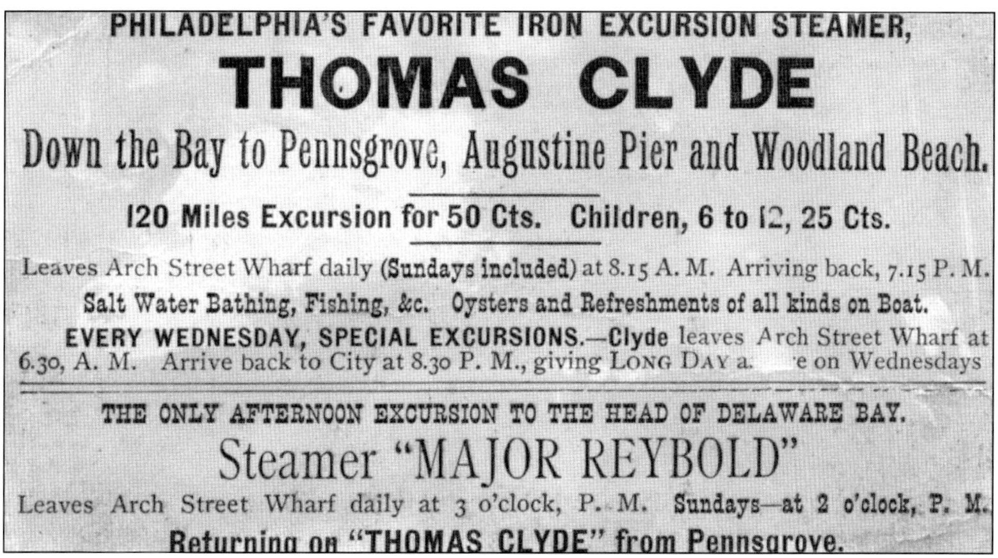

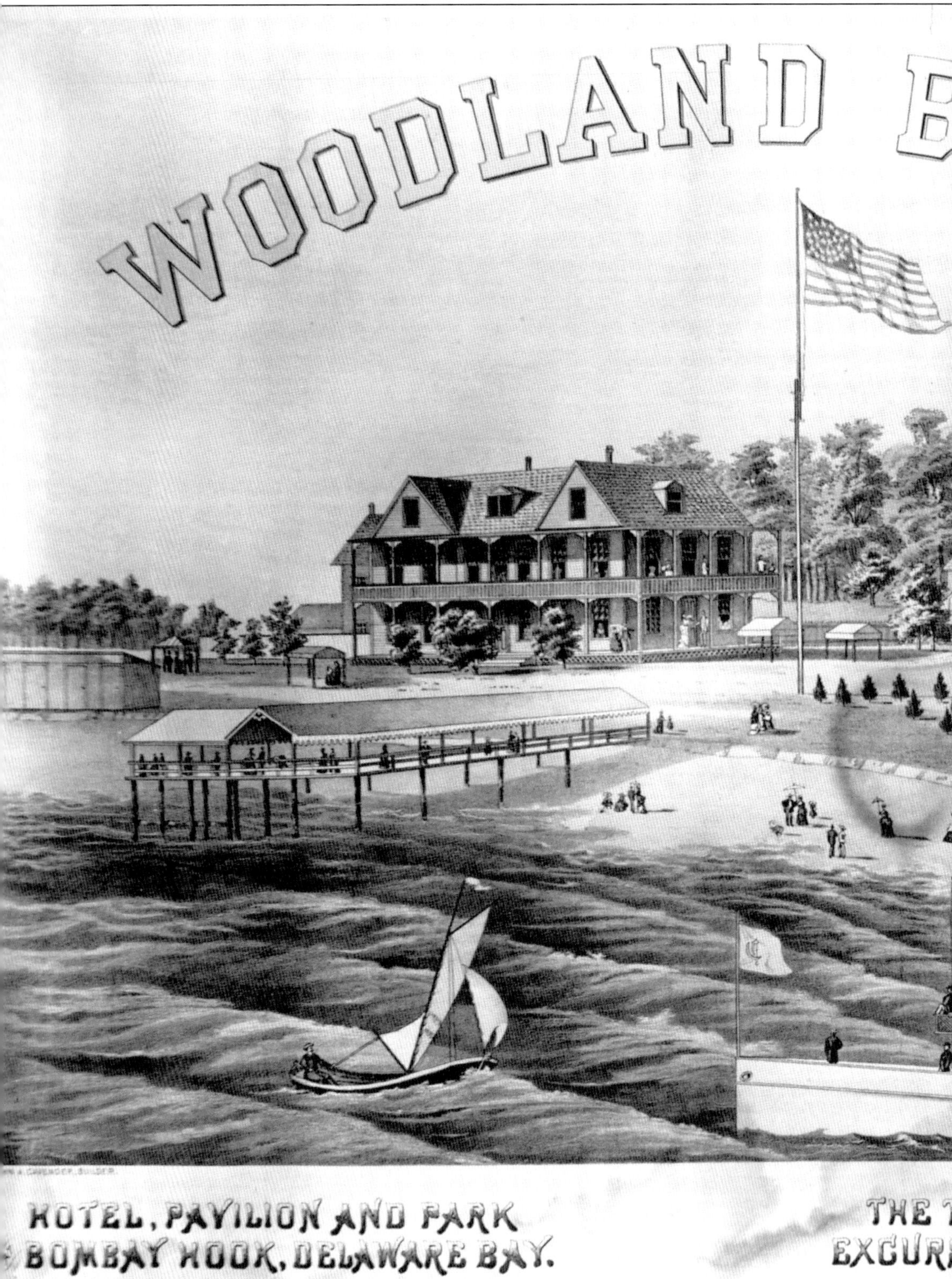
WOODLAND
HOTEL, PAVILION AND PARK
BOMBAY HOOK, DELAWARE BAY.
THE

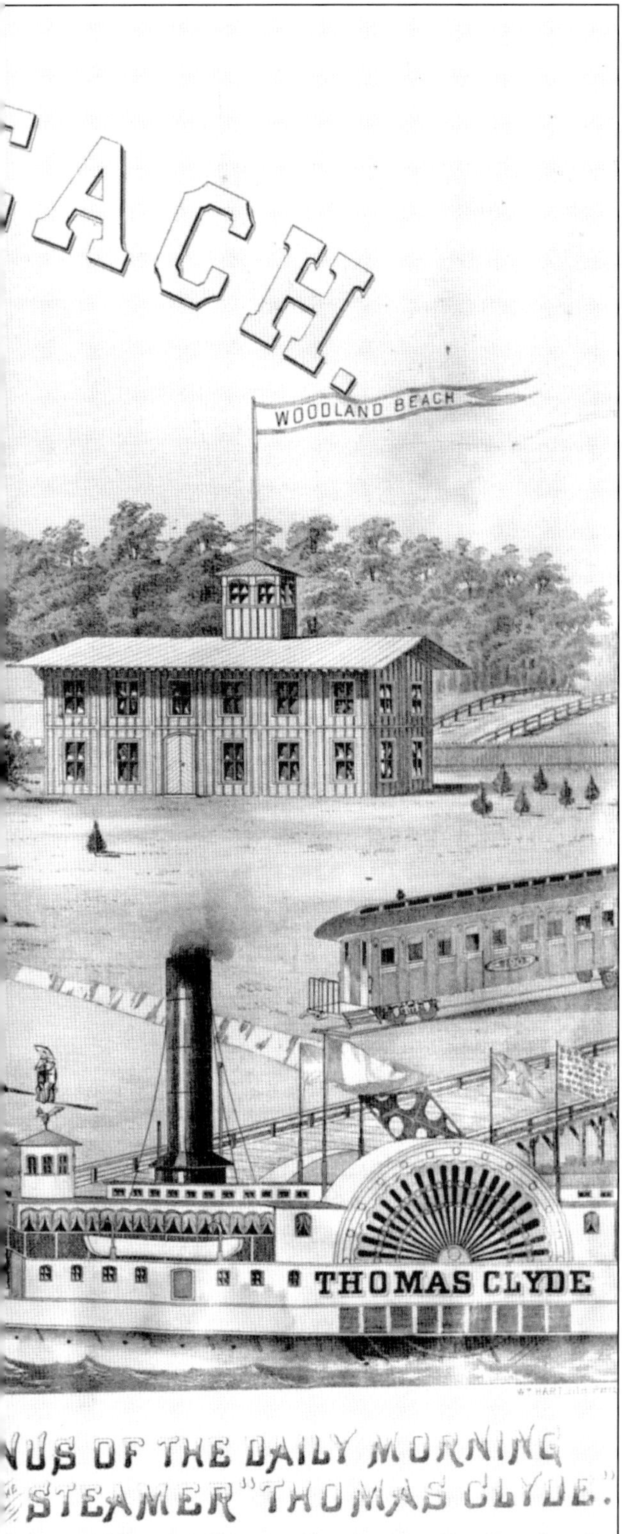

In the 1870s, James Spruance was forced to sell some of his property holdings to cover debts. William Reybold, the son of Philip Reybold, purchased all 540 acres of the Pearsons Cove Farm for $5,000 in 1879 from trustee John H. Hoffecker. William was the president of the steamboat company that built and captained steamers to transport their huge crop of peaches. Woodland Beach was a perfect opportunity to continue to grow not only the peach crops, but also the income of the steamer. Reybold improved upon the resort and employed many capable persons to run the daily operations. George Millington, who also owned the Capital Hotel in Dover, managed the resort for Reybold while Lucious P. Campbell was in charge of the Woodland Beach Hotel. Reybold also made an agreement for the Smyrna and Delaware Bay Railroad Company to run a daily train from Clayton to the Woodland Beach pier terminus.

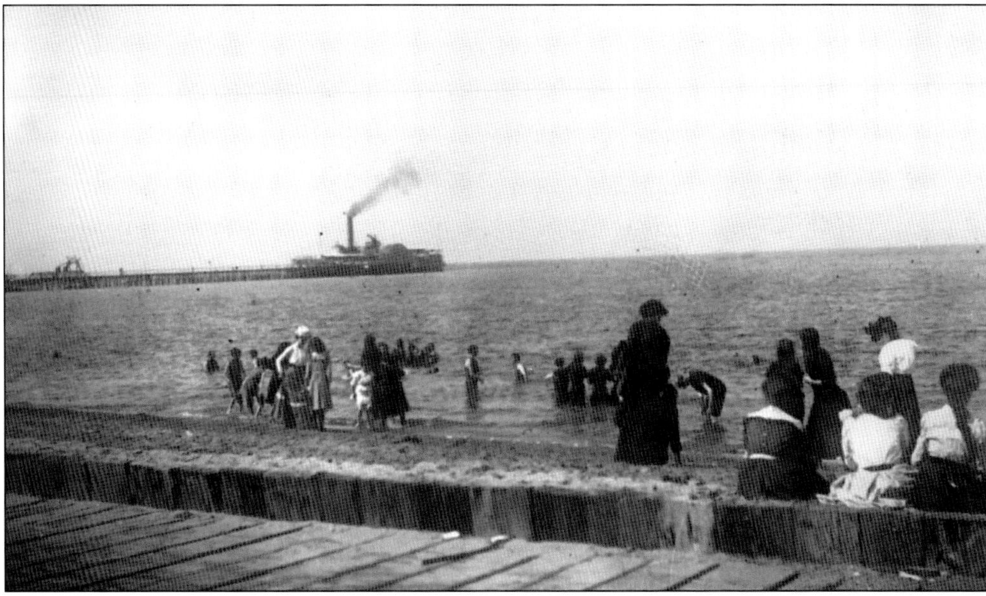

It was said that it was not uncommon for the unloading of all the passengers and luggage from such ships as the *Thomas Clyde* to take three hours. The ships were popular, packed with people, luggage, produce, and other exports heading north. In 1884, William Reybold also purchased prime real estate at Collins Beach. When he resold it in 1886, his terms stated that no ship excursions could be made there for seven years. This was insurance to keep Woodland Beach booming. Above, Victorian-style bathing suits can be seen as vacationers dipped into the Delaware Bay in August 1900, with the *Clyde* in the background of the long pier. The photograph below shows passengers lining up to board the famous *Clyde* at the end of their stay. (Both, courtesy of the Duck Creek Historical Society.)

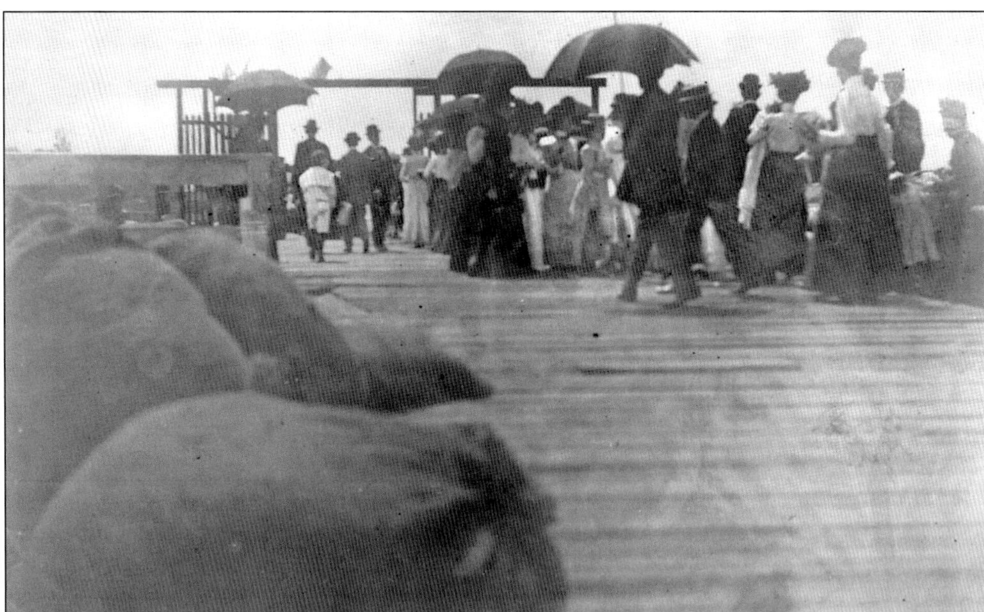

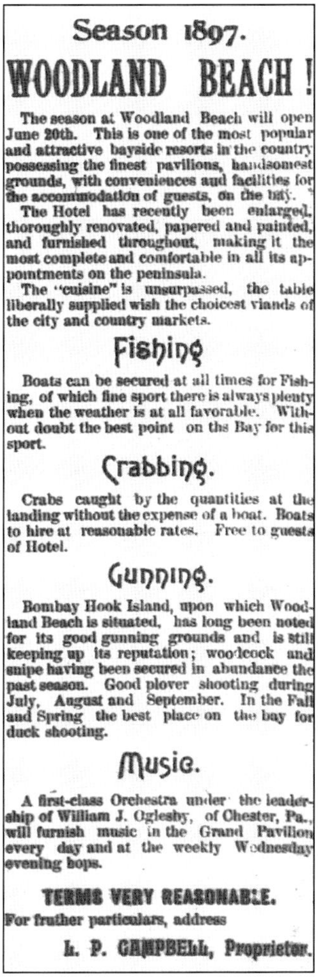

Season 1897.

WOODLAND BEACH!

The season at Woodland Beach will open June 20th. This is one of the most popular and attractive bayside resorts in the country possessing the finest pavilions, handsomest grounds, with conveniences and facilities for the accommodation of guests, on the bay.

The Hotel has recently been enlarged, thoroughly renovated, papered and painted, and furnished throughout, making it the most complete and comfortable in all its appointments on the peninsula.

The "cuisine" is unsurpassed, the table liberally supplied wish the choicest viands of the city and country markets.

Fishing

Boats can be secured at all times for Fishing, of which fine sport there is always plenty when the weather is at all favorable. Without doubt the best point on the Bay for this sport.

Crabbing.

Crabs caught by the quantities at the landing without the expense of a boat. Boats to hire at reasonable rates. Free to guests of Hotel.

Gunning.

Bombay Hook Island, upon which Woodland Beach is situated, has long been noted for its good gunning grounds and is still keeping up its reputation; woodcock and snipe having been secured in abundance the past season. Good plover shooting during July, August and September. In the Fall and Spring the best place on the bay for duck shooting.

Music.

A first-class Orchestra under the leadership of William J. Oglesby, of Chester, Pa., will furnish music in the Grand Pavilion every day and at the weekly Wednesday evening hops.

TERMS VERY REASONABLE.

For fruther particulars, address

L. P. CAMPBELL, Proprietor.

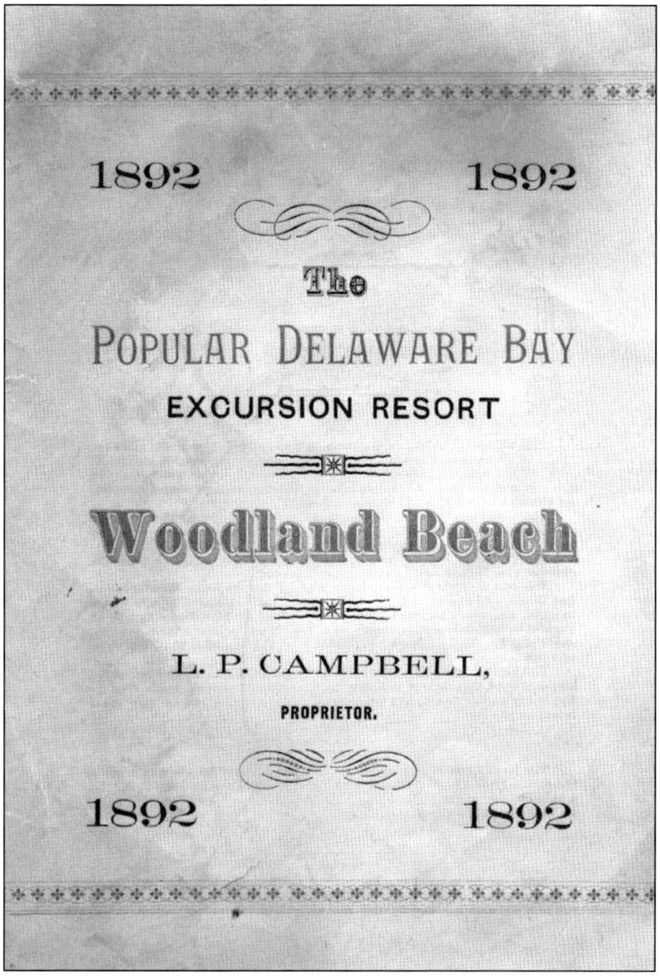

In 1892, Lucious P. Campbell was the proprietor of the Woodland Beach Hotel. He ran advertisements in the *Smyrna Times* and printed his own leaflets for distribution. He boasted of the many amenities available at Woodland Beach, especially that of the newly expanded hotel and 24-acre park filled with trees behind the hotel for retreating pleasure. Campbell and his family rented a house on the edge of the resort town for years before eventually purchasing the house and land in 1897. He ran the hotel until near his death in 1911, when he left his 1,000-acre Bombay Hook farm property to his wife, Anna. His son, James D. Campbell, worked as a teacher in the one-room schoolhouse that operated for a short time at Woodland Beach. (Right, courtesy of the Duck Creek Historical Society.)

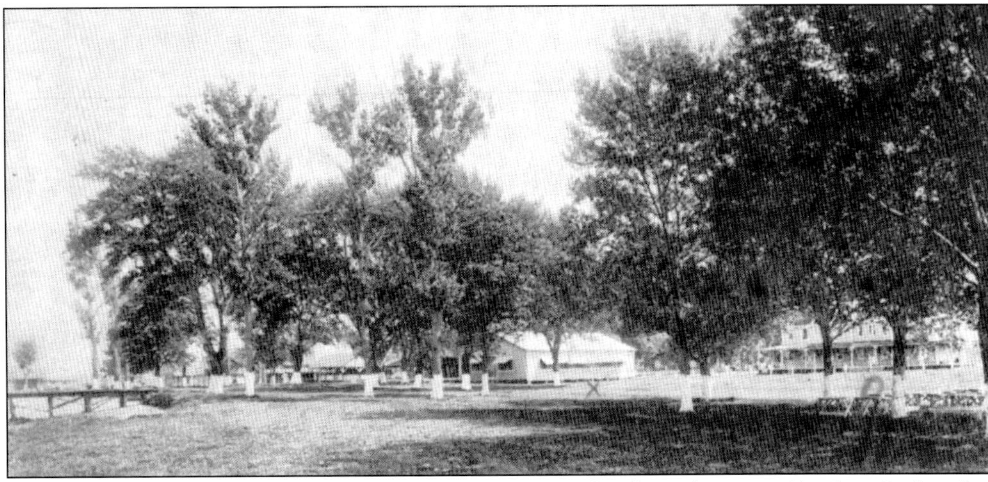

After William Reybold's death, his two sons sold the Woodland Beach resort. Absalom Codery first purchased the property and then quickly resold it to James R. Mott. Mott moved to Delaware from Atlantic City, New Jersey, with his wife, Annie, in the late 1800s. Mott, who previously worked as a developer, came to Woodland Beach with big plans. Just before Reybold's death, Mott was doing some work for him at the resort. Already a very popular and profitable resort during Reybold's ownership, Mott built and fixed up existing cottages and planned for a grand amusement park, creating the heyday times so fondly referred to today. After a storm washed out much of Collins Beach to the north, Mott purchased the remnants of the Collins Hotel and floated it down the Delaware Bay to add to his existing accommodations, wasting no opportunity to create a more impressive resort. Pictured above is the substantial Woodland Beach Hotel and dance hall.

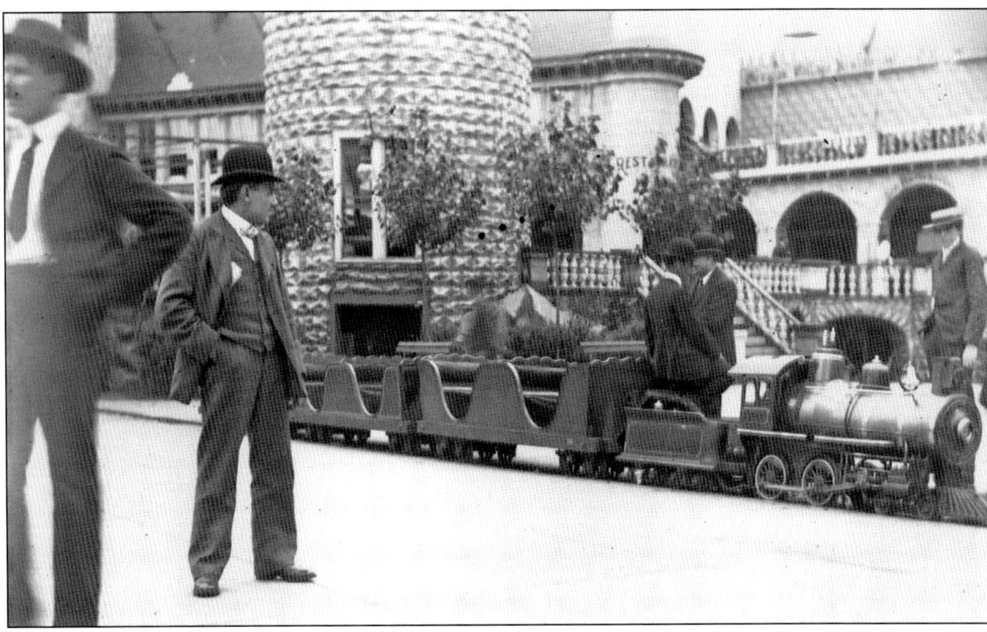

On the 1900 census, Mott listed "amusements" as his employment. And amusements he delivered. He installed a merry-go-round, a rumored roller coaster, and a toboggan slide. It is said that without seeing the rides at Woodland Beach, one would never believe they existed. That included a ride called the Razzle Dazzle and a miniature train run on steam power, similar to the one above. It cost 5¢ to enjoy the rides; they were immensely popular during the summer months.

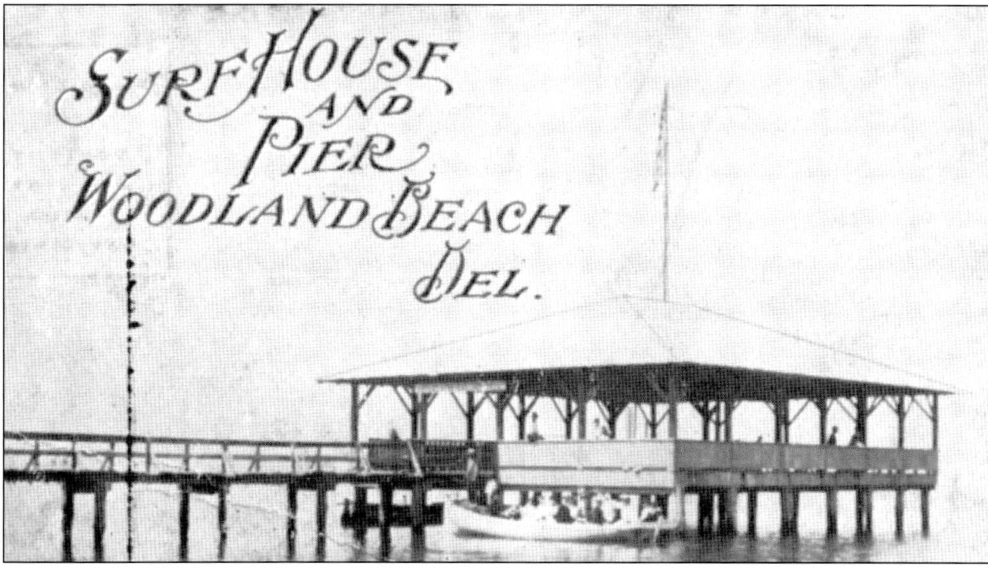

The Surf House and Pier were just one of the many draws of the resort. One dance hall was installed near the hotel and another overlooking the water on a pier. James Mott even put in a bowling alley. There was absolutely something for everyone at the Woodland Beach resort.

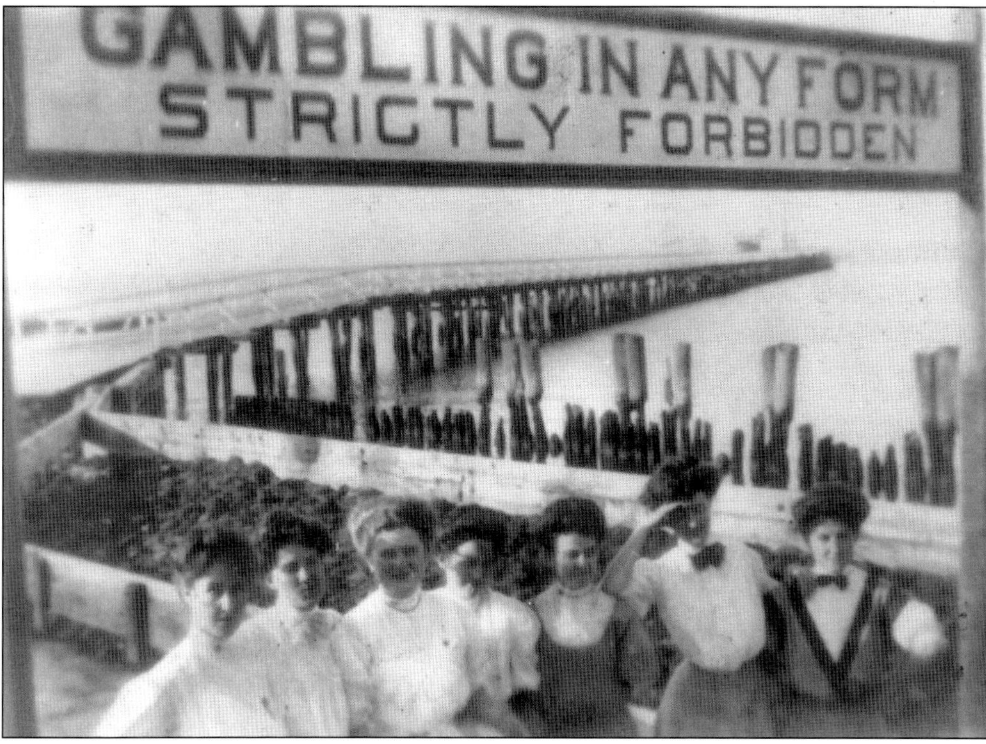

Many rumors swirled concerning the resort and the immoral behavior that may have occurred. Some speculated that gambling and drinking went on at Woodland Beach during Prohibition. However, it clearly posted that gambling was strictly forbidden. Others claimed that bootleggers from Jersey brought liquor into the resort by boat. Reportedly, they were met with a barrage of gunfire from federal agents. (Courtesy of Roy James Jr.)

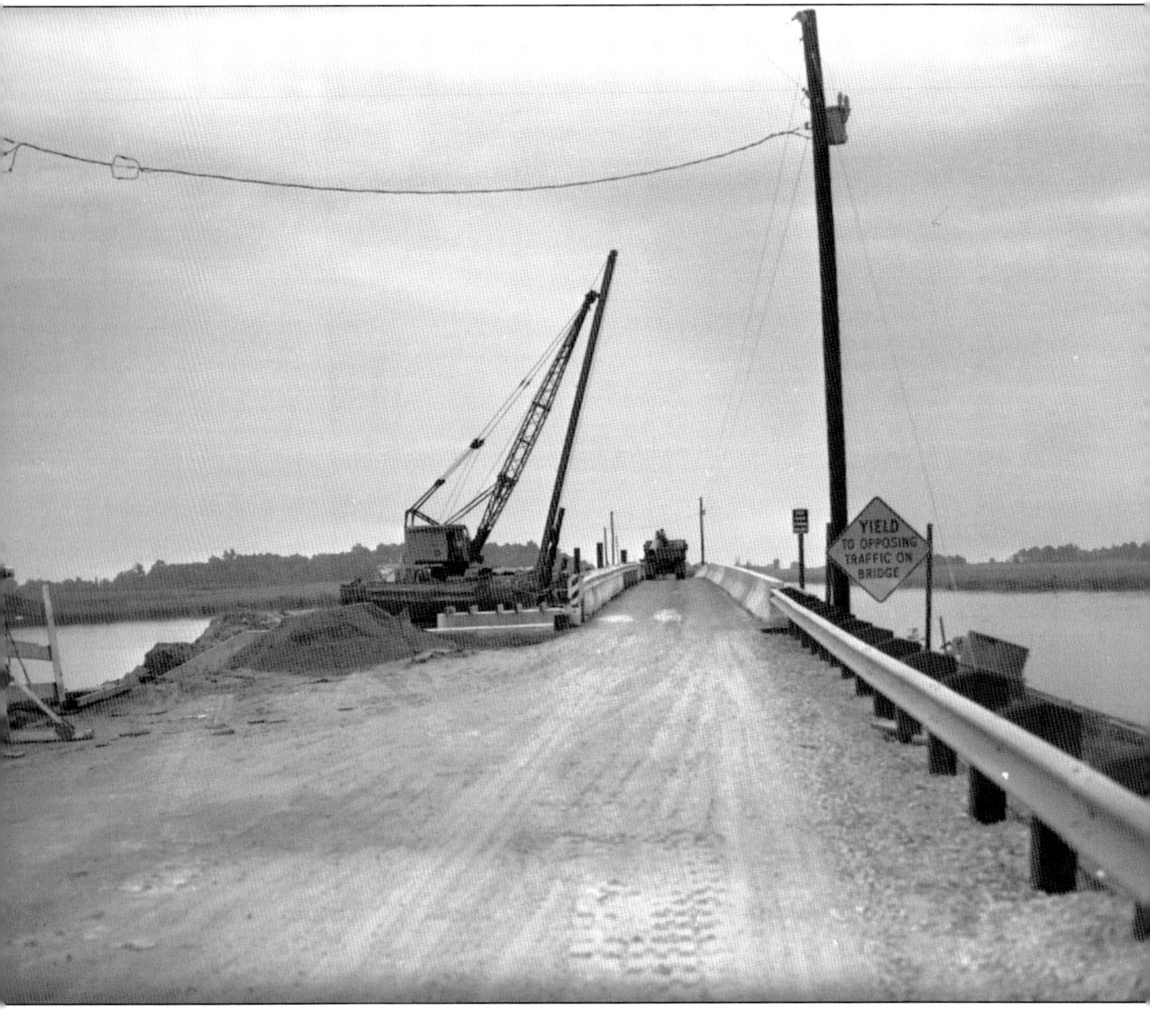

In 1914, yet another grand storm washed out the only road into Woodland Beach again, virtually cutting the small community off from the outside world. Finally, James Mott decided to invest $42,000 of his own money and, with some help from the government, rebuild the road with the hope that the resort town could be revived. Ultimately, it was never what it once was again. The roadway and bridge into the community continued to be a problem and is still being repaired on a regular basis by the now caretaker, the State of Delaware.

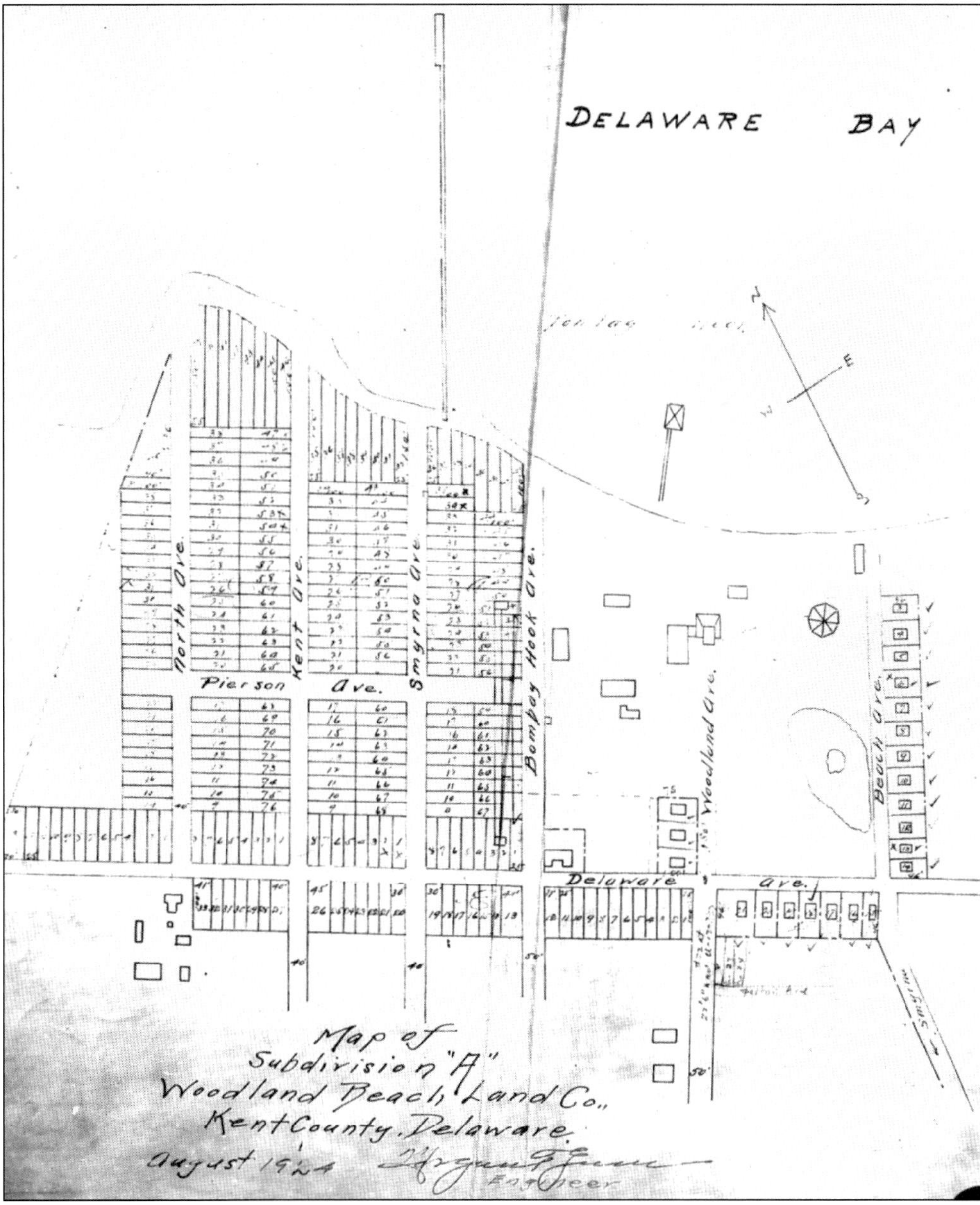

Over the years, the roller coaster prosperity at Woodland Beach was nearly lost and then rebuilt several times. After the road destruction in 1914, there was a sharp decline in tourists to the beach community. The railroad had long since ceased and the steamships, no longer popular, stopped arriving. Small bungalows still lined the streets for visitors, but Mott began to sell off lots as part of a subdivision for his new Woodland Beach Land Company after several unsuccessful attempts at convincing business owners within the community to purchase the grounds. Soon, Mott retired to Florida, leaving the old resort ruins to a real estate company.

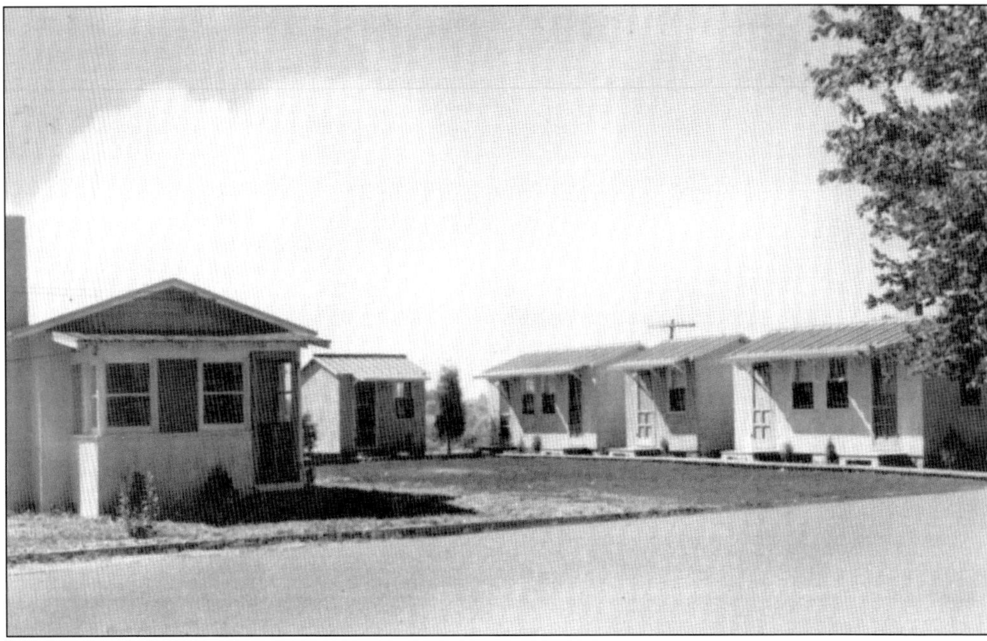

Woodland Beach saw a surge of new interest from fisherman starting in the 1930s. Cottages still for rent into the 1950s were some of the small bungalows built by Mott while he waited for his resort to reemerge after 1914. Mostly under the ownership of realtors, the cottages worked well for crabbers, fishermen, and lovers of the coast during the second revival of the community.

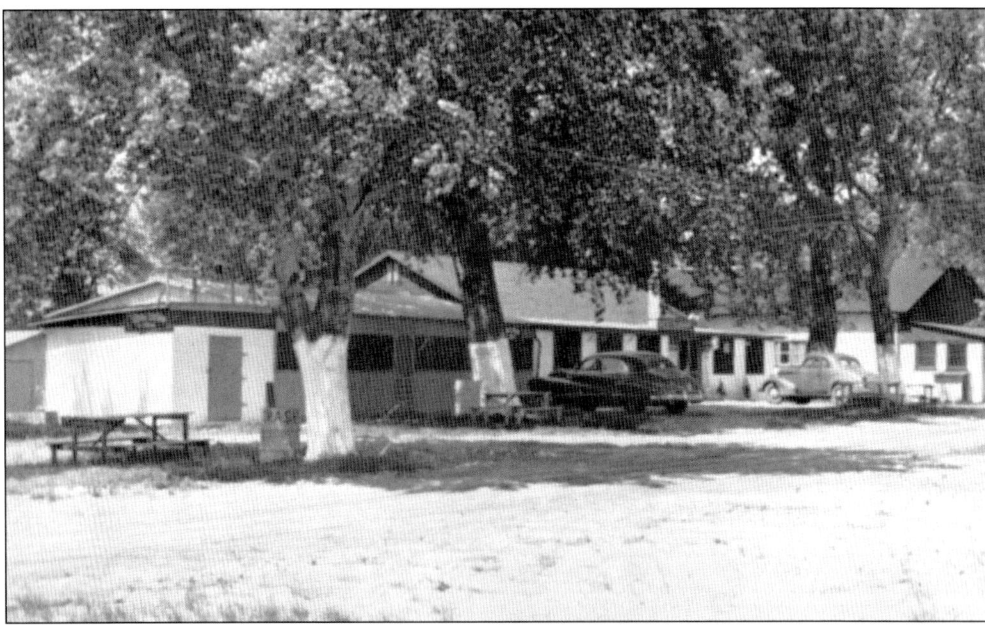

A dance hall called the Coliseum Night Club continued into the 1950s as part of a restaurant. Many came for sunshine and seafood dining in the casual atmosphere on summer evenings. Families traveled from Smyrna to enjoy a day of crabbing, picnicking, and dinner at one of the seafood houses at Woodland Beach. (Courtesy of Brooks Keen.)

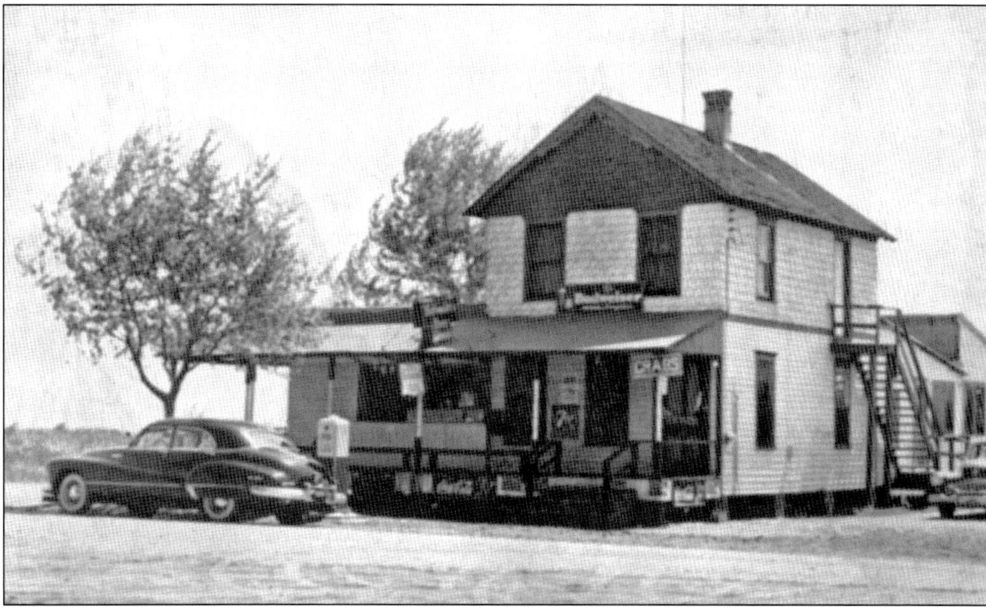

Blendt's Place is a seafood restaurant in the well-known last building on the right located on the main avenue. The restaurant was famous for steamed crabs and seafood as well as sandwiches. More than food, Blendt's carried fishing supplies, and it was noted, "Harry delights in helping fishermen." Blendt's Place was open all year.

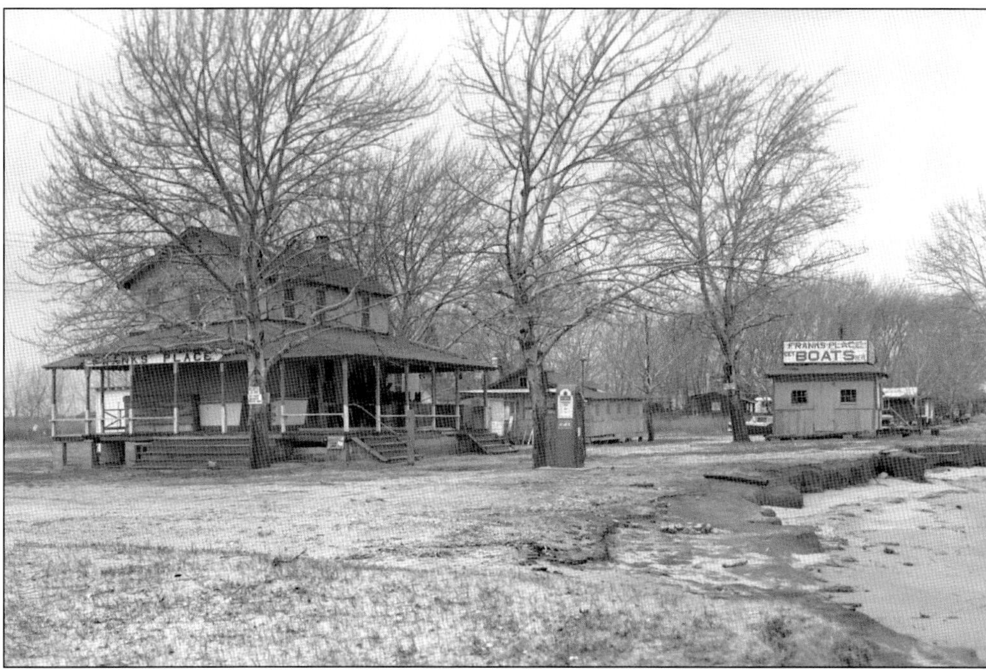

Frank Burrows of Kenton owned and operated Frank's Place for over 30 years with his wife, Ruth Burrows. They operated a general store, sold bait, and rented out boats for visitors to Woodland Beach. At the height of their business, they had 270 boats, all of which would be rented out by 4:00 a.m. on a summer Saturday or Sunday. Eventually, Burrows sold his business to a retired couple from New Jersey.

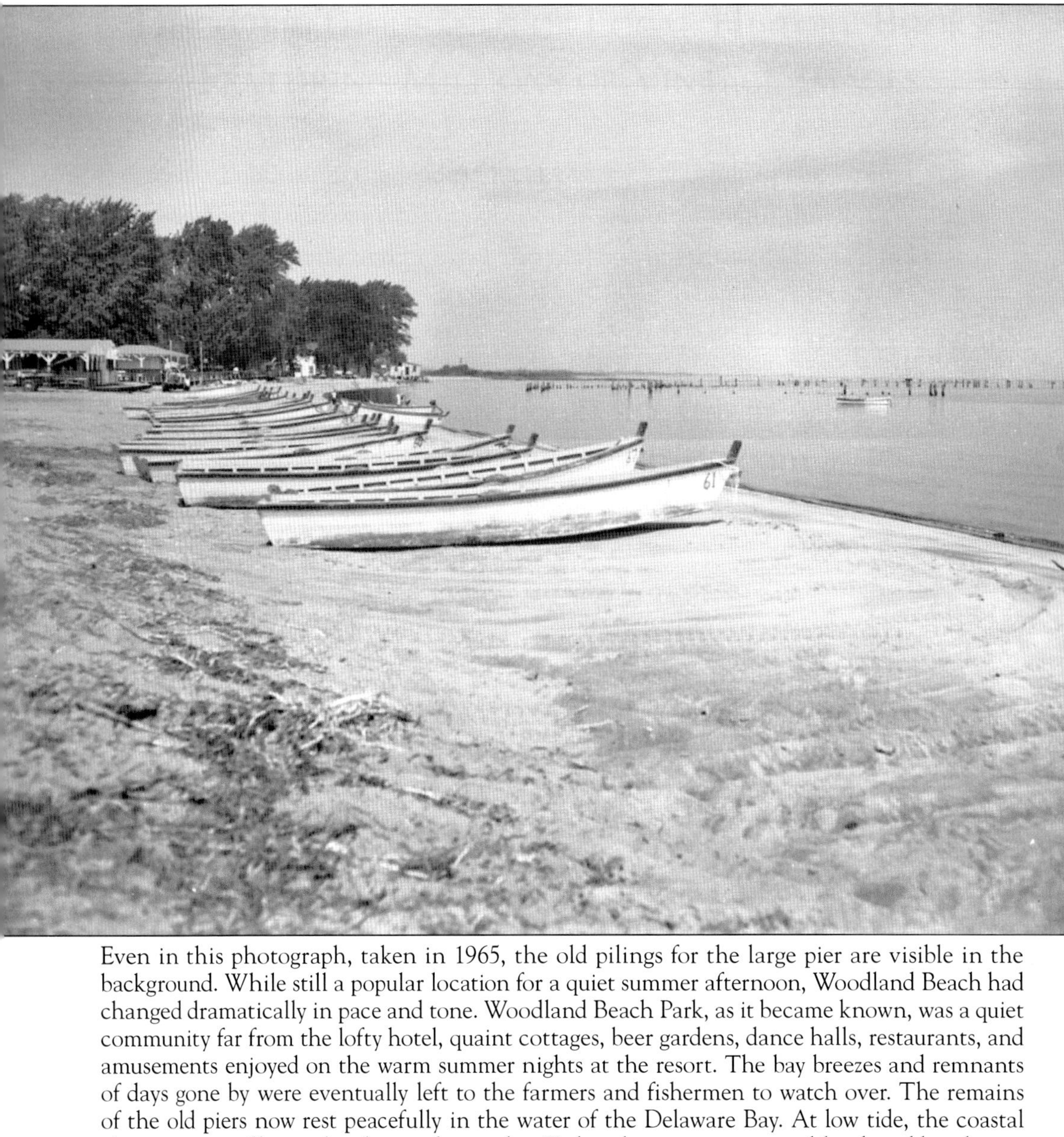

Even in this photograph, taken in 1965, the old pilings for the large pier are visible in the background. While still a popular location for a quiet summer afternoon, Woodland Beach had changed dramatically in pace and tone. Woodland Beach Park, as it became known, was a quiet community far from the lofty hotel, quaint cottages, beer gardens, dance halls, restaurants, and amusements enjoyed on the warm summer nights at the resort. The bay breezes and remnants of days gone by were eventually left to the farmers and fishermen to watch over. The remains of the old piers now rest peacefully in the water of the Delaware Bay. At low tide, the coastal observer can still spot the ghosts of yesterday. Today, the waterways, marshland, and beach area at Woodland Beach are owned by the State of Delaware, while the middle and lower portion of Bombay Hook is a National Wildlife Refuge.

INDEX

DISCOVER THOUSANDS OF LOCAL HISTORY BOOKS FEATURING MILLIONS OF VINTAGE IMAGES

Arcadia Publishing, the leading local history publisher in the United States, is committed to making history accessible and meaningful through publishing books that celebrate and preserve the heritage of America's people and places.

Find more books like this at
www.arcadiapublishing.com

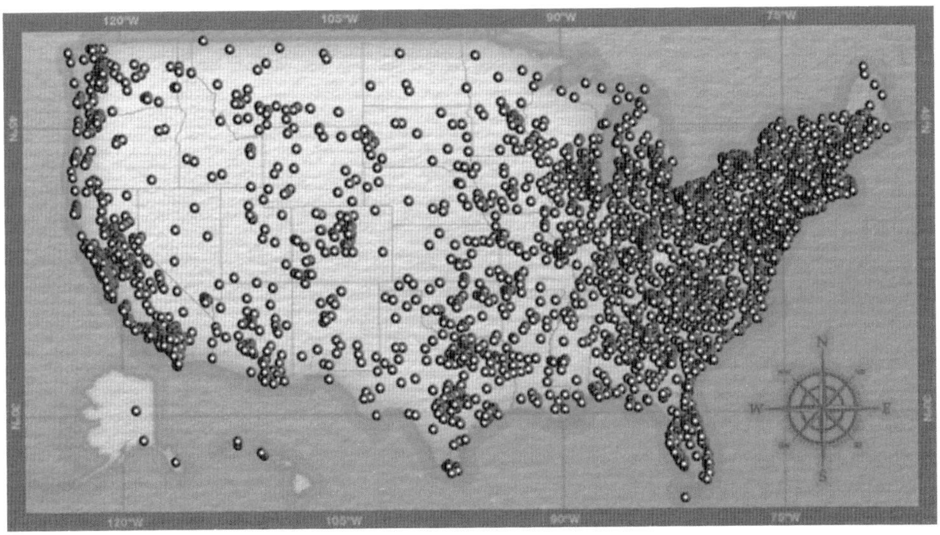

Search for your hometown history, your old stomping grounds, and even your favorite sports team.

Consistent with our mission to preserve history on a local level, this book was printed in South Carolina on American-made paper and manufactured entirely in the United States. Products carrying the accredited Forest Stewardship Council (FSC) label are printed on 100 percent FSC-certified paper.

MADE IN THE USA